Life and adventures
of the celebrated bandit
Joaquin Murrieta
His exploits in the state of California

Recovering the U.S. Hispanic Literary Heritage

Board of Editorial Advisors

Life and adventures
of the celebrated bandit

Joaquin Murrieta

His exploits in the state of California

Ireneo Paz

Translation by Francis P. Belle

Introduction by Luis Leal

Introduction translated by
Francisco A. Lomelí and Miguel R. López

Recovering the U.S. Hispanic Literary Heritage

Arte Público Press
Houston, Texas

This volume is made possible through grants from the Rockefeller Foundation.

Recovering the past, creating the future

Arte Público Press
University of Houston
452 Cullen Performance Hall
Houston, Texas 77204-2004

Cover design by Adelaida Mendoza

Paz, Ireneo, 1839–1924.
    [Vida y aventuras del más célebre bandido sonorense Joaquín Murrieta. English]
    Joaquin Murrieta, California outlaw / Ireneo Paz : English translation by Frances P. Belle ; introduction by Luis Leal.
        p.   cm.
    ISBN 1-55885-277-8 (pbk. : alk. paper)
    1. Murrieta, Joaquín, d. 1853. 2. Revolutionaries—California Biography. 3. Mexicans—California Biography. 4. Outlaws—California—Biography. 5. Frontier and pioneer life—California. 6. California—History—1850–1950. 7. California—History—1846–1850. I. Title.
F865.M96P3913   1999
979.4'04'092—dc21   99-39122
                                                                          CIP

1 2 3 4 5 6 7 8 9   10 9 8 7 6 5 4 3 2 1

To the memory of the Mexican
gambusinos *in northern California*
—L. L.

Table of Contents

Introduction by Luis Leal

Introduction

The Pastoral Myth

The eighty years of the history of Upper California as part of Mexico, from 1769 (the first land expedition by Gaspar de Portolá and Fray Junípero Serra) until 1848 (the California Gold Rush), has been called the "Pastoral Age." The structural base of the period was the *latifundio,* the large landed estate whose social and cultural center was situated in the large houses of the so-called *ranchos.* Historians such as Hubert Howe Bancroft, with his book *California Pastoral, 1769–1848* (1888); novelists, especially Helen Hunt Jackson with her *Ramona* (1884); and the films of Hollywood have all mythologized that culture, so that today we commonly accept their depiction of the restful and pleasant life of old California, where all social problems were resolved by Zorro, that mysterious and powerful character who was a sort of Hispanic Batman.

The origin of the *ranchos* may be found in the land grants given to the first settlers by the Spanish Crown in the eighteenth century. When Upper California ceased to be a province of New Spain and became part of the Republic of Mexico, the ranches multiplied as a result of the appropriation of the mission lands carried out by the central government in 1838. Land owned by the missions was auctioned off and passed into the hands of well-to-do families.

From 1848 on, as the Californios were being stripped of their property, the *ranchos* disintegrated, and the groups that had provided manual labor—cowboys, laborers, shepherds, servants—moved to the urban centers or began to work in the mines; some of them joined the gangs of bandits that were beginning to form. As Joseph Henry Jackson observes, "These thousands of vaguely employed Mexicans found themselves displaced persons . . . [and] could rarely find anything to do but the most menial work. Others simply took what they needed as they could find it, and if this meant living off a society which, as it seemed to them, had refused them support, why that was how it was. It is easy, then, to see how, in the mind of the Spanish-Californian, patriotism was equated with outlawry" (1955: xvii).

Gold Fever

Gold was discovered in Upper California on January 24, 1848, a few days before the signing of the Treaty of Guadalupe Hidalgo. The discovery, however, did not become public until after February 2, the date of the signing of the treaty. The first flakes were discovered by a carpenter, James Wilson Marshall, while building a mill for John Augustus Sutter on his ranch in Coloma. During the first few months of 1848, the only prospectors were Anglos. Soon, however, the news of the discovery reached the entire globe, prompting an extraordinary influx of miners into California, which, at its peak in 1852, reached more than 100,000 (Nicholson 1990: 38). The first to arrive were the Sonorans, whose number increased to such a degree that the settlement where they lived was called Sonora or Sonorita. The presence of the Sonorans was of great benefit to the Anglo miners, who learned from them the methods of extracting gold by sluicing as well as panning, methods that had been used in Mexican mines since time immemorial. Attracted by the gold, other Latin Americans, particularly from Peru and Chile, soon arrived in Upper California. The theory of Joaquín Murrieta's Chilean origins may be due to the arrival of some miner by that last name.

With the arrival of miners from other Latin American countries and other regions, Anglos became a minority, with the resulting rivalries and inevitable racial conflicts. John Rollin Ridge tells us: "The country was then full of lawless and desperate men, who bore the name of Americans but failed to support the honor and dignity of that title" (1955: 9).

To protect the Anglos, the state government passed Draconian laws against the foreign miners, among whom were a number of Mexicans born in California before 1848 and who, according to the Treaty of Guadalupe Hidalgo, were to be considered citizens of the United States. In 1850 an unfair Foreign Miner's Tax Law was passed, aimed at Mexicans and other Latin Americans. The law required all foreign miners to pay a very high fee for annual licenses that prevented them from realizing any return. Historians would denounce the law as unfair and offensive. According to one, T. H. Hittell, the law was hated primarily because the agents in charge of enforcing it were paid their salary from the money they collected from the miners (cited by Jackson 1955: xvi). Unable to fight against the law in the courts, many "foreign" miners left the country after 1852. That was not the case with those of European origin, who were considered "Americans." Others affected by the law joined the large number of bandit groups. The stereotype then created of the Mexican as a *bandido* has yet to disappear, since it was promoted first by the so-called dime novels and then all over the world by the Hollywood westerns. The newspapers became alarmed by the success of the well-organized groups of bandits, whom they referred to as "cut-throats," and urged the government to protect "decent citizens" from their attacks.

Social Bandits?

In his book *Bandits*, Eric Hobsbawm defines a social bandit as a person whom the government persecutes as a criminal, but whom the public considers a hero (1969:13). Social bandits, according to Hobsbawm, appear only in pastoral societies; they have no revolutionary ideology nor plans of social reform. However, they do correct injustices committed against the poor and helpless, succeeding sometimes in becoming a part of larger social movements and thus achieving some changes in society.

As an example of the social bandit who joins a political/ revolutionary cause, Hobsbawm mentions the case of Francisco Villa. Joaquín Murrieta, on the other hand, died too young and too soon after his appearance in the public eye to have joined any such cause. In fact, no such cause arose after 1848 in California. But Murrieta was a "social bandit" to whom one can attach all the characteristics Hobsbawm mentions. In the introduction to his book *Legends of the California Bandidos*, writer Angus MacLean says, "From this distance in time [1977], it is hard to separate the *revolucionario* from the *bandido*. In fact, many of the south-of-the-border bandits of the gold rush years would seem to have gotten their start in the insurrections down in Mexico, before transferring their talents to Alta California" (1977: vii).

I
The Historical Joaquín

Antecedents

If it is difficult to separate the mythical from the historical elements present in all oral or written narratives, the task becomes nearly
impossible when one is dealing with a figure like Joaquín Murrieta.
In his case, myth and legend have fed history much more than the
reverse. Nonetheless, we will try to outline the relationship between
myth and history in the tangled case of this young miner who was
unknown before 1853, but who, a few years after his supposed death
on July 24 of that year, became the most outstanding of California's
popular heroes. We'll begin with the hypothesis that Murrieta was a
historical figure who was born in Sonora and lived in California.
From there we'll examine the process by which a myth was created
around that figure, as much in the popular imagination as in literature,
theater, folklore, and film.

The name Joaquín has a long tradition in California history. It
appears in various places as early as the eighteenth century, when the
first land expeditions to Upper California began. In the expedition led
by Juan Bautista De Anza was the family of José Joaquín Moraga,
which included a son named Gabriel. It was he who gave the name of
San Joaquín to one of the rivers in the state. There is also a San
Joaquín County, a town of San Joaquín, and, finally, the San Joaquín
Valley where the story of the hero unfolds. Joaquín was a very common given name among the Californios. In the later twentieth
century, both the name and story were revived among Chicanos with
the publication in 1967 of the epic poem *Yo soy Joaquín* by Rodolfo
"Corky" Gonzales.

When the Name Joaquín Came to Mean *Outlaw*

The name Joaquín was first used in the newspapers to refer to
Mexican bandits, though without identifying any one of them by a
surname, between 1850 and 1851. In 1852 when the newspapers
began to publish complaints about the so-called Mexican bandits,
they had no concrete information as to whom those "bandits" might
be, although it was rumored that one was named Joaquín. As late as

January 29, 1853, the ironically named *San Joaquín Republican* newspaper, of Stockton, published one of those alarming notices:

FROM CALAVERAS
[Per Brown's Express]

It is well known that during the winter months a band of Mexican marauders have infested Calaveras county, and weekly we receive the details of dreadful murders and out-rages committed in the lonely gulches and solitary outposts of that region. The farmers lost their cattle and horses, the trader's tent was pillaged, and the life of every traveler was insecure [....] The band is lead [sic] by a robber, named Joaquín, a very desperate man, who was concerned in the murder of four Americans, sometime ago, at Turnerville. (Latta 1980: 37)

All the abuses, assaults, robberies, and murders that occurred were shortly attributed to Joaquín, who quickly became a mythical fig-ure capable of appearing in different places at the same time. Although journalists came to realize that they were dealing with more than one Joaquín, the popular imagination quickly identified them all with the name of only one, Joaquín Murrieta. Nevertheless, little or almost nothing was known of Joaquín's private life before he was identified with the head put on public display in Stockton, California, on August 12, 1853—or before John Rollin Ridge published his biography.

Principal Sources for the Study of Joaquín Murrieta

In one of the first studies on the historical basis of Murrieta, researcher May S. Corcoran ("Robber Joaquín" 1921) has gone to the extreme of attempting to exclude all information except what appears in the official statutes of the State of California for 1853—the year Joaquín was supposedly murdered—along with the oral testimony of a contemporary of Murrieta, Captain William J. Howard, an assistant to Harry Love, the leader of the posse of "Rangers" that attacked and killed two men they identified as Joaquín Murrieta and his compan-ion, "Three-Fingered Jack."

Corcoran begins her short article by stating that the information

WILL BE
EXHIBITED
FOR ONE DAY ONLY!

AT THE STOCKTON HOUSE!
THIS DAY, AUG. 12, FROM 9 A. M., UNTIL 6. P. M.

THE HEAD
Of the renowned Bandit!

JOAQUIN!
AND THE
HAND OF THREE FINGERED JACK!
THE NOTORIOUS ROBBER AND MURDERER.

"JOAQUIN" and "THREE-FINGERED JACK" were captured by the *State Rangers*, under the command of Capt. Harry Love, at the Arroya Cantina, July 24th. No reasonable doubt can be entertained in regard to the identification of the head now on exhibition, as being that of the notorious robber, *Joaquin Murietta*, as it has been recognised by hundreds of persons who have formerly seen him.

Cartel: "The head of the renowned Bandit!
And the hand of Three Fingered Jack!"

concerning Murrieta that appears in California history books is not reliable. She mentions two historians of the nineteenth century, Hubert Howe Bancroft and Theodore H. Hittell, whose work she rejects because they say too little or because what they do say can be refuted in light of official documents or the testimony of eyewitnesses. She adds that the works of other writers (whom she doesn't mention) are so extravagant that they cannot be believed. Of course, the same could be said of the very sources that Corcoran uses—that is, the official statutes and whatever information Howard was able to recall thirty years after the fact. Corcoran does not mention the principal source of information concerning Joaquín Murrieta, which is the biography by journalist John Rollin Ridge, *The Life and Adventures of Joaquín Murrieta*, published in 1854, one year after the death of Joaquín. However, she concludes her work with yet another legend, as we shall see later in this study.

A number of other researchers have also tried to solve the problem of the life of Murrieta. Among these is Remi Nadeau, the author of an article published in 1963 ("Joaquín—Hero, Villain or Myth?") and a book, *The Real Joaquín Murieta, California Gold Rush Bandit: Truth v. Myth* (1974), in which the author reconstructs the adventures—or rather the series of crimes—of "Joaquín" (not necessarily Murrieta), according to reports in the newspapers of San Francisco, Sacramento, and other cities during 1852 and 1853. More than a means of reconstructing history, these news reports appear to be the very source of the myth of Joaquín Murrieta. "From those sources . . .," writes Nadeau, "there emerges a Joaquín who terrorized Amador, Calaveras, and probably Mariposa counties for just two months—January to early March, 1853" (1963:19). According to the historical information collected by Corcoran, Nadeau, Frank Latta, Manuel Rojas, and other researchers, these reports of Joaquín's activities are based on data not always reliable.

The investigator most interested in reconstructing the life of Murrieta has been Frank F. Latta, whose *Joaquín Murrieta and His Horse Gangs* (1980) is an exhaustive compilation of reports, photographs, documents, facts, and so forth, surrounding Murrieta, his family, his friends and companions, his adventures, and his death. Latta spent his life gathering information, interviewing possible Murrieta descendants, relatives, and acquaintances, both in California and in northern Sonora (where, according to the author, Murrieta was born). Latta is also the only researcher who includes a version of the story in which Murrieta's death comes not at the hands of Love and his rangers, but later and under very different circumstances. It is also Latta who suggests why nothing more was known of Murrieta after he was supposedly killed by the Rangers. Unfortunately, Latta's extensive information is poorly organized.

In Mexico, the principal researcher into the life of Murrieta is Manuel Rojas, whose *Joaquín Murrieta, "El Patrio": El Far West del México Cercenado (Joaquín Murrieta, "the Native": Mexico's Mutilated Far West)* appeared in its third edition in 1992. Rojas's information and the numerous illustrations he presents reflect his extensive work in the region of Sonora where Murrieta was born, as well as his firsthand knowledge of the primary sources. That Murrieta is considered a historical figure is evident in the articles that appear in a number of dictionaries, including the *Diccionario Porrúa de historia, biografía y geografía de México* (1964), and the *Columbia Encyclopedia* (5th ed., 1993).

First Reliable Identification

It was in the announcement of the exhibition of the head "of the well-known robber Joaquín Murrieta" on August 12, 1853 in Stockton, California, that Murrieta was identified for the first time as the leader of a band of outlaws accused of various robberies and other crimes.[1] But Ridge was the first to reconstruct—or invent, according to some critics—the life and adventures of the best-known popular hero among both Californians and Chicanos.

The complete name "Joaquín Murrieta" first appeared in the San Francisco newspaper *Alta California* on December 15, 1852.[2] After that date there are frequent references to the activities of Joaquín in the newspapers. The first murder attributed to him (he was known in Los Angeles as a horse thief but not as a murderer) was that of General Joshua H. Bean (brother of Roy Bean, the famous judge of Wild West lore), which occurred in San Gabriel (near Los Angeles) on November 7, 1852. Was the perpetrator of this crime the same Joaquín who was at the same time roaming far to the north in San Joaquín Valley? According to Nadeau, "there is no sure way to connect Joaquín Murieta, the Los Angeles horse thief, with Joaquín, the terror of the placers" (1974: 32).

In January of 1853 a bandit named Joaquín appeared near San Andreas. "No last name was given in newspaper accounts," says Remi Nadeau. "Like Joaquín Murieta, he was young and he liked to collect other people's horses. But he also preyed on the Chinese miners, robbing them when he chose, and killing them indiscriminately" (1963: 19). On the twenty-first of that month, the *San Joaquín Republican* attributed several homicides to Joaquín; on January 23, at the Bay State Ranch near San Andreas, a Mexican being held for horse theft was rescued by three Mexican riders. After defeating their pursuers, they arrived at Yackee Camp, firing at every American they could find; on the twenty-seventh there was word of Joaquín's presence at the gold mines. The news, according to the *San Joaquín Republican*, was conveyed by two persons: a Mr. Stevens, and an unknown French Canadian. It seems that these were mere rumors. By the first week of February, the district was in flames. On the seventh, a member of the gang, allegedly Joaquín's brother, was captured and hanged at Angel's Camp. Joaquín traveled northward with his men, and according to newspaper accounts, he rode through the streets of San Andreas "at a quick gallop and shot three Americans as he passed through the streets" (Nadeau 1963: 19). On February 8 they attacked a camp of Chinese miners near Big Bar on the banks of the Cosumnes River, where they killed six people and took $6,000. On the twelfth of the same month, near Fiddletown, three members of the gang were surprised and forced to flee on only one horse, two of them mounted and the other on foot, clinging to the horse's tail. When Joaquín's band robbed a German traveler north of Jackson, a posse of twenty men rode out of town and encountered four of them, including Joaquín himself, near a chaparral-covered hill. One of the four was killed, and Joaquín was wounded on the cheek, "which could account for later descriptions of him specifying a scar on the right cheek" (Nadeau 1963: 20). In the testimony of Deputy Philemon T. Herbert, there is mention of a "robber Joaquín," but without reference to a specific person. But in the government document of May 17, 1853, the name *Murietta* finally appears, heading the list of the five Joaquíns accused of banditry. That the last name is misspelled indicates the scant knowledge about the life of Murrieta.

Frank Latta's book includes photocopies of the main newspapers of the period that refer to Joaquín, as well as a "gang roster" of sixty-two persons associated with Murrieta.

II
Biography

From Sonora to California

We can reconstruct the life of Joaquín with information from various sources, including news reports of the period, the biography by John Rollin Ridge, as well its imitators and translators, and also the principal studies on Murrieta by Jackson, Latta, Nadeau, Rojas, and so forth.

Ridge wrote the first biography. He indicates that Joaquín was born in Sonora, Mexico. It was not until "C. M." [Carlos Morla] published his 1867 Spanish translation, taken from the French translation by Robert Hyenne, which in turn had been taken from the *Police Gazette* version of 1859, that anyone claimed Joaquín was born in Chile. All of the American and Mexican critics state that he was born in Sonora, although not all of them mention the actual place of birth. Not even the 1904 translation published in Mexico City by Ireneo Paz mentions the name of the town. Not until recently have biographers given the name of a town. Manuel Rojas, in his book *Joaquín Murrieta, "El Patrio": El Far West del México cercenado* (3rd ed., 1992), after mentioning sites suggested by various other critics, states that "Joaquín Murrieta was born in the Villa de San Rafael 'El Alamito,' in the district of Altar, Sonora, México, and the date of birth, pending actual documentation, must have been between 1824 and 1830" (1992: 36). Frank Latta, in *Joaquín Murrieta and His Horse Gangs* (1980), tells us that "*El famoso* Joaquín was born on El Camino Real [...] in a stone house near the left bank of Arroyo de los Alamos in Pueblo de Murrieta located about 50 miles south of the picturesque old Colonial mining town of Real de los Alamos" (1980: 127). The *Diccionario Porrúa* states that Joaquín was born "in the Rancho del Salado near Alamos, Sonora" (1964: 991). It is interesting to note that in Chile the belief persists that Joaquín was born in the town of Quillota, twenty miles south of Valparaíso.[3]

Nor are Murrieta's biographers in agreement as to the date of Joaquín's birth, although all of them (with the exception of the *Diccionario Porrúa*) put it between 1824 and 1832. John Rollin Ridge is the first to mention Joaquín's age. He tells us that in 1850, when he was working in the Stanislaus mines, he was eighteen years old (1955: 8), which means that he was born in 1832. However, he also states that when he died in July of 1853, he was twenty-two years old, which means that he was born in 1831. Both the *Police Gazette* edition (1859), as well as that of Ireneo Paz, published in 1904, state "In 1845 Joaquín left his home town in Sonora to seek his fortune in the Capital. He was then sixteen years old" (1953: 5). From this we may deduce that he was born in 1829. The authors of the *Columbia Encyclopedia* article, although unsure of the date, suggest the year 1829:

> **Murrieta or Murieta, Joaquín** (1829?–1853), California bandit, b. Mexico. From 1849 to 1851 he mined in the California gold fields. After he and members of his family had been mistreated by American miners and driven from their claim, he became the leader of a band of desperadoes. For two years his robberies and murders terrorized California, until the legislature authorized Capt. Harry Love, deputy sheriff of Los Angeles Co., to organize a company of mounted rangers to exterminate Murrieta's band. Surprised at his camp near Tulare Lake, Murieta was shot, and most of his followers were killed or captured. Romanticization of his career began with the publication (1854) of John R. Ridge's *The Life and Adventures of Joaquín Murieta*.

The *Diccionario Porrúa*, no doubt in error, gives the year as 1809:

> **Murrieta, Joaquín** (1809–?) Rebel and outlaw. b. in the Rancho del Salado, near Alamos, Sonora. He went to California during the Gold Rush. In 1849 he began to suffer mistreatment by the American authorities, which had recently seized that territory from Mexico. Reacting against the abuses, he decided to take revenge and his rebellion led to his career as an outlaw. A very popular figure in Sonora. (1964: 991)

All other biographers, however, agree that Murrieta was born between 1824 and 1832.

Little is said about Joaquín's youth in his native town. According to Ridge, the young Joaquín had a gentle personality. Those who knew him as a student spoke favorably of his generosity and his noble character. According to the same biographer, when Joaquín was still a youth, he felt an urge for adventure, and at eighteen years of age he traveled to the gold mines of California in quest of fortune. He was, according to Ridge, of medium height, slender but with a well-proportioned body, "and active as a young tiger" (1955: 8). His skin tone was neither very dark nor very light, but was clear and brilliant, and his appearance was extremely handsome and attractive. His large black eyes, blazing with the enthusiasm of his ardent nature, his strong and well-formed mouth, his well-shaped head, his long and shining black hair, his silvery voice full of generous expressions, the frank and cordial comportment which distinguished him, won for him the sympathy of all with whom he communicated, and he enjoyed the respect and confidence of the entire community of which he was a part (Ridge 1955: 8–9). That characterization that Ridge made of Murrieta, pointing out his physical and moral characteristics, reappears in the San Francisco *Police Gazette* version and in the subsequent French and Spanish translations.

Ridge, Murrieta's first biographer, does not mention Joaquín's trip to the Mexican capital in 1845, an episode added by the anonymous author of the 1859 edition, and that was included in all the Spanish translations. We are told that Joaquín went to Mexico City to seek his fortune. He carried with him a letter for a Señor Estudillo, a friend of his father. This gentleman placed him as horse trainer in President Santa Anna's stables. However, Joaquín did not remain long in this position due to a conflict with another horse trainer, a young man named Cumplido. The problem was resolved by means of an equestrian competition in which the youths demonstrated their riding skills by jumping over a five-foot fence. Joaquín's horse touched the fence when a friend of Cumplido's waved a handkerchief just as the rider was flying over the fence. Angered by this incident, Joaquín returned to Sonora.

Another adventure not found in Ridge is Joaquín's 1848 trip to San Francisco in search of his brother Carlos, who had lived in California for several years. Not finding his brother there, Joaquín returns to Sonora, "where he was soon married to a very beautiful young woman named Carmen Félix" (Paz 1953:7). One year later he received a letter from his brother Carlos asking him to travel to the San José Mission, where gold had been discovered. Joaquín must postpone his trip for ten months due to the illness of his father. Finally, he makes the journey to California, accompanied by Carmen.

Two days after arriving in San Francisco, he finds his brother. According to Ridge, it is not Carmen but Rosita Félix who accompanies Joaquín. In *California Pastoral,* historian Herbert Howe Bancroft includes this stereotypical and romantic tale:

> Joaquín, when in his seventeenth year, became enamoured of the beautiful dark-eyed Rosita Félix, who was of Castilian descent, and sweet sixteen; she returned his passion with all the ardor of her nature. Her hard-grained old father on discovering this amour flew into a rage, and would have vented it upon the boy had he not taken flight. Rosita followed her lover to the northern wilderness, assisted him in his efforts at honest living, attended him through all of the perils of his unlawful achievements, and finally, when death so early severed them, returned to the land of her childhood, and under the roof of his parents mourned her well-beloved through long dreary years. (1888: 646)

In the *Police Gazette* version and its translations, Carmela (or Carmen in the Spanish translations) is raped and murdered by a group of Anglo miners. This incident changes Joaquín's character, and he swears revenge on the murderers. He spends the rest of his brief life searching for them to exact revenge, and at last succeeds. But his actions make him into a feared and hunted criminal, for which he soon pays with his life. In Ridge's version, however, Rosita does not die. After Joaquín's death she returns to Sonora, where she lives for many years with her family. Ridge ends with the following paragraph:

> Of Rosita, the beautiful and well-loved of Joaquín, nothing further is known than that she remains in the Province of Sonora, silently and sadly working out the slow task of a life forever blighted to her, under the roof of her aged parents. Alas, how happy might she not have been, had man never learned to wrong his fellow-man! (1955: 159)

The Metamorphosis

Joaquín's peaceful and benevolent nature, in Ridge's description, changes completely as a result of the violence suffered at the hands of Anglo miners. Ridge states (and his imitators repeat) that people who knew him before the incident doubted that he could be the same person. The other aspect of his character, that of the bloodthirsty bandit, is the one found in nearly all of the novels written by Anglo writers, as well as in the work of scholars who have taken an interest in his life. Even a critic such as Dr. Raymund Wood accepts the idea of Joaquín's ferocity. He tells us that, according to the "legend," Murrieta wanted only to kill the twelve miners who had raped and murdered his wife. But then he adds:

> The plain fact of the matter is that he was the leader of a gang of cut-throats, who committed untold murders and robberies in the Mother Lode, and were responsible for innumerable thefts of horses and cattle in the plains. (Mariana 1970: 10)

The First Adventure

Horace Bell, in his *Reminiscences of a Ranger* (1881), recounts the following episode, considered to be the first one attributed to Murrieta. According to Bell, during the fall of 1851 Joaquín and his men stole twenty-nine horses in East Los Angeles and drove them north. By the time they reached the Tejón Pass, the owners of the horses, who were also Mexican, were in pursuit. Murrieta's band was stopped by the Tejón Indians, who took some of the horses while the rest were recovered by their owners. According to Bell, the Tejón chief and some of his people stripped Joaquín and his men, flogged them, and finally let them go. In *The Robin Hood of El Dorado: The Saga of Joaquín Murrieta, Outlaw of California's Age of Gold* (1932)—considered a novelized biography by some critics—Walter Noble Burns retells this story, but adds rhetorical effects that highlight the humorous aspects of the incident.

The Pursuit

In 1853, public ignorance about the identity of Joaquín was such that some citizens proposed the government should offer a reward of five thousand dollars for the capture, dead or alive, of any criminal named Joaquín. Since the name Joaquín was common among the Mexicans residing in Upper California, the idea was absurd. Nevertheless, the legislature took the proposal seriously, and Philemon

T. Herbert, a representative of Mariposa County, presented a bill on March 28, 1853, which proposed that a reward of five thousand dollars be offered for the capture or the killing of the thief named Joaquín.[4]

The committee in charge of military affairs approved the motion, but the Assembly tabled it as a result of opposing arguments made by Assemblyman José M. Covarrubias. Although Covarrubias was in the minority, his arguments were substantial and sufficient to convince members of the Assembly that the bill was unfair. Covarrubias argued that a price would be put on the head of a person who was presumed to be guilty, without ever presenting the case before a jury; and that rumors and news reports were insufficient evidence of his guilt: Unless Joaquín possessed supernatural powers, it was impossible for him to be in very distant places at the same time. In addition, there were various honorable individuals in California, including descendents of old families, who happened to be named Joaquín, such as Judge Joaquín Carrillo of Sonoma, as well as others no less reputable. Despite the arguments presented by Covarrubias, less than two months later, on May 4, 1853, Senator Wade went before the State Legislature to make a request on behalf of the citizens of Mariposa County that a responsible person be authorized to organize a party of twenty or twenty-five well-armed and well-equipped men for the purpose of arresting Joaquín and his thieves. At last, after endless debate in the Assembly and the Senate, the wishes of the "honorable citizens of Mariposa County" were fulfilled, and the following statute was approved and enacted on May 17, 1853:

Harry S. Love is hereby authorized and empowered to raise a Company of Mounted Rangers not to exceed twenty men, and muster them into the service of the State for the period of three months, unless sooner disbanded by order of the Governor, for the purpose of capturing the party or gang of robbers commanded by the five Joaquíns, whose names are Joaquín Muriati (*sic*), Ocomorenia, Valenzuela, Botellier and Carillo (*sic*), and their band of associates.[5]

The Death of Joaquín

Love and his followers went in search of "Joaquín," blamed for any number of assaults and murders, beginning in 1852. The newspapers had stirred up the populace against the "Mexican bandits" supposedly led by Joaquín. An editorial published in the San Francisco newspaper *Alta California* noted, "Every murder and robbery in the country has been attributed to 'Joaquin.' Sometimes it is Joaquín Carrillo that has committed all these crimes; then it is Joaquín something else, but always 'Joaquin'" (J. H. Jackson, 1955: xxvi). To restore calm, the State Legislature issued the above-mentioned order, which was signed by Governor John Bigler on May 17, 1853. It authorized Captain Harry Love, whom Hubert Howe Bancroft called "a law-abiding desperado," (1888:649) to capture, with the aid of his rangers, all five Joaquíns. The governor himself offered a reward of $1,000.

On July 24, 1853 Captain Love was at the head of his Rangers when they confronted a group of Mexicans at Arroyo Cantúa, near Tulare Lake. The leader of the Mexicans found some of Love's questions offensive and refused to answer them. Suddenly, pistols and rifles were drawn, and there ensued a battle to the death. Two of the Mexicans were shot dead, two were arrested, and the rest escaped. One of those arrested was drowned during the journey to the Mariposa jail; the other man was delivered to the sheriff and then lynched by a mob. One of the men who died in Arroyo Cantúa was said to be Joaquín Murrieta—his was the first name to appear on the arrest warrant. The other was "Three-Fingered Jack," the alias of one Manuel García, who was missing two fingers on one hand. The one they called Joaquín was beheaded. For its preservation, as proof of death, the head was taken to the nearest town, Rootville (known today as Millerton), on the San Joaquín River. There it was placed into a jar that was filled first with whiskey and later with alcohol. The same was done with the hand of García (his face had been destroyed). Some people denied that it was Joaquín's head; others claimed that it did indeed belong to a Joaquín Valenzuela, but not to Murrieta. Still others said that it looked like the head of an Indian.

It is not known which of the Rangers killed Joaquín. It could have been William W. Byrnes, who claimed he knew Joaquín and identified him when he was seated by the campfire before he attempted his escape on horseback. Other authors say that it was William T. Henderson or John A. White. Latta offers the following assessment:

According to Henderson's statement in the *Fresno Expositor*

[Nov. 12, 1897], he was the man who killed the man the Rangers represented as Joaquín Murrieta. Henderson also stated that John A. White [....] also shot Murrieta once. This account the author [Latta] has found to be accepted by pioneers who had talked with many of the Rangers over the period of 50 years. William Howard stated the [*sic*] "Joaquín" was killed by White, leaving Henderson entirely out of the picture. Howard claimed to have been present when the killing took place and should have known the facts. The opinion of this author [Latta] is that Howard ignored the part played by Henderson. (1980: 348)

III
Translation and Plagiarism of Ridge's Work

John Rollin Ridge and His Work

Very little information exists about the life of John Rollin Ridge (1827–1867). The earliest known facts about him are from the brief editor's preface to the first edition of his book. Ridge was a journalist and poet of Cherokee ancestry. He was born in Georgia; his grandfather, Commander Ridge, had sent his son, John Ridge, to New England to continue his studies. In Connecticut, John married a young Anglo woman, whom he took to live with his family in Georgia. The future biographer of Joaquín Murrieta was born there in 1827.

A few years later, after gold was discovered on Cherokee land, the U. S. government forced the Cherokee tribe to leave Georgia. They were resettled west of the Mississippi River by the administration of President Andrew Jackson. During the migration to "Indian territory," Ridge's father and grandfather were killed by partisans who opposed the abandonment of their lands in Georgia. His mother sent young John Rollin Ridge to New England for his education. However, he soon returned to Fayetteville, Arkansas, where she had settled after the dispute between the two tribal groups.

As a young man, Ridge killed a man who was apparently sent by his father's enemies to provoke him. He was forced to hide in Springfield, Missouri, and in 1850 he moved on to California. Life in San Francisco and the surrounding towns was not very favorable to him. He worked as a miner, a businessman, an employee of Yuba

From John Rollin Ridge ("Yellow Bird"),
Life and Adventures of Joaquín Murieta (1854)

County, and finally as a journalist. In San Francisco he wrote for the magazine *The Pioneer,* which published his poems and articles.

Ridge did not enjoy much success as a poet and journalist, being only one of many contributors in San Francisco's journalistic corps. Upon its 1854 publication, *The Life and Adventures of Joaquín Murrieta, the Celebrated California Bandit* was reviewed by only one or two newspapers. Ridge's name did not appear among lists of the best-known writers of the period, and he complained about his financial difficulties.[6] On October 9, 1854, he wrote to his cousin, Stand Watie of Oklahoma, asking him for help to establish himself as a journalist, and telling him that he had not made his fortune with the book on Murrieta because the publisher, W. B. Cooke, had stolen the proceeds after selling seven thousand copies of the book, leaving Ridge and others "to whistle for our money" (Lee and Little, 82). But Ridge's misfortune did not end there. In 1859 an anonymous author plagiarized his book and published it in ten installments in the *Police Gazette* of San Francisco and also in book form. That version was then plagiarized by others in Spain, France, and Chile; and although there is much of Ridge's work in these plagiarized editions, the reader is unaware that she or he is reading the words of "Yellow Bird" (Ridge's Cherokee name, which identified him as the author of the book). During this time his book was not translated *directly* into Spanish, although Ridge's words did appear in pirated Spanish translations and plagiarized editions.

In 1871, seventeen years after its original publication, Fredrick MacCrellish published an authorized "third" (actually a second) edition of Ridge's work under the title *The History of Joaquín Murieta, the King of California Outlaws, Whose Band Ravaged the State in the Early Fifties.* This included revisions and minor changes by Ridge.[7] But misfortune did not allow Ridge to see the new edition. He died on October 5, 1867 (Nadeau 1974: 121).

In his posthumously published prologue, Ridge alludes to a pirated edition of his work. Though he doesn't directly mention the *Police Gazette* version, he is surely referring to it. He writes:

A spurious edition [of my book] has been foisted upon unsuspecting publishers and by them circulated, to the infringement of the author's copyright and the damage of his literary credit—the spurious work, with its crude interpolations, fictitious

additions, and imperfectly designed distortions of the author's
phraseology, being by many persons confounded with the
original performance. (Walker, 1939: 257)

This "third" edition (1871) of Ridge's book, like the first, is
extremely rare. Fortunately, it was reprinted in Hollister, California,
in 1927 by the editors of the *Evening Free Press* newspaper, who
included with it the story of another famous hero of California,
Tiburcio Vásquez. The title of this volume no longer highlights
Murrieta, but rather the period *California's Age of Terror: Murieta
and Vásquez*.

As with many other writers, Ridge did not achieve recognition
until many years after his death, through the numerous novels that
imitated his, and the various plays, stories, poems, and films inspired
by his work. In 1955, in honor of the hundredth anniversary of the
first edition, the University of Oklahoma Press issued a well-prepared
edition based on the first, with a scholarly introduction by historian
Joseph Henry Jackson that gathered an extensive body of information
regarding the works on Murrieta.

Critics often ask: Why did Ridge choose to write a book about a
little-known Mexican outlaw? His interest in the Mexicans of
California may have been the result of his sympathy for them and of
finding their story similar to that of his own family in Georgia. Both
had been deprived of their lands. Like them, Ridge had undoubtedly
suffered discrimination. It may be that Ridge saw in Murrieta the hero
who had not emerged to defend his own people. The editor of the first
edition observes:

> [Ridge's] own experiences would seem to have well fitted
> him to portray in living colors the fearful scenes which are
> described in this book, connected as he was, from the age of
> seventeen up to twenty-three, with the tragical events which
> occurred so frequently in his own country, the rising of fac-
> tions, the stormy controversies with the whites [....] and all
> the consequences of that terrible civil commotion which fol-
> lowed the removal of the Cherokee Nation. (1955:2)

According to the scholarly study by Franklin Walker (1939), the
differences between the first and second edition of Ridge's book may

be found primarily in the effort to document the facts of the narrative, in the development of certain adventures, and in the greater amount of detail provided.

Ridge's Work Plagiarized

There is no real problem with regard to the first two editions of Ridge's work. In 1859, however, a pirated edition by an anonymous author appeared in the San Francisco magazine *California Police Gazette*. It is sufficient to compare one or two paragraphs to see the plagiarism:

> Ridge: Joaquín Murieta was a Mexican, born in the province of Sonora of respectable parents and educated in the schools of Mexico. (1955:8)

> *Police Gazette:* Joaquín was born of respectable parents in Sonora, where he received a good education. (facs. ed. 1969:1)

> Ridge: It became generally known in 1851 that an organized *banditti* was ranging the country; but it was not yet ascertained who was the leader. (1955: 14)

> *Police Gazette:* It became generally known, in 1851, that organized *banditti* were ranging the country, and that Joaquín was the leader. (facs. ed. 1969: 7)

When the *Police Gazette* version was published, Ridge informed the Grass Valley press that it was a pirate edition (Walker 1937: 257). Nevertheless, it was ironically this version and not Ridge's that spread Murrieta's fame to the world, and especially to Europe and Latin America. This pirate edition introduced certain variations that help us trace the origin of later editions. One of these changes is Joaquín's female companion, whose name is "Rosita" in Ridge's work but "Carmela" in the pirate edition, although here she appears as Joaquín's wife rather than as his companion. Also, when she dies, she is replaced by another character, "Clarina," who does not figure in Ridge's original. This pirate edition, known as "Carmela-Clarina," is the one that was translated, first into French and later into Spanish, and made Murrieta known in Europe and the Hispanic world. Some critics combine the two versions of 1854 and 1859; for example, Dr. Raymund F.

Wood, in his pamphlet *Mariana la Loca* (1970), states: "One such young man from Sonora was a certain Joaquín Murrieta, who came to California with his young wife Rosita (or Carmela, if we follow the later, 1859, version of Ridge's original story)" (1970: 4). In the first place, Rosita was not the wife of Joaquín, but rather his friend or companion. Carmela is his wife in the 1859 version, in which Rosita does not appear. When he attempts to give the date of Joaquín's arrival in California, Wood follows the 1859 version, according to which the year is 1849 or early 1850 (1970: 4). Ridge does not mention the year of Joaquín's arrival in California. He states only that by the spring of 1850 he was working in the gold fields of Stanislaus. In the 1859 version and its translations, Joaquín comes to San Francisco in early 1848, searching unsuccessfully for his brother Carlos. He then returns to Sonora and marries Carmela (or Carmen). One year later he receives a letter from Carlos asking him to join him immediately at San José Mission because great quantities of gold have been discovered in the mountains. But due to the illness of his father, Joaquín is not able to join his brother until ten months later.

Wood also confuses the death of Rosita with that of Carmen. According to Ridge, Rosita did not die; after Joaquín's death, she returned to Sonora. Ridge's work ends with the paragraph quoted earlier, in which the author imagines Rosita in Sonora and he laments her misery, using her to introduce a moralizing ending typical of the literature of the period. Carmela, on the other hand, does die after being raped while Joaquín was unconscious from a blow received from the Anglo miners. When he regains consciousness and sees the body of his wife, he swears vengeance. Wood converts this scene into a tragedy similar to that of Pyramus and Thisbe:

> When it was over Rosita recovered her senses, realized what had happened, saw that her husband was, she believed, lying dead in a pool of his own blood, and, unwilling to live any longer, reached across the floor for the dagger that she had worn in her dress and plunged it into her heart. The men, somewhat sobered by this suicide, were about to leave the cabin when Joaquín, who was not dead, began to stir. (*Mariana* 1970: 8)

Hyenne's title page: *El bandido chileno Joaquín Murieta.*

The Translations

In Paris in 1862, the publishing house Lécriban et Toubon, Libraires, Rue du Pont-Lodi, published *Un Bandit Californien (Joaquín Murieta)* by Robert Hyenne, a writer who had authored a number of books, including *La Pérouse, Aventures et Naufrages* (1859), *William Palmer, Empoisonneur et Faussaire*, followed by *Une Affaire d'or, Episode de la Vie Californienne* (1860). The book on Murrieta was published without indicating its nature as a translation, and with a warning that "All reproduction, including partial reproduction, is forbidden." But the book is a translation of the *Police Gazette* version—which in turn is a plagiarism of Ridge. Here are the first paragraphs of each:

> Ridge: Joaquín Murieta was a Mexican, born in the province of Sonora of respectable parents and educated in the schools of Mexico. (1955: 8)

> *Police Gazette*: Joaquín was born of respectable parents in Sonora, Mexico, where he received a good education. (1969: 2)

> Hyenne: *Joaquín reçut le jour au Mexique. Sa famille, originaire de la Sonora, et fort honorable sus toutes les rapports, le fit élever dans su ville natale, où reçut un excellente éducation.* [Joaquín first saw the light of day in Mexico. His family, originally from Sonora and very respectable in every way, educated him in a proper manner, and he had excellent teachers.] (1862: 2)

In 1867, Chilean journalist and translator Carlos Morla Vicuña (1846–1901) published a Spanish translation of Hyenne, which was very popular and was re-edited a number of times, in some cases with slight variants. We know that Morla translated various works. Without mentioning Hyenne's *Murrieta*, Raúl Silva Castro tells us that Morla was "a journalist in his youth, and chose to become a translator after translating Longfellow's *Evangeline*" (1961).[8]

The critic Ricardo Donoso, in his prologue to the translation by Carlos Morla that was published in the literary supplement of *Excélsior*[9] under the title of "Vida y aventuras de Joaquín Murrieta," and without mentioning the first edition of the translation by Carlos Morla, notes that "the second edition of this version is from 1874, the third from 1879, and so on, to a total of fourteen editions" (32). The third edition is mentioned in the *Anuario de la prensa chilena, 1877–1885*, of the National Library of Santiago:

> *El bandido chileno Joaquín Murieta en California*, by Robert Hyenne. Translated from the French by C. M. Third edition. Santiago de Chile: The Republic Press of Jacinto Núñez. June 1879, 270 pp. "The first edition was printed in 1867 and the second in 1874. The initials of the translator correspond to Carlos Morla Vicuña."[10]

The first to copy the translation by Morla was Carlos Nombela y Tabares (1836–1919), who included most of it in his two-volume novel (1,127 pages) *La fiebre de riquezas: Siete años en California* (The Fever of Riches: Seven Years in California). In 1970 Professor Luis Monguió published a study of Nombela's novel in which he quotes portions to prove that the part that refers to Murrieta may be traced to the English edition published in the *Police Gazette*. Professor Monguió undoubtedly was unaware of Morla's Spanish version. The following is an example taken from Nombela's novel that is almost identical to the Spanish translation of Hyenne:

> Hyenne: "This is how my career of killing began!" he [Murrieta] said. "Here I have one of my attackers at my feet," he continued. "Now that I have taught my heart and my hand what they must do, I swear that I will not rest until I have annihilated the very last of these villains." (Acha/Maucci p.15)

> Nombela: "This is how I have begun my vengeance! . . . Here is one of my oppressors . . . one of my tormentors, breathless at my feet! . . . Now that my heart and my hand know what they must do, I must allow them no peace; I must not permit them a moment of rest until I have annihilated the last of these villainous tyrants!" (I, 443-4; quoted by Monguió, p. 246)

Although we lack conclusive information, we believe that the edition published with no date at Biblioteca Hércules in Barcelona by one "Professor Acigar," under the title *El caballero chileno bandido de California: Unica y verdadera historia de Joaquín Murieta*, is the same one that Morla published, which is the only one in which Murrieta appears as a Chilean. Also in Barcelona, "V. Acha" published *El bandido chileno Joaquín Murieta en California,* under Hyenne's name but without the name of the Spanish translator or a date of publication. We may suppose that this is the same translation done by Carlos Morla. This Spanish translation was already known in California in 1881, the year in which another Spanish version appeared in *La Gaceta* of Santa Barbara. This was an incomplete version because the weekly newspaper folded on July 20 of that year. On the front page of the final edition, number 106, we find the following note: "Due to the suspension of publication, *La Gaceta* is obliged to skip from chapter IX to chapter XXIV of *La vida y aventuras de Joaquín Murrieta* and to scenes of plundering and bloodshed by the bandits, and acts of valor and cunning by their leader."[11]

According to Charles W. Clough in his notes to the reprinting of the *Police Gazette* edition of Murrieta by Francis P. Farquhar, the Spanish translation of Hyenne's text, in which Murrieta appears as a Chilean, was completed in 1870, but this appears to be an error, for no known edition exists for that date.[12] Jackson suggests that these pirate editions in Spanish were copied from a Chilean magazine, and therefore Murrieta becomes a Chilean. It seems that Jackson did not know the complete history of the Spanish editions, even though in his book *Bad Company* he reproduces the illustrated cover of one of them, which is attributed to R. Hyenne. That illustrated edition was reprinted in Mexico City by V. Acha and Maucci Hermanos, crediting Robert Hyenne as the author, but with a different illustration on the cover and, as is the case with all of these editions, no publication date. Nor does Jackson mention the Chilean edition of 1906, published by the Centro Editorial of *La Prensa* in Santiago in which the name of the translator is given as "C. M.," the initials of the Chilean playwright Carlos Morla.

Ireneo Paz

In 1904, in his print shop in Mexico, Ireneo Paz published the *Vida y aventuras del más célebre bandido sonorense Joaquín Murrieta: Sus grandes proezas en California,*[13] a version that has been attributed to him since the book does not give the author's name. In 1925 Frances P. Belle published an English translation as if the author were Ireneo Paz, and since then the book has been attributed to Paz. The title, *Life and Adventures of the Celebrated Bandit Joaquín Murrieta: His Exploits in the State of California,* is followed by the phrase, "Translated from the Spanish of Ireneo Paz by Frances P. Belle."[14] What Paz had done was merely retouch the text to recover the Mexican nationality of Murrieta, which is why he added *sonorense* to the title—a word that appears in none of the other Spanish editions translated from French, or directly from English. If we compare the texts of Paz, Hyenne, *La Gaceta* of Santa Barbara of 1881, and the original texts in English by Ridge, it is easy to verify that Ireneo Paz's text is a rehashing of the earlier versions. All begin by giving information about the birthplace of Joaquín:

Ridge: Joaquin Murieta was a Mexican, born in the province of Sonora of respectable parents and educated in the schools of Mexico. (1955: 8)

Police Gazette: Joaquin was born of respectable parents in Sonora, Mexico, where he received a good education. (1969:2)

Hyenne: Joaquín first saw the light of day in Mexico. His family, which was originally from Sonora and very respectable in every way, raised him in his native town, where he received an excellent education. (p. 5)

La Gaceta (Santa Barbara): Joaquín was born in Mexico: his family, originally from Sonora and respectable in every way, raised him in his native town, where he received a good education (2.98 [1881]: 1).

Paz: Joaquín Murrieta was born in the Republic of Mexico. His family, originally from Sonora, and respectable in every way, raised him in his native town, where he received a good and conscientious education. (1953: 5)

These (non-Ridge) quotations, and the editions themselves, have, as we have said, a common source in the pirated English edition of the *Police Gazette* magazine, through which we find that the version published by Ireneo Paz is almost identical to that of *La Gaceta* of 1881. Ireneo Paz published his life of Joaquín in 1904, undoubtedly moved by a desire to make him Mexican once again. But in spite of his efforts, belief that Murrieta was a Chilean has persisted, as we can see in the work of Pablo Neruda.

In his study "Literatura hispana de y en los Estados Unidos," Octavio Paz affirms that "The cycle of Joaquín Murrieta begins one year after his death with the novelized biography *Life and Adventures of Joaquin Murieta, the Celebrated California Bandit* (San Francisco, 1854). The author, an adventurer and journalist named Yellow Bird, was also known as John Rollin Ridge. He was the son of a Cherokee chief and a white woman. Ridge's book was followed by others. At first, Joaquín was a Mexican from Sonora, and he figured as such in the first Spanish narrative of his adventures: *Vida y muerte del más célebre bandido sonorense, Joaquín Murrieta* (México, 1908). The author of this text was my grandfather, Ireneo Paz. In passing from English to Spanish, Joaquín acquired an 'r' in his surname: Murrieta. The character was destined to have, like so many heroes, an uncertain origin" (1987: 55).

IV
Joaquín Murrieta as Myth

Preliminaries

To what can we attribute the sudden transformation of Joaquín into a mythical character? Undoubtedly, one factor was the dramatic exhibition of his head in Stockton, San Francisco, and other California cities, and another is the biography published by John Rollin Ridge one year after these events.

But it is also due to the example of romantic European heroes to whom the writers compare him. Among the titles of the works dedicated to him, we find *The Fra Diavolo of El Dorado*, *The Robin Hood of El Dorado*, and *Joaquín, the Claude Duval of California*, this latter a novel in which are mentioned other famous romantic bandits including Jonathan Wild, Rinaldo Rinaldi, Cartouche, and Schneitzer. In the introduction to his version of Murrieta's story, Hyenne not only compares him to these European figures but claims that Joaquín surpasses them: *"Malgré le renom que possède en Italie Fra Diavolo, malgré la reputación bien établie des Cartouche et des Mandrin de notre pays, il nous faute pourtant avoner que Joaquín Murieta, le bandit Californiene, les a tout surpassés"* (2) [Despite the fame of Fra Diavolo in Italy, and despite the well-established reputation of the Cartouches and the Mandrins in our own country, we must nevertheless avow that Joaquín Murieta, the California bandit, has surpassed them all].

The American historian Hubert Howe Bancroft compares him to none other than Napoleon. In *California Pastoral*, he states: "The terms *brave, daring, able* faintly express his qualities. In the cañons of California he was what Napoleon was in the cities of Europe" (1888: 645). Besides, California did not have a popular hero like Davey Crockett, who had sacrificed his life in the Alamo for Texas independence.[15]

How can we explain the fact that it was Murrieta and not one of the other four Joaquíns (Carillo, Ocomorenia, Botellier, Valenzuela) who became the most famous popular hero in the history of California? One expert historian, Jackson, explains:

California might have developed its own folk hero sooner if gold mining had been a more romantic business. [...] A hero hip deep in an icy mountain torrent is only a chilly hero at best [....] California's folk hero, then, if there was to be one at all, had to be something other than a symbolic enlargement of the patiently grubbing, ragged, homesick, and fever-ridden "honest miner."

There had long been such another figure embedded in folk memory. [....] He was, in every land, the man who took from the rich and gave to the poor [...] In California, in the fifties, no such hero existed, but that did not matter. Ridge obligingly fashioned one in the image men have always liked for their folk heroes—that of the Romantic Bandit—let him a name, gave him substance and fixed him forever in print. (1955: xx)

As we shall see later, other circumstances besides Ridge's work helped to create the legend of Joaquín Murrieta. His was the first name of those on the arrest warrant. Nevertheless, there is no doubt that the exhibition of the head, along with Ridge's work, published one year after the death of the popular hero, spread the fame of Joaquín Murrieta throughout the United States, and he came to symbolize the resistance of the Mexican people in California, who considered him not a bandit but a defender of a culture on the verge of disappearing.[16] The people knew that Joaquín Murrieta was a reality. However, the many fictitious stories about his life and adventures have caused that historical reality to be questioned, attributing the existence of Murrieta to the work of Ridge, whom some have considered to be the creator of Joaquín Murrieta as legendary hero.

In his first chapter, Ridge mentions the names of the five individuals named Joaquín, having taken them, we suppose, from the statute promulgated on May 17, 1853. According to Ridge,

There were two Joaquíns, bearing the various surnames of Murieta, O'Comorenia, Valenzuela, Botellier, and Carillo [*sic*]—so that it was supposed there were no less than five sanguinary devils ranging the country at one and the same time. It is now fully ascertained that there were only two, whose proper names were Joaquín Murieta and Joaquín Valenzuela, the latter being nothing more than a distinguished subordinate to the first, who is the Rinaldo Rinaldi of California. (1955: 7)

The creation of the myth of Joaquín Murrieta is started by the Mexican people of California. Dr. Raymund Wood, in his *Mariana la Loca* (1970), observes:

[A]mong these descendants of the old Spanish families he was something of a hero, and was admired for his bravery in revenging himself on his Yankee oppressors. These Californios might not, in theory, approve of his cattle thefts, and still less did they approve of the murders that he and his gang committed, but they were generally willing to provide a fresh mount for any Mexican who seemed to be in a hurry to avoid his gringo pursuers, without asking too many questions (1970: 15).

After the death of Joaquín, Ridge, as well as his imitators, collected information about the hero directly from the people as well as from the newspapers. On April 18, 1853, the *Daily Herald* of San Francisco published a story from its correspondent in Monterey, California, to the effect that Joaquín visited a rancher in the Salinas Valley, to whom he recounted his misfortunes, telling him that he was robbed, had lost more than $40,000, and had been pursued and beaten in the mines. In May of 1854, a story about Joaquín was published in the only issue of the *Pacific Police Gazette* magazine (now lost); on July 9 of the same year, the magazine *California Police Gazette* began publication of the story, "Joaquín, the Mountain Robber! Or, The Guerilla of California" (of which only four chapters appeared).[17] None of these early narratives gives the complete name of the character. At the same time, speeches, conversations, and arguments are put into Joaquín's mouth. In the following example from Ridge (appropriate for a novel, but not for a biography), Joaquín tells his old acquaintance Joe Lake:

"Joe," said he, as he brushed a tear from his eyes, "I am not the man I was; I am a deep-eyed scoundrel, but so help me God! I was driven to it by oppression and wrong. I hate my enemies, who are almost all of the Americans, but I love *you* for the sake of old times. I don't ask you, Joe, to love me or respect me, for an honest man like you cannot, but I do ask you not to betray me. I am unknown in this vicinity, and no one will suspect my presence, if you do not tell that you have seen me. My former good friend, I would rather do anything in the world than kill you, but if you betray me, I will certainly do it." (1955: 50)[18]

The myth gained strength immediately following the death of the supposed Joaquín Murrieta. We find the first signs of it in that no one was certain whether the person whom Love and his men killed at

Arroyo Cantúa was in fact Joaquín Murrieta. The only proof that Love had was the head, preserved in whiskey. To collect the reward offered by the state, he had to gather the testimony of people who said that they had known Joaquín, and that the head in Love's possession was that of the bandit.

The information that Love's assistant, Captain William J. Howard, gave to the scholar Corcoran seems suspicious to us, although he himself assured that many of the fabulous stories told about Murrieta had no merit. While nothing was known about Murrieta's family,[19] Howard claimed that he had the opportunity to meet his wife and had lived near her for a long time when he was camped in Hornitos. According to him, she was a very beautiful woman and was known by the name of Reina (that is, Queen) for her beauty and regal manners (Corcoran, 1921: 4 3rd col.). Later we shall see why the information given by Howard concerning Murrieta's wife is baseless.

Three important elements in the creation of the myth were the incredible ability of Joaquín to escape every ambush; his simultaneous presence in distant locations, and his death, which the popular imagination, the true creator of the myth, denies: Joaquín did not die, he went to Sonora. In 1856 the *Sentinel* of Santa Cruz published a report that Joaquín Murrieta had returned to Mexico, where he was seen by a person who had known him in California. In 1879 the *Alta California* repeated the same story, adding that Joaquín talked about the death of Murrieta so that he could live in peace. In 1932 Walter Noble Burns, author of the novel *The Robin Hood of El Dorado*, placed the following legend on the reproduction of the announcement of the exhibition of Joaquín's head in San Francisco:

> Evidence of the terror that the celebrated bandit, Joaquin Murrieta, created in California in 1850–1853. Thousands flocked to see the head of this desperado, who is known to have murdered more than 300 men, who plundered American miners on a state-wide scale, whose band pillaged ranches and settlements with a terrible suddenness. Long after he was killed by Harry Love's Rangers, many Californians believed that he had escaped and would return to harass the state. After 80 years, Murrieta's notoriety still lives in the West. (1932)

In 1939 Wade Wilson said that when he was the president of the Chamber of Commerce of Sonoma, a Mexican who was investigating the life of Murrieta had visited him and told him that the dead man was not Joaquín, but a cousin of the real Murrieta, who had died in Mexico. As late as 1970, Dr. Raymund F. Wood, in his *Mariana la Loca*, tells us that "additional testimonies have recently come forward that seem to support the opinion that Murrieta was not killed in the San Joaquín Valley—that he was in another part of the state at the time and that he later quietly went to Sonora, his native state, where he lived for many years, surrounded by riches and splendor, and was recognized by at least one Californian, Ramón Solórzano; that he may have returned to visit California incognito because he was identified by Pierre Reynaud of Placerville in the 1870s; and that he finally died of old age in Sonora" (14). That these and other legends have grown around the figure of Joaquín Murrieta indicate his strong presence in the popular imagination.

In his introduction to the 1955 edition of Ridge's book, historian Joseph Henry Jackson expressed the following opinion, which, because of the author's reputation, exerted a strong influence on later writers on Murrieta:

It is not going too far to say that in this little book Ridge actually created California's most enduring myth. It is true that in the early years of the gold rush there was a Murieta. But it was Ridge's *Life* of that outlaw, as preposterous a fiction as any the Dime Libraries ever invented, that sent this vague bandit on his way to be written into the California histories, sensationalized in magazine pieces and books in several languages, and eventually to be made the subject of a "biography" which was brought to the motion-picture screen. (1955: xi–xii)

This is not Jackson's first reference to the fictional nature of Ridge's book. In 1939, when he published the first of his several studies of Murrieta, included in *Bad Company*, Ridge's work was considered more of a biographical novel than a biography because it is, according to Jackson, "nine-tenths pure invention." Nevertheless, Jackson praises Ridge for creating the historical as well as the mythical character. According to Jackson, "It is not too much to say that

Ridge, in his preposterous little book, actually created both the man, Murieta, and the Murieta legends as these stand today" (1977:15). That "literary" creation was accepted as true, says Jackson, when the historians Bancroft and Hittell included the exploits of Murrieta in their books. Other scholars do not accept Jackson's position. Remi Nadeu, for example, says: "It has been claimed by literary scholars that Ridge created Joaquín 'practically out of whole cloth' [Jackson's phrase]. This is not really the case. It is clear that he used some, though probably not many, of the Joaquin reports in contemporary newspapers" (1974: 118). Others, such as Frank F. Latta, go even further and study Murrieta as a totally historical figure, with ancestors and descendants who still live in the state of Sonora. And in Ireneo Paz's *Vida y aventuras del más célebre bandido sonorense Joaquín Murrieta: Sus grandes proezas en California*, published in Los Angeles in 1919, we find this concluding phrase: "As an interesting detail, we add that presently living in the city of Los Angeles, Cal. are Rosa, Herminia, and Anita Murrieta, children of Antonio, the brother of Joaquín Murrieta" (128).

The Head of Joaquín and the Hand of Jack

To prove the identity of the head that Bill Byrnes—one of the bloodiest Rangers who had accompanied Love—had cut from the body of one of the four dead men, Captain Love, as we said, had to obtain testimonies from people who claimed to have known Murrieta. According to three survivors of the killings, the severed head was not that of Joaquín Murrieta, but of Joaquín Valenzuela. The newspaper *Alta California* stated that the head was not that of Joaquín, the "roving, daring, formidable, murderous, ubiquitous, sharp-shooting and notorious Mr. Joaquín, of whose exploits we have heard so much" (Nadeau, 1974: 98). Nevertheless, Love forced two prisoners taken during the skirmish to confess, under threat of death, that the head belonged to Joaquín Murrieta. They did so, but even that did not save them from death at the hands of the Rangers. *Alta California* did not hesitate to say, however, that the head might have been that of "some *hombre* who had the misfortune to be born a Mexican" (Nadeau, 1974: 99).

Because he found it necessary to defend himself against accusations of deceit, Love began to gather testimonials in the town of

JOAQUIN'S HEAD!!

IS TO BE SEEN

AT KING'S,

CORNER OF HALLECK AND SANSOME STS.,

OPPOSITE THE AMERICAN THEATRE.

ADMISSION $1. _____ au18 tf

The following is one of the many affidavits, certificates, INC., proving the identity of the Head:

STATE OF CALIFORNIA—COUNTY OF SAN FRANCISCO, ss: Ignacio Lisarraga, of Sonora, being duly sworn, says:— That he has seen the alleged head of Joaquin, now in the possession of Messrs. Nuttal and Black, two of Captain Love's Rangers, on exhibition at the Saloon of John King, Sansome street. That deponent was well acquainted with Joaquin Murrieta, and that the head exhibited as above is and was the veritable head of Joaquin Murrieta, the celebrated Bandit. And further says not.

IGNACIO LISARRAGA.

Sworn to before me, this 17th day of August, A. D., 1853.

CHAS. D. CARTER, Notary Public.

From *The San Francisco Herald,* Aug. 20, 1853.

Quantzburg, where he exhibited the head of the supposed Joaquín. All who signed the testimonials, however, referred to a certain Joaquín that they had known or heard about, or were told of his exploits. Others said they had met him in places that, according to the historical records, Joaquín had never been. Three witnesses signed with an "X," without having read the contents of the testimonial. In Stockton, when Love exhibited the head, a priest, Dominic Blaine, said that he had met Joaquín in the Mines Hotel of that city. No one, however, swore to having seen Joaquín commit a crime.

As if to confirm the rapidly developing mythical aspect of Joaquín, Murrieta himself supposedly wrote a letter to *The San Francisco Herald*, in which he said: "I still retain my head, although it is proclaimed through the presses of your city that I was recently captured" (Nadeau, 1974: 103). It was said that Murrieta himself had visited the exhibition of "his head." What must he have felt upon seeing it in a jar? And what were his thoughts about having to pay a dollar to see it? Here myth passes into the realm of the fantastic, of macabre humor.

The myth of the head of Murrieta did not end in 1853. On the contrary, it has gained strength over the years. In 1879 the Nevada City *Transcript* published an item about an alleged sister of Joaquín, who said that the head she had gone to see was not that of her brother. According to an item titled "Joaquín Murieta Lore" that appeared in the *Oakland Tribune* on February 20, 1949 (reprinted in the *Western Folklore* review), Wade Wilson says that in 1905 he saw the supposed head of Joaquín Murieta in San Francisco's Jordan Museum, and he remembers that the features more closely resembled those of an Indian than of a "Castilian." He adds that in 1932 he had spoken to George Barron, head of the De Young Museum in San Francisco's Golden Gate Park, who told him that he had investigated the story of Murrieta and that three responsible persons, from three different regions of southern California, had told him that they had known Murrieta and had seen him after his alleged death. Barron also assured Wade that the head that had been on display at the Jordan Museum was that of an Indian, and bore no resemblance to the real Murrieta. Barron also believed that when Murrieta had "completed his mission" in California and had escaped to Mexico, another man had taken his place and carried on his feats.

Murrieta: Mexican or Chilean?

A controversy has existed for years as to the birthplace of Joaquín Murrieta, with some insisting that he was from Sonora, Mexico, others (among them the poet Pablo Neruda) claiming that he was Chilean. According to his first biographer, John Ridge, Murrieta was Mexican, having been born in the province [*sic*] of Sonora of well-to-do parents, and educated in the secondary schools of Mexico (1955: 8). Murrieta appears as Chilean *only* in Morla's translation and its subsequent reprintings. In 1904 Ireneo Paz retouched that text for the purpose of restoring Murrieta's Mexican nationality, which is why he added to the title the word *sonorense*, a word that does not appear in any of the other Spanish or Chilean editions translated from the French. If we compare the texts of Paz, Hyenne, *La Gaceta* of Santa Barbara of 1881, and the English originals, it is easy to verify the birthplace of Joaquín:

Ridge (1854): Joaquin Murieta was a Mexican, born in the province of Sonora of respectable parents and educated in the schools of Mexico (1955: 8).

Police Gazette (1859): Joaquin was born of respectable parents in Sonora, Mexico, where he received a good education (1969: 2).

Hyenne (1862): Joaquin first saw the light of day in Mexico. His family, originally from Sonora and very honorable in every respect, raised him in his native town, where he received an excellent education (1862: 2).

Morla (1867): Joaquín was born in Santiago. His family, which was from the same city and respectable in every way, gave him a fine education, and he had excellent teachers (Acha, p. 5).

La Gaceta of Santa Barbara (1881): Joaquín was born in Mexico: his family, originally from Sonora and very respectable by all accounts, raised him in his native town, where he received a good education (2.98, 1881, 1).

Paz (1904): Joaquín Murrieta was born in the Republic of Mexico. His family, originally from Sonora, and respectable in every way, raised him in his native town, where he received a good and conscientious education (1953: 5).

The following example confirms that Murrieta was Mexican, not Chilean. Ridge does not mention this adventure; it appears in the first edition of the *Police Gazette,* thus indicating that the Spanish translators used that particular edition.

Police Gazette: Shortly after his arrival at the City of Mexico, he called upon one of his father's old friends, Señor Estudillo, and presented a letter of recommendation. El Señor received him warmly and soon obtained for him a situation as a groom in the magnificent stables of President López de Santa Anna (1969: 2).

Hyenne: Upon his arrival in Mexico he called on Señor Estudillo, an old friend of his father, and presented him with a letter of recommendation that earned him a fine reception from that gentleman. Soon his protector obtained for him a position as a trainer in the fine stables of President López de Santa Anna (1862: 2).

Morla: His father having died by that date [1845], Joaquín went to stay at the home of an old family friend, Señor Estudillo, and the good man gave him an excellent welcome. Soon his protector obtained for him a position as an officer in one of the regimental guards that escorted President Bulnes (Acha, p. 5).

La Gaceta of Santa Barbara: In 1845 Joaquín left his native land and went to seek his fortune in the capital [....] Upon arriving in Mexico City he went to the home of an old friend of his father, a Señor Estudillo. He delivered to him a letter of introduction and was very well received by that gentleman.

Soon his protector secured for him a position as a groom in the stables of President López de Santa Anna (1881: 1).

Paz: In 1845 Joaquín left his home in Sonora to seek his fortune in the capital [....] Upon arriving in Mexico City, he went to the house of an old friend of his father, a Señor Estudillo, and presented him with the letter of introduction, whereupon he was very well received by that gentleman. Soon his protector had obtained for him a position as a groom in the stables of President López de Santa Anna (1953, 5).

It is obvious that Joaquín Murrieta could not have been Chilean and Mexican at the same time, since it is not possible that Señor Estudillo could have placed Joaquín in the service of both Bulnes and Santa Anna at the same time, although both presidents were in power in 1845. The quote and the editions themselves have a common source: the English edition that appeared in *Police Gazette* magazine, by means of which we discovered that the edition published by Ireneo Paz is almost identical to that of *La Gaceta* of 1881. Ireneo Paz published his life of Joaquín in 1904, moved undoubtedly by the desire to reintegrate him into Mexico. Despite his effort, the belief that Murrieta was Chilean has persisted, as we can see in Neruda, who says that:

The ghost of Joaquín Murieta continues to traverse the Californias [....] When he left Valparaiso in search of gold and death, he did not realize that his nationality would become split and his personality scrutinized and reduced to shreds. He did not know that his memory would be decapitated, as he himself was by those who brought him to injustice.

But Joaquín Murieta was Chilean.

I have seen proof. But the purpose of these pages is not to prove facts or shadows. (1966: 10)

Without a doubt, Joaquín Murrieta was Mexican and not Chilean. It was Carlos Morla Vicuña who, with a stroke of the pen, created the myth of Joaquín Murrieta's Chilean nationality.

V

Joaquín Murrieta in Narrative Fiction

Ridge Viewed as Fiction

Despite his short life and his brief career, Joaquín Murrieta has served as a central subject for historians, novelists, playwrights, and poets to produce a fair number of works. Many are the historians from California who mention him, the poets who invoke him, and the novelists who have transformed him into a mythical hero. Although historical information about Murrieta is scarce, the novels in which he appears as the main character are many; and the same can be said of other artistic forms such as drama and poetry.

In narrative fiction, Joaquín first appears in the story "Joaquín the Mountain Robber, or the Bandits of the Sierra Nevada," which the *Pacific Police Gazette* published in May of 1854. In July of that year, the *California Police Gazette*, in its first two issues, included the first four parts of the story "Joaquín, the Mountain Robber! Or, The Guerilla of California."[20] This title suggests that it is the same as the piece in the *Pacific Police Gazette*, a point that cannot be clarified until copies of this newspaper are found. What we do know is that in these early stories about Joaquín, the hero is not identified with the last name of Murrieta. But here the theme of revenge already appears. If the complete name of Joaquín Murrieta is not found in these stories, we do find it a month later in the work by Ridge, although spelled with one *r*.

Much discussion has been generated about the problem of historical veracity in this author's work. For some, it is a simple novel, a fiction created by Ridge. J. H. Jackson, for example, accepts the idea that Murrieta, as a man of flesh and blood, existed but that Ridge's biography is mere fiction:

It is true that in the early years of the gold rush there was a Murieta. But it was Ridge's *Life* of that outlaw, as preposterous a fiction as any the Dime Libraries ever invented, that sent this vague bandit on his way to be written into the California histories. (1955: x–xii)

And later, he adds:

His [Ridge's] narrative, masquerading as fact, was an obvious fiction, abounding in "conversations" between Murieta and his men in secret caves and the like; it was built frankly to the traditional Robin Hood blueprint. (xxvii)

Kent L. Steckmesser shares the same opinion about Murrieta and another popular hero, Billy the Kid. To create his work, he says, Ridge uses a very common trick, pretending to write a true story when what he does is use folkloric elements and imitate the melodramatic episodes of the dime-novel variety, as well as putting elegant discourses into the hero's mouth and the presence of acts and provocations vividly imagined (1912: 77-8). These and other historians consider Ridge as the creator of the legend of Murrieta, not as his biographer. Possible fictitious sources are cited, such as the letters of Dame Shirley (a pseudonym of Louise Amelia Knapp Smith Clappe), in which the flagellation of a "Spanish" person is described and his vow to take revenge. That anonymous Spaniard (a Mexican?), we are told, becomes Joaquín Murrieta. This possible influence was first observed by Franklin Walker (*Frontier,* 1939) and later commented by Jackson (1977: 333), who suspects that Ridge, while writing his novel, read Clappe's letters in the offices of the newspaper *Pioneer,* where they first appeared and where Ridge was a contributor.

Another influence in Ridge's work was the legend of Robin Hood and, according to Carlos Cortés, "of all the Chicano bandits [Murrieta] is the one that most resembles Robin Hood, because just like him, he is the protagonist of a legend that is much better known than the true story" (115). Besides, the most popular novel about Joaquín published in the twentieth century, that of Burns, has precisely this title: *The Robin Hood of El Dorado.* Jackson, as we already saw in the previous paragraph, believed that the work of Ridge "was built frankly to the traditional Robin Hood blueprint, [....] to capture an audience that loves a shocker" (1955: xxvii).

Already in his short preface, the editor of the first edition had said that "Yellow Bird" (the name under which Ridge published the work) "has not thrown his book to the world without care, without authority of his assertions. In general, it will be seen (what is said) is strictly true" (1955: 4). In the 1871 edition, sporadic reference is made to sources of information not cited in the first edition, perhaps in response to those who doubted the veracity of the narrated events. He mentions on page 12, for example, the newspaper *Marysville Herald* of November 13, 1851, to indicate where he obtained the news of the killing of the seven men. On page 21, he adds that the narrated circumstance was told by "a man called Brown, a close friend of Joaquin, with whom the bandit spoke very frankly." At the end of the work, he also reproduces various testimonies that accompanied the head exhibit, vouching for its authenticity. Despite that attempt to document some events, the 1871 edition is closer to fiction than that of 1854.

This second edition was the source that the renowned historian Herbert Howe Bancroft used in his work *California Pastoral*. In the chapter on the Californian bandits, we read: "Allow me to present some of the most famous highway robbers who have, without any doubt, as much right to figure in the pages of history as those who become famous robbing without stepping outside the accepted norms of society" (1888: 644-5). Bancroft presents Murrieta as a historic person without questioning his existence. In order to describe him, he uses Ridge's work without ever mentioning it.

Imitators and Embellishers

The life of Murrieta soon passes from history to literature, either in novels, theater, or poetry. It is of interest to note that in various novels and in Howe's play, the conflict is not between Murrieta and his men and the Anglo-Americans, but rather between Joaquín and the treacherous schemers among Mexicans and Californians.

From the numerous plagiarized texts and translations of Ridge's work by Hyenne, Nombela, Acigar, Morla, Paz, Bell, etc., fictitious novels have been produced, the majority based on the 1859 edition published by the *California Police Gazette*, with the addition here and there of some episodes that have been invented or taken from other novels on popular heroes, according to the concept of the traditional stereotype. Among the most important are those by Henry Llewellyn Williams (1865), Joseph E. Badger (1881), Charles Caldwell Park (1912), Ernest Klette (1928), Walter Noble Burns (1932), Dane Coolidge (1939), and Samuel Anthony Peeples (1949).

The first, *Joaquin, the Claude Duval of California, or the Marauder of the Mines* (1865), was published anonymously but has been attributed to Henry Llewellyn Williams. The conclusion of this work—which Jackson called "a fearfully bad novel" (1955: xl)—is not about Murrieta's death at the hands of Captain Love, but rather tells how he drowned in a lake when the boat he was in sank. That the novel is one more of the many plagiarized texts is confirmed by the following quote regarding Joaquín's birth and education, with its gratuitous commentary:

He was born in Sonora's capital, in Mexico, of a family respectable enough, and sufficiently well off to give him a good education, as education went in that priest-ridden country. (Jackson 1977: 332)

The work, however, is of interest because in it Joaquín is compared to Claude Duval, the famous English outlaw of the seventeenth century. Kent L. Steckmesser, who has compared the legends of Murrieta and Billy the Kid, the famous New Mexican bandit, observes that "English Restoration highwayman Claude Duval is the favorite" (77, n.3).

The two novels by Joseph E. Badger were the most read since they formed part of the "Beadle's New York Dime Library" series. In the first, *Joaquín, the Saddle King* (1881), Murrieta is a young blond Spaniard who supported the Texan revolutionaries and later fought on the side of the North Americans in the war of 1847. Someone asks him why he adores the North Americans and Joaquín answers: *"Ah! porque son muy hombres; he vivido con ellos, he comido, peleado y cabalgado con ellos. Estoy orgulloso de que sean mis amigos. Cómo deseo que fueran mis compatriotas"* (Paredes 1973: 182) (Oh, because they are true men; I have lived with them, eaten with them, fought and ridden with them. I am proud to count on their friendship. How I wish they were my compatriots). Thus Murrieta becomes again, in Badger's novel, a hero of *all* North Americans.

What these novelists of popular works accomplish is to recreate episodes already found in Ridge's work included in the *California Police Gazette* edition. In his second novel, *Joaquin, the Terrible,*[21] for example, Badger narrates the encounter of Joaquín with his brother Carlos, a character who does not appear in Ridge but does figure in the *California Police Gazette* version and its translations. But only this much is said: that *"dos días después de su llegada (a San Francisco), paseándose en uno de esos ricos salones destinados al juego que había en la plaza pública, encontró a su hermano"* (Morla, ed. Acha: 9; Paz 1953:8) (Two days after his arrival [in San Francisco], strolling through one of those rich saloons designated for gambling that are found in the public square, he found his brother.) That encounter, occupying less than three lines, is the source for the first three chapters of Badger's novel in which Carlos wins an enormous amount of money in John Vanderslice's Wheel of Fortune saloon. He develops the scene by giving names to various secondary characters: for example, the gambling table attendant Diego Cagatinta; Carlos's wife, Nicholasa; and a Mexican at the service of Vanderslice whom others call Pepe the Creeper, a repulsive man—described as having the features of a rat—hired by Vanderslice to kill Carlos to steal the gold he has earned while thinking he is Joaquín, given the strong resemblance. At the moment Carlos leaves the gambling saloon, they try to kill him, but thanks to the warning of Nicholasa, Joaquín kills Pepe and saves the life of Carlos without realizing he is his brother. That is how they find each other.

In truth, the first narrators reveal very little about Carlos. They opt to inform us that after the encounter with his brother Carlos, whom he tells of the plundering of his lands, Joaquín leaves his wife, Carmen, at the Mision de Dolores under the care of an old friend of his brother, Mr. Manuel Sepúlveda, and he leaves with his brother to Sacramento, where they purchase horses to go to Hangtown (Placerville). Carlos meets Flores, with whom he goes out for a night stroll. They are detained and hanged, accused of having stolen the horses they had bought. Horrified, Joaquín returns to Sacramento with a desire to take revenge, and that is all.

On the other hand, in Badger the main part of the novel is dedicated to Carlos. In reality, all of it is impregnated with cruel scenes. Secondary plots also appear, for example, the love conflicts between Joaquín and Vanderslice, the latter turning out to be a Mexican named Don Manuel Cumplido, a rival of Joaquín's in Mexico for Carmela's love. The other conflict is betwen Carlos and Raymond Salcedo, a Californio contending for Nicholasa's love. Joaquín's enemies are not the Anglos, but rather Salcedo, who pursues Carlos until he manages to kill him; and Cumplido, who manages to avenge himself against

Introduction   liii

Joaquín by inciting the miners against him. The novel ends when Joaquín discovers the bodies of Carlos and Flores (Flórez) hanging. Horrified, he returns to the mining camp, where he is accused of having stolen his galloping mare and is beaten up. In the last chapter, Carmela is raped by the Anglo miners, and among them we find the Mexican Vanderslice. Before they leave, they set fire to Joaquín's cabin.

Another popular novel in which great empathy is expressed for Joaquín is one written by "Carl Gray" (a pseudonym of Charles Park), titled *A Plaything of the Gods* (1912). In his *The Popular American Novel, 1865–1920* (1980), critic Herbert F. Smith states that Park tries to justify Joaquín's conduct and to show how just his actions were in imposing his own brand of justice. He also observes that although the novel follows the Robin Hood model, it is even closer to the one in which the anti-hero is revered, a technique well illustrated in the film *Bonnie and Clyde* (1980: 95).[22]

Walter Noble Burns

In general, these first novels—known as "dime novels" for their original cost, although the price went up to fifteen cents and then a quarter—"had nothing to do with the real Joaquín and were simply capitalizing on the fame achieved for him by the earliest tales," as Nadeau has observed (1974: 125). The same does not occur with Walter Noble Burns's work, in which new details about Murrieta are introduced, as collected from the newspapers of that time. Nevertheless, these cheap novels (in both price and quality) prepared the terrain for Murrieta's reception by the readers of the twentieth century, whose interest in the "Gold Rush" hero experienced a renaissance in the fall of 1919 with the story of Joaquín published by Frederick R. Bechdolt in the popular magazine *Saturday Evening Post*. "The Bechdolt story in that widely read medium was enough to start a whole new cycle of Murieta writing" (Jackson 1955: xli).

But it was the novel by Walter Noble Burns and the film based on it that renovated the interest in Murrieta. According to Jackson, after the work by Ridge, Burns's novel is the one that contributed most to establish the image of Joaquín in the imagination of the North American. Much of the novel's success is due to its title and to the movie that was filmed in 1939. Jackson, obsessed with the idea that

Murrieta was a product of the myth created by Ridge, points out:

> Murieta was no Robin Hood [....] but Ridge had made him
> one, and most of the writers since had fallen in with the nat-
> ural pattern. [....] And it was the obvious thing for the public
> at large, which obstinately wanted a hero, however imagi-
> nary, to accept this estimate. To combine the idea of Robin
> Hood with the ever-magical words "El Dorado" was an
> admirable stroke of promotional genius. (1977: 37)

These words were published in 1939, in the first study that
Jackson dedicated to Murrieta; in 1955, he attributes the similarity
between Joaquín and Robin Hood, as already seen, to the imitation of
the narratives dedicated to the English bandit.

Burns initiates his work by addressing the different spellings of
Joaquín's last name, while concluding that he accepts the spelling as
"Murrieta" because it was the one used by Ireneo Paz and the translator Bell. Besides, he adds, "this spelling was pronounced correct by
don Antonio Coronel, once mayor of Los Angeles, who knew the
family, and it is the spelling that was used by Rosa, Herminia, and
Anita Murrieta, who formerly lived in Los Angeles and were the
daughters of Joaquín's brother Antonio" (3). After that clarification,
Burns provides a laudatory characterization of Joaquín. Among other
things, he mentions his face "of ivory pallor such as you might have
expected if his hair had been golden and his eyes blue" (5), which
contradicts Latta's later claims that Joaquín had blue eyes. Burns
goes on to say that Joaquín distinguished himself with noble dignity:

> An *hidalgo* touch in his grave dignity, his punctilious politeness
> and his air of proud reserve. A calm thoughtful countenance
> that indicated a cooly poised character. Quiet, frank, unpre-
> tentious. Honest. Known as a square gambler and a square
> man. Not averse to a glass of wine. Considered a good dancer.
> A lively, agreeable companion. Some humor and laughter in
> him. Even tempered . . . .(5)

According to Burns, Joaquín and Rosita Carmel Féliz were born
in Real de Bayareca between Arizpe and Hermosillo. Joaquín elopes
with his girlfriend Rosita to prevent her father, Ramón Féliz, from

marrying her to the landowner don José González. Contrary to what Ridge says, however, they got married the following day in Arizpe, and they came to Los Angeles, where Joaquín worked as a horse breaker in a circus act. After different jobs in various parts of California, they settled in Saw Mill Flat, where they arrived during the spring of 1850. According to the *Corrido de Joaquín Murrieta*, Joaquín had learned English with his brother Carlos, but Burns claims he didn't speak a word of English[23] when he left Sonora. By the time he arrived at the gold mines, Burns says he spoke it like a native, without any accent (9). It is in Saw Mill Flat that five Anglo miners attack Rosita, who dies. Joaquín swears to take revenge and kills all five.

Following Ridge's lead, Burns does not present his work as a novel, but as a biography. Nevertheless, he goes beyond what Ridge had done when he places footnotes to document his words. When he narrates the incident of Rosita's rape, he states that the information was obtained from the miner Frank Wilson, a friend and neighbor of Joaquín and Rosita who had helped them:

> My account of this affair is based on a story supposed to have been told originally by Frank Wilson. It was corroborated with some difference in detail by Lewis Page, a resident of Saw Mill Flat at the time, who told it to his daughter, Miss Marian Page, still living a half mile from the scene of the occurence. (11)

As third-hand information, this fails to convince a well-informed reader of all its claims. At the other extreme, we find declarations and confessions put in Joaquín's mouth, as he narrates his own life:

> I located first near Stockton, but I was constantly annoyed and insulted by my neighbors and was not permitted to live in peace. I went to the placers and was driven from my claims. I went into business and was hated by everyone in whom I trusted. [....] I then said to myself, I will revenge my wrongs and take the law into my own hands. (161)

But it is the life of Robin Hood that shapes the novel by Burns, as we can see in this passage through the voice of the omniscient narrator:

Myth and fable have enveloped him [Murrieta] with the rose
and purple of a mountain seen from far off. The murderous
robber has become a picturesque figure of fantasy, high
souled, as chivalrous as he is brave riding forth merrily with
a plume in his hat and a roguish sparkle in his eye to a thousand madcap adventures. He makes love with the gallantry of
a cavalier. He flings away his gold at the gambling table with
princely abandon. He is a protector of women. He robs the
rich and gives to the poor [....] He is a Robin Hood of El
Dorado. The live oaks, digger pines and manzanita thickets
of the Sierra foothills are his Sherwood Forest; and Three
Fingered Jack, Claudio, González, Valenzuela,—as atrocious
knaves as ever cut a throat—lack only jerkins of Lincoln's
green, long bows and cloth-yard arrows to be the Little John,
Allan-a-Dale, Will Scarlet and Friar Tuck of his roystering
crew. (40)

It was Burns's novel, and the film based on it, that made Murrieta
known to new generations that were already well acquainted with the
myth of Robin Hood.

Adolfo Carrillo

To date, no other novelist has exceeded Burns in the re-creation
of Joaquín's life. Prior to Burns's novel, however, a native of Jalisco,
Adolfo R. Carrillo (1865–1926) had published a short story titled
"Joaquín Murrieta," included in his collection *Cuentos californianos*,
a work published in Los Angeles around 1922. Carrillo, a journalist
exiled during the Porfirio Díaz dictatorship (1876–1910), had lived in
San Francisco during the first years of the century, and he later occupied a position in the Mexican Consulate in Los Angeles.

In his short story about Murrieta, divided into four parts, Carrillo
presents some biographical facts about Joaquín that do not appear
anywhere else, making us suspect that he had knowledge of some
documents unknown today. For example, he tells us that his house
was situated in the hills of Oleta in Amador County, five *leguas*
(leagues, or three and one-half miles) from the Sacramento River, that
his mother Juanita and his sister Dorotea "*de quince abriles*" (fifteen
Aprils or years old) lived with him, that Joaquín was twenty-two

years old, and that he had been a cowboy back in Sonora "*y por eso como jinete no había quien le igualara*" (89)[24] (and that is why as a rider there was no one who could match him). Furthermore, it is not his friend nor wife, but his sister Dorotea who is raped by Anglo miners, led by an ex-prisoner named Pat King, "*escapado de los calabosos de Australia*" (90) (an escapee from the dungeons of Australia). Dorotea dies and Joaquín swears to avenge her.

In the second part, which is very short, Carrillo states that Joaquín, whose "*nombre se evoca hoy mismo con estremecimiento de pavura*" (91) (name is remembered today with terrifying fear), carried out his first act of vengeance by killing Pat King and the miners accompanying him. Joaquín is joined by "*Jaime Rivera, cuatrero y abigeo, conocido con el apodo Three Fingers [sic] Jack, su lugarteniente*" (91) (Jaime Rivera, horse thief and cattle rustler, known by the nickname Three-Fingers Jack, his second lieutenant). According to Latta's informants, there was a José Rivera who was identified as the cook of Joaquín's group, known for being "a(n) honest, hardworking man" (1980: 130). Therefore, he cannot be the same one who appears in Carrillo's short story. Three-Fingered Jack has been identified as Manuel Duarte, and never as Jaime Rivera.

In the third part of the story, Carrillo discusses the organization of Joaquín's gang, among which there are three characters not mentioned by Latta: Mateo Riestra, "alias *El Tecolote, quien jamás dormía*" (alias "The Owl," who never slept); Pedro Morales, *El Chato* (Pug-Nose), "*de ferocidad tigresca y puntería mortífera*" (of a tiger-like fierceness and a deadly aim); and Pablo Escontría, *El Madrugador* (The Early Riser), who "*mataba con su cuchillo de monte sin bajarse del caballo*" (92) (killed with his mountain knife without getting off his horse). The reward offered for Joaquín's head by the governor is greatly exaggerated to fifty thousand dollars. Carrillo describes the encounter of Murrieta and his forty men with Sheriff Medon's posse "*que al frente de doscientos jinetes quiso envolver a Joaquín en su guarida de Fresno*" (93) (who attempted to encircle Joaquín by fronting him with some two hundred riders at his hideout in Fresno). Medon, a character unknown to the biographers of Murrieta, is defeated, and Three-Fingers kills him, cutting off his head.

The fourth and final part of the story recounts the encounter of Joaquín with Lina Solano, his first love, whose kiss seals his death. Here, Carrillo introduces historical figures, such as members of the famous Vallejo family. Joaquín attends a dance to celebrate the wedding of María Vallejo, niece of general Guadalupe Vallejo. There he dances with Lina, falling in love instantly. Jack does not care for Lina because she belongs to a family of renegades, given that her uncle *"fue uno de los que entregaron California a los gringos"* (96) (was one of those who surrendered California to the gringos). Three-Fingers' suspicions come true for Lina betrays Joaquín, who is surprised by three hundred cavalry men on the plains of La Mora in the Sapo ravine. The sheriff, here named Lewis Hamlin, orders Joaquín and Three-Fingers to surrender, but the latter answers: *"Los mexicanos no se rinden! ¡Mueren! y para que no cayera vivo en manos de sus enemigos, le disparó (a Joaquín) un tiro en la frente, dándose él mismo un pistolazo"* (97) (Mexicans do not surrender! They die! and so that he [Joaquín] would not fall into the hands of his enemies, he shot him in the forehead, then shot himself with a pistol). The bodies are taken to Colosa, where Murrieta's head is severed, *"que después fue exhibida en uno de los museos de San Francisco. ¡Todavía se encuentra allí, en urna de dorado vidrio, la inanimada reliquia de época tormentosa y siniestra, símbolo mudo de una rebeldía sanguinariamente sublime!"* (97) (which was later exhibited in one of the museums of San Francisco. It is still there in a golden glass urn, the inanimate relic of a turbulent and sinister period, a silent symbol of a bloody and sublime rebellion!). Without a doubt, Carrillo, having lived in San Francisco, visited the museum where Joaquín's head was exhibited, inspiring him perhaps to write the story.

VI
Joaquín Murrieta in Poetry

The Nineteenth Century: Miller and Stewart

The first poet who gave expression in verse to the life and adventures of Murrieta was Joaquín Miller (1837-1913), the name under which Cincinnatus Hines (or Heine) Miller is known, an author of the "long and very bad poem," according to Jackson (1955: xxvi), titled "Joaquín Murietta." The latter is included in the collection *Joaquín et al* from 1869, published in Oregon, and then later in *Songs of the Sierras* from 1872, a book which appeared in London in 1871. When the poem was published, his friends started calling him "Joaquín," and Miller accepted the name, under which he is known.

Miller was born on a farm near Liberty, Indiana. At the age of fifteen he went with his family to live in Oregon. With a fancy for adventure, he abandoned his family and headed to California in search of gold in the same year Murrieta was killed. It was there that he published a letter in defense of the rights of Mexicans, for whom he always showed sympathy, and which he expressed in 1869 in the poem he devoted to Murrieta, and in his novel *The One Fair Woman,* published in London in 1876, in which the character as an observer is named Murietta.[25] In the long poem by Miller (30 pages), Murrieta gallops and gallops on his horse until he is fatally wounded and goes on to die in a church, where a priest cares for him:

Death has been in at the low church door,
For his foot-prints lie on the stony floor. (Frost 57)

Rather than a character, Miller's Joaquín appears to be a shadow. As Frost says, "The actual Joaquín Murietta is scarcely in the poem, even in the slightest detail" (58). He's right. One of the few direct references to Joaquín is the following, expressed in a context in which the romantic motif of ruins appears:

Some joints of thin and chalk-like bone,
A tall black chimney, all alone
That leans as if upon a crutch,
Alone are left to mark or tell,
Instead of cross or cryptic stone,
Where Joaquín stood and brave men fell.
(*Poems* II, 128)

One of the few physical characteristics mentioned by the poet is a scar on the face, "A brow-cut deep as with a knife," a characteristic referred to by subsequent authors but absent in Ridge.

Some writers have criticized Miller for glorifying Murrieta. According to Nadeau, "Miller went even further than the others in purifying Joaquín as a kind of Galahad." As Joaquín breathes his last, Miller writes: "Here lies a youth whose fair face is/ Still holy from a mother's kiss" (1974: 126). Although the poem, as already pointed out, was criticized for its length and poor composition, there is no doubt that it has had influence on other writers. In Miller's case, however, the influence of his poem has not been as important as the poet's adoption of the name Joaquín, under which he published his works.

In 1882 Marcus A. Stewart published a long narrative poem titled *Rosita: A Californian Tale,* in which the character created by Ridge as Joaquín's female friend appears as the wife of Ramón, one of the many subordinates of Murrieta. Stewart suggests that Murrieta did not die but instead returned to Sonora where he lived long and happily. The place where he goes with his friend Marie is not specified since it is only mentioned that he went to live "in a land/ Far south of California's strand"—that despite the poet's reference to Joaquín's head being exhibited in Jordan's Museum in San Francisco. The idea that Joaquín did not die at the hands of Love's Rangers was common in California. As late as 1980, Latta wrote: "Captain Love held in his hands the head of a *blacked-eyed, shock-black haired California Indian* named Chappo, that later was to be identified as the head of Joaquín, el Famoso" (ll). And, according to the same author, Joaquín had blue eyes: "He was decidedly blond, blue-eyed" (ll). As we know, the idea that Joaquín did not die was common in the oral tradition.

The Twentieth Century: Gonzales and Elizondo

In Chicano literature the presence of Joaquín Murrieta reaches its highest expression in the epic poem *I am Joaquín/ Yo soy Joaquín* (1967),[26] by Rodolfo "Corky" Gonzales. The poetic voice, the "I" of the title, identifies himself with a mythic Joaquín. *"Yo soy Joaquín,"* affirms Luis Valdez with his deep voice in the filmed version of the poem. But, we ask ourselves in this poem: Who is Joaquín? As a historical/mythic character, Joaquín has been transformed in the poem into a symbol of the Chicano—the only Chicano hero at the level of art. Joaquín is a synthesis of various popular heroes and anti-heroes found in Mexican and Chicano cultures. The poetic voice, however, is personified by the figure of Joaquín Murrieta:

I rode the mountains of San Joaquín.
I rode east and north
     as far as the Rocky Mountains,
          and
all men feared the guns of

Joaquín Murrieta.
I killed those men who dared
to steal my mine,
    who raped and killed
    my love
        my wife. (44)

For the first time in literature, Joaquín is identified with mankind—and with the culture of Mexico—as he elevates the Chicano people, exalting their values and merits. He directly identifies himself with six popular Mexican heroes. Three are indigenous and from the period prior to the conquest; another, Juan Diego, also indigenous, pertains to the colonial period. Finally, two are revolutionaries from the twentieth century:

I am Cuauhtémoc,
proud and noble,
    leader of men,
(....)
I am the Maya prince.
I am Nezahualcóyotl,
    great leader of the Chichimecas. (16)
(....)
I am faithful, humble Juan Diego. (42)
(....)
        I am Emiliano Zapata! (34)
        I am . . . the apostle of democracy,
        Francisco Madero. (40)[27]

Another type of identification, at a secondary level, is one made indirectly. When Joaquín states "I am Cuauhtémoc," the hero in the poem embodies the Aztec hero, but in the present. The same does not occur in the case of Hidalgo, where the duality does not disappear. In this case, the poetic voice is transferred to a mythic past and becomes identified with the clergy, the Spanish government, and the military that fought against Hidalgo. What we hear is the voice of a Spaniard, a royalist who is not a supporter of independence. But it is also the voice of Hidalgo, and hence the duality. Hidalgo, as the *criollo* that he was, was also of Spanish lineage:

> I sentenced him
>   who was me.
> I excommunicated him, my blood.
> I drove him from the pulpit to lead
>   a bloody revolution for him and me . . .
>   I killed him. (26)

Hidalgo's head, couched in mythic time, lives and waits for the historical events which the insurgents were unable to accomplish on the battle fields to materialize. Joaquín and all the revolutionaries wait alongside the head:

> His head,
> which is mine and of all those
> who have come this way,
> I placed on that fortress wall
> to wait for independence. (26)

The same occurs with the other heroes who together with Hidalgo fought to create a nation—Morelos, Matamoros, Guerrero—with whom Joaquín also lived and died as a comrade, without embodying them. He does the same with the Niños Héroes in Chapultepec (young cadets who purportedly leaped to their deaths wrapped in the Mexican flag), at whose side he faced death by plunging headlong with the Mexican flag, the ultimate symbol of Mexican identity, serving as their shroud.

In Juárez's case, the identification is at times direct, at other times indirect, with the latter prevailing. Joaquín is not Juárez, although he did participate in his heroic campaigns:

> I fought and died
>   for
>   Don Benito Juárez
> guardian of the Constitution. (30)

Joaquín admires Juárez for not giving away a single inch of Mexican soil, unlike Santa Anna, with whom Joaquín does not identify:

And this giant
    little Zapotec
        gave

not one palm's breath
of his country's land to
kings or monarchs or presidents
of foreign powers. (33)

On one occasion, however, Joaquín is Juárez. But here the use of the imperfect tense rather than the present, as in the case of Cuauhtémoc and Zapata, creates a temporal distance:

I was he
    on dusty roads
        on barren land
as he protected his archives
as Moses did his sacraments. (30)

The identification with Villa is always indirect. There is no doubt that Joaquín is not Villa because he is mentioned as a companion of the military leader, from whom he maintains a certain distance:

I am Joaquín.
I rode with Pancho Villa,
        crude and warm . . . (34)

On the other hand, the identification with Zapata, who reclaims his land, is absolute. After a close identification with him, Joaquín yields his voice to this hero from the south:

I am Emiliano Zapata.
    "This land,
        this earth
            is
                OURS." (34)

The direct or indirect identification with the popular Mexican heroes represents only one of the two faces of Joaquín. Anti-heroes such as Hernán Cortés, Porfirio Díaz, and Victoriano Huerta provide the other face. The identification with Hernán Cortés is not with the conquerer himself, but instead with his sword, which symbolizes destruction of the indigenous cultures:

> I am the sword and flame of Cortés
> the despot. (16)

To counteract the shock of identification with the conquerer, immediately afterward there appears the symbol that unites the Aztecs who were conquered by Cortés with present-day Mexicans:

> And
> I am the eagle and serpent of
> the Aztec civilization. (16)

While most prominent in the poem, the identification of Joaquín with Mexican heroes, anti-heroes, and symbols is not the only one. Not surprisingly, he also identifies himself with popular Chicano heroes such as Elfego Baca and the Brothers Espinoza from the San Luis Valley, who establish a parallel with the Mexican heroes. But the central identification that structures the entire poem is naturally with Joaquín Murrieta:

> Hidalgo! Zapata!
> Murrieta! Espinozas! (48)

The syncretic cultural images give form to another type of identity—the one that involves the gods, the people, the national symbols, and nature. Here the antithetical images and concepts multiply. Joaquín is Mayan prince but also Christ; he is pagan but also Christian; he is the sword of Cortés but also the Aztec eagle and serpent; he is tyrant but also slave; he is the Virgin of Guadalupe but also Tonantzin; he is a rural policeman but also a revolutionary; he is Indian but also Spaniard; he is *mestizo* but also *criollo*; he is soldier but also *soldadera* (soldier woman); he is a farmworker but also a boss. But he is, above all, the Chicano people—a product of racial, social, and cultural synthesis. The Chicano is a descendant of racial admixture; he is the representative of the true cosmic race of which

Vasconcelos speaks. He is also the heir of the rich Mexican culture that the Chicano has managed to sustain despite his precarious economic situation:

> My fathers
> have lost the economic battle
> and won
> the struggle of cultural survival. (6)

Nonetheless, it is evident that Joaquín finds his identity, more than anything else, in the indigenous peoples, the farmworker, and the poor:

> I am the mountain Indian,
>   superior over all. (39)
> Here I stand
> poor in money,
> arrogant in pride
> (....)
> My knees are caked with mud.
> My hands calloused from the hoe. (64-6)

After this retrospective overview of history, the poetic voice returns to the present to reaffirm its identity with the long-suffering Chicano people, be they in jails or on battlefields in France, Korea, or Vietnam. Although poor, he finds pride, bravery, and faith in the future:

> The odds are great
> but my spirit is strong,
>   my faith unbreakable . . . .(100)

Joaquín, then, collects all the aspects of Indo-Hispanic culture and concludes by identifying himself with his people: the Mexicans, the Spanish, the Latino, the Hispanic, and the Chicano: all forming one culture out of eclectic features. Joaquín is Yaqui, Tarahumara, Chamula, Zapotec, mestizo, Spanish, Mexican, Latino, Hispanic, Chicano,

> or whatever I call myself,

I look the same
I feel the same
        I cry
and
sing the same. (98)

With this poem, Gonzales defined Chicano culture as a living continuation of Mexican culture and the Chicano as its racial descendant. Gonzales's poem changed the ideology of the Mexican American, transforming him into a Chicano with a new vision of social and philosophical position.

I am the masses of my people and
I refuse to be absorbed.
        I am Joaquín. (100)

Another Chicano poet who has concerned himself with Murrieta is Sergio Elizondo. In his *Perros y antiperros; una épica chicana* (1972), he devotes two poems to him: *"Murrieta en la loma"* (Murrieta on the Hill) and *"Murrieta, dos"* (Murrieta, Two). After a brief introduction, in which the poetic voice describes a muleteer equipped with a rope, a hat, and *huaraches* passing over a hill, the hero himself begins to speak, explaining that he is carrying a load to Santa Barbara. He describes himself:

Soy callado, hombre de paz
pero en la cintura me fajo
un cuchillo cebollero . . . (1972: 62)

[I am a quiet man of peace
but on my belt I strap
an onion-cutting knife . . . .]

Soon, however, he is transformed into a mythic person:

Hace cien años que vivo,
Califas es mi casa
y en México está mi Tata. (1972: 62)

[I have lived for a hundred years,
Califas (California) is my home
and my Tata (father) is in Mexico]

As a good Catholic, he is protected by Baby Jesus:

En mi católica fe
vivo yo y mi amor;
el Santo Niño me guacha
día y noche;
por el camino real . . . (1972: 62)

[In my Catholic faith
live both my love and I;
the Holy Child watches over me
day and night
Along the royal road . . .]

In *"Murrieta, dos"* the voice of Murrieta continues to portray itself, except that he is now an orphan or "son of Malinche" who does not come from Mexico. He is a character lost in time and space:

No vengo de ninguna parte,
a ninguna parte voy . . .
(1972: 65)

[I come from nowhere,
nowhere do I go . . .]

Without a personality, he is a solitary man; he is a nobody, and he is alone. Only nature accompanies him. Furthermore, he is immaterial. On the other hand, he tells us that he is:

De nada estoy hecho, por eso soy. (1972: 64)
(Of nothingness I am made, therefore I am.)

At the end of the poem, however, he identifies with Joaquín—or, rather, other people identify him with Joaquín:

¿Qué soy?
Dicen que soy Joaquín—
Murrieta me llaman.
(1972: 64)

[What am I?
They say I am Joaquín—
Murrieta they call me.]

Thus, Joaquín becomes dust, a shadow, and nothingness.

VII
Joaquín Murrieta in Theater and Film

In Nineteenth-Century Theater

In 1858, a year before the pirated version of Ridge's work appeared in the *California Police Gazette*, Charles E. B. Howe published in San Francisco a dramatic work in five acts, *Joaquín Murieta de Castillo, the Celebrated California Bandit.*[28] In this first dramatization of the life of Joaquín Murrieta, a few small changes are introduced. For example, Murrieta's lover, Rosita, is called Belloro, a name created by two words, the English "bell" and the Spanish "*oro*" (gold), thus producing a bilingual image of a "golden bell." Howe also added a few characters, among them Ignacious, who briefly appears in the first act,[29] and Juan Gonzalles (*sic*), Belloro's brother. According to Jackson, Howe's play greatly popularized the anecdote in which Murrieta, upon reading the government proclamation offerring to pay five thousand dollars to anyone who delivers him dead or alive, writes at the bottom of the text: "I'll pay ten thousand. Joaquín." While Howe gave this story currency, the anecdote is already in Ridge (1955: 68). Notable in the play is the presence of García (Three-Fingers), in this case as Joaquín's enemy who is in love with Belloro. Here, as in Badger's work, Murrieta's enemies are not Anglos but Mexicans.

In his "New Light on Joaquín Murrieta" (1970), Dr. Raymund F. Wood tells us that Professor Ray P. Reynolds found the unpublished diary "A Reconnaissance from Guaymas, Sonora, Via Babispe to

Franklin, Texas," written in 1872 by Albert Kimsey Owen, founder of the Colonia Topolobampo in northern Sinaloa. Owen recounts that on November, 3, 1872, the "melodrama" *Joaquín Murrieta* was represented in Hermosillo, Sonora, by the actor Don Gabutti.[30] Owen gives a detailed description of the work, which is transcribed by Dr. Wood. It is Owen's opinion that Murrieta was from the district of Hermosillo and that his two brothers were still living in Buena Vista in 1872, on the banks of the Río Yaqui. According to Owen, Gabutti in his tragedy presents Joaquín as "a hero of the first water." At the end of the play, he states, the only person left alive is the prompter. Here he adds an interesting note regarding the audience's reception of the tragedy. Owen comments:

> It meets the applause of the Mexicans and it is said to excite them to such frenzy that the Americans and even other foreigners are afraid of venturing in the building, and for days after the performance *gringos* are likely to be insulted on the streets of Hermosillo. (Wood, "New Light" 58-9)

There is no information available regarding the sources used by Gabutti to write about Murrieta's deeds. Wood speculates that Gabutti knew Howe's play, a theory impossible to prove. Nor is there any biographical data on Gabutti. Not a single copy of the play is known to exist.

Twentieth-Century Theater: The Chilean Perspective

The interest of the Chilean playwright Antonio Acevedo Hernández, author of *Joaquín Murieta: Drama en seis actos* (Joaquín Murieta: Drama in six acts), published in Santiago in 1936 by the magazine *Excélsior*, a doubtless result from the popular translation of Ridge's work by Carlos Morla. Acevedo Hernández (1886–1962) belonged to a group of playwrights that renewed the Chilean theater. His works are uniformly somber and pessimistic, whether of a rural nature (*Árbol viejo,* or Old Tree; 1930) or set in the urban slums (*Almas perdidas,* or Lost Souls; 1917). He also wrote a novel, *Pedro Urdemalas* (1947).

In Acevedo Hernández's drama, Murrieta is, of course, Chilean. In the anonymous introduction, titled "*Joaquín Murieta, el buscador de oro y de justicia*" (Joaquín Murieta, the seeker of gold and justice), one can observe that Murrieta has again become current as a result of the movie that appeared the same year as Acevedo Hernández's play. To the anonymous writer of the prologue, the moviemaker has restored the reputation of the famous highwayman from California by projecting his figure on the screen. He insists, naturally, on the Chilean origins of Joaquín: "Murieta, an audacious and unwavering Chilean, moved to Mexico, which explains why many think he was Aztec" (1936: 1). The only novelty in this short prologue is the note about Hyenne, who is said to be a citizen of the United States. Also of interest is the quote credited to the Peruvian poet José Santos Chocano, who characterized Pancho Villa as a "divine outlaw," an epithet that is applied to Murrieta. According to the drama by Acevedo Hernández, Murrieta is "a kind of anti-imperialist outlaw comparable to Pancho Villa and all who raised their rifles to defend [against] the greed of the north" (2).

The play in six acts follows closely Joaquín's deeds, according to Morla's translation. Nevertheless, he introduces some new characters, such as Fred, a North American who criticizes Chileans for "all being bandits . . . . restless and gamblers" (1936: 5). Joaquín defends Chile as a "country of free men" (5). Other variants are also introduced in the biography of Joaquín, who after being whipped by the Anglo miners, affirms: "That day I was also whipped, I, who in my country had been an officer in an army that has never been defeated . . . ." (1936: 6). This insult makes him hate the Anglos, about whom he says: "I have seen them and I have learned to despise them with all of my soul, to hate them with all my might. You treat us as slaves, so we must defend ourselves" (1936: 6).

In the fifth act, a new character, Mariquita, an aggressive Chilean woman, is introduced, and Joaquín appears dressed as a Chilean *huaso* (cowboy). Three-Fingers is also Chilean and knows how to sing, as we can see in this quatrain:

> *Mi pueblo es el más valiente*
> *Chile es la tierra más bella*
> *y una esplendorosa estrella*
> *fulgura sobre su frente.* (1936: 19)

[My people are the bravest,

Chile is the most beautiful land
with a shining star
radiating over its forehead.]

An exotic note is found in the presence of an Italian character, Don Antonio, who states: "I am a bandit. I was with Carlotti in the Abruzzos." He also adds: "Gentlemen, I have always been a *brigantti* (bandit), a good *brigantti,* Carlotti's companion, an admirer of Luis Candelas, of the children of Ecija and of Joaquín" (1936: 20, 21).

The last act takes place on the U.S.-Mexico border where Joaquín dies—instead of in Arroyo Cantova, as in the historical version. Harry Love appears with another character, Tomás Gatica, who knows Murrieta and betrays him. Love's people kill Joaquín and Three-Fingers. The drama ends with these words: "He was not a bandit, he was a superior man!"

One of Acevedo Hernández's objectives was to remind the Latin American countries of Simón Bolívar's idea that they have to unite to defend their rights. Joaquín says that he is not a bandit but a great member of the parliament:

Joaquín: Esto es lo que tiene que hacer la América Española si no quiere perderse: unirse, ir hacia Bolívar, formar una sola y gran potencia que contrarreste la acción de todos los dominadores irrazonados. (1936: 23)

Joaquín: This is what Spanish America has to do if it does not want to lose: unite, move towards Bolívar, and form a single great power to counteract the actions of all the unreasonable, dominating conquerers. (1936: 23)

Pablo Neruda is the most important writer who has devoted a literary work to Joaquín Murrieta. In 1966, the Santiago, Chile, publishing house Zig-Zag published Neruda's cantata in verse *Fulgor y muerte de Joaquín Murieta* (Splendor and Death of Joaquín Murieta). The work was presented by the Instituto de Teatro of the Universidad de Chile on October 14 of the following year in the Teatro Antonio Varas of Santiago, under the direction of Pedro Orthous, with the music by Sergio Ortega. Two texts of the cantata exist, one from Zig-Zag, and the libretto published by Editorial

Losada in the second volume of the *Obras completas de Pablo Neruda* (1968; Complete Works of Pablo Neruda).

According to Manuel Rojas, Neruda's work was presented in Mexico City in December 1976: "The U.C.C.T. (Union of Theater Critics and Commentators) of Mexico City unanimously gave *Fulgor y muerte de Joaquín Murieta* its award as the 'Best New Theater Work' by Pablo Neruda, and directed by Merino Lanzilotti" (1992: 78).

In his foreword, Neruda tells us he has proof that Joaquín Murrieta was Chilean, but that his objective is not to prove the hero's nationality, but rather to keep his name alive, because "they want to erase him from the map" (1966: 11). He rejects the theory of the "seven" (*sic*) Joaquíns, which he considers "another way to dissolve the rebel" (1966: 11). By studying this rebel, he was able to participate vicariously in his person, and that is why he gives a "testimony of the brilliance of that life and of the existence of that death" (1966: 11).

In his preface, Neruda explains that his work is "tragic but it is also written partly in jest. It is trying to be a melodrama, an opera, and a pantomime" (1966: 15). He goes on to provide the director with brief instructions in which he suggests, among other things: "If it is possible, include a film crew." The major interest if the 1966 edition lies in the illustrations from the period of the "gold rush" and from the covers of various books dedicated to Murrieta.

The action of the cantata is developed in six scenes. The first dramatizes the departure of Murrieta from Quillota to the port of Valparaíso, where Three-Fingers awaits him. This is in the year 1850. The two future bandits set out on their trip to California, accompanied by the customs employee Reyes and Teresa. According to Neruda's instructions to the director, in the second scene "a sailboat should appear continuously [. . . .] during the trip of the schooner" (1966: 15). During the voyage, "Joaquín, a tamer of horses, took Teresa, a peasant woman, as his wife" (1973: 36). The third scene takes place in San Francisco in the tavern "El Fandango," where the confrontation begins between Chilean, Mexican, Peruvian, and Argentine miners and the Rangers. When asked "And how is it going for those from Mexico?" an anonymous miner answers: "We barely earn enough for one *enchilada*" (1973: 62). They all request *chicha* (an alcoholic beverage made from fermented corn), but a Ranger tells them: "You are now in California. There is no *chicha* here. In

California you must have whisky" (1973: 64).[31] Humor, at the expense
of Chileans, emerges when they ask for whisky with "water-closet."
Immediately afterwards, the first tragic note is introduced in the form
of the death of twenty miners, seventeen Chileans, and three
Mexicans. A Chilean asks, "And why did they kill them?" The
Mexicans accompanying them affirm, "It is because we are not fair-
skinned!" (1973: 70). The second tragic note is the death of Teresa in
the fourth scene foretold by the poetic voice:

> *Salió de la sombra Joaquín Murieta sin ver que una rosa de
> sangre tenía en un seno su amada y yacía en la tierra extran-
> jera su amor destrozado.*
>
> *Pero al tropezar en su cuerpo tembló aquel soldado y besan-
> do su cuerpo caído, cerrando los ojos de aquella que fue su
> rosal y su estrella, juró estremecido matar y morir persi-
> guiendo al injusto, protegiendo al caído.* (1973: 110, 112)

> [Joaquín Murieta came out of the shadows without seeing his
> beloved holding a rose of blood on her bosom, his shattered
> love resting in peace in a foreign land.
>
> But upon stumbling across her body, that soldier trembled,
> kissing her fallen body, closing the eyes of she who had been
> his rosebush and his shining star, shaking, he swore to kill
> and die hounding the source of injustice while protecting the
> downtrodden.]

The revenge by General Murrieta—as the Indian Rosendo
Juárez[32] calls him—is dramatized in the subsequent scene, titled "El
fulgor de Joaquín" (The Brilliance of Joaquín). This fifth scene opens
with a *canción masculina* (masculine song), a song similar to the
Corrido de Joaquín Murrieta:

> *Con el poncho embravecido
> y el corazón destrozado,
> galopa nuestro bandido
> matando gringos malvados.* (1973: 120)

[With his enraged poncho
and his heart shattered,
our bandit gallops
killing villainous gringos.]

The female chorus sings a lament for the death of Joaquín, which includes the following verses:

Con una rosa en la mano
ha muerto Joaquín Murieta
. . . .
para que no resucite,
le cortaron la cabeza
al muerto, en el cementerio. (1973: 156)

[Joaquín Murieta has died
with a rose in his hand
. . . .
to prevent his resurrection,
they cut off the dead man's
head at the cemetery.]

His head, according to the Neruda's cantata, was exhibited in a cage and not in a jar in alcohol. The shack owner announces the exhibition, shouting for all to hear, while resorting to a bilingual discourse similar to the one used today by Chicano poets:

Entrad here a my *barraca*   [Enter here in my shack]
for only twenty cents.
Here is Joaquín Murieta,
aquí está el tigre encerrado.   [here is the tiger locked up.]
(1973: 158)

The people pay him homage and propose to steal "the captain's head [. . .] and even though he died without confession, he ought to be buried according to his religion" (1973: 166). Joaquín's head speaks at the cemetery, and says, among other things:

¿Pero cómo sabrán los venideros,
entre la niebla, la verdad desnuda?

De aquí a cien años, pido, compañeros
que cante para mí Pablo Neruda. (1973: 172)

[But how will the newcomers know,
amidst the fog, the naked truth?
One hundred years from now, I ask, fellow companions,
that Pablo Neruda sing for me.]

The cantata ends with the poet's voice, which states:

Alabado sea, que sea alabado tu nombre, Murieta.
[Blessed be, blessed be thy name, Murieta.]

This work by Neruda has brought the Californian hero prestige beyond the American border. His influence can be found in the work *"Estrella y muerte de Joaquín Murieta"* (Star and Death of Joaquín Murieta), a libretto by Pável Grushkó for the rock-opera by Alexie Ribnikov, a part of which was published in the journal *Plural*, preceded by an interview by Carlos Espinosa Domínguez of Grushkó, titled *"De la crónica de bandidos al tema revolucionario actual"* (From the Chronicle of Bandits to a Contemporary Revolutionary Topic).[33]

The Chileans Acevedo Hernández and Pablo Neruda are not the only playwrights who have represented the figure of Joaquín Murieta on stage, although they are the ones of the greatest renown. Other theatrical works exist but are difficult to locate—for example, that of Brígido Caro, titled "Joaquín Murrieta," presented in Los Angeles during 1930s.[34] In 1989 the Universidad Autónoma de Ciudad Juárez published in its "Cuadernos Universitarios" the play *Joaquín Murrieta, obra de teatro* (Joaquín Murrieta, a Work of Theater), by Oscar Monroy Rivera. More recently, Manuel Rojas, a scholar of Murieta, presented a theatrical work in Ciudad Juárez about the life of "El Patrio" (Native Son).

In Film

The first film about Murrieta, *The Robin Hood of El Dorado*, appeared in 1936, based on the eponymous 1932 novel by Walter Noble Burns. It was directed by William Wellman, and starred Warner Baxter as Murrieta. Other players included Ann Loring,

Margo, Bruce Cabot, and J. Carrol Naish. This film helped to establish the mythical figure of Murrieta in the minds of not only U.S. moviegoers but the Mexican people as well. Even intellectuals such as José Vasconcelos discussed it.

Vasconcelos's *Breve historia de México* (Brief History of Mexico) doesn't take its information from the dime novels, or even from *The Life and Adventures of Joaquín Murrieta* by John Rollin Ridge ("Yellow Bird")—but rather from the film. Vasconcelos accepts without question the film version of the life of Murrieta and describes his adventures step by step, interweaving commentaries about Mexican politics.

> *Pero aun con (la presencia de Murrieta) los bandidos andan sin programa. Parecen cabecillas mexicanos que gritan frases de tal o cual plan, pero no entienden lo que dicen ni tienen capacidad para llevarlo adelante, si el azar les depara el triunfo.* (1944: 396)

[But even with (Murrieta's presence) the bandits operate without a plan. They seem to be Mexican ringleaders who blare out phrases of this or that idea, but don't understand what they say, nor do they have the capacity to carry it out if fate grants them a victory.]

Although Vasconcelos claims the film is "an extraordinarily significant fiction," he adds almost immediately that Murrieta is a "historical character more or less modified in the film version, but eminently representative" (1944: 385). He continues to describe the main scenes of the film thus:

> *A Murrieta le roban la tierra, le violan a la mujer recién casada. Un amigo yankee generoso se ofrece a patrocinar sus reclamaciones. [...] Poco después, Murrieta es azotado por un grupo de linchadores. Un bandido lo recoge y, por fin, lo hace jefe del pequeño grupo que aterroriza la comarca ....*

> *Una noche, Murrieta asalta y comienza a robar, ya no de los norteamericanos, sino al grupo de hacendados mexicanos que celebraba una junta para ver el modo de defender sus tierras*

de los negociantes yanquees que las usurpan. (1944: 385-6)

[Murrieta's land is stolen from him, his newly wed wife is raped. A generous Yankee friend offers to sponsor his claims. [....] Shortly thereafter, Murrieta is whipped by a lynch mob. A fellow bandit helps him and at the end he is made chief of the small group which terrorizes the town . . . .

One night Murrieta strikes again and initiates a stealing spree, no longer from the North Americans but from a small group of Mexican landowners, who hold a meeting to find a way to defend their lands from the Yankee businessmen who usurp them.]

Other American films on the life and adventures of Joaquín Murrieta are those starring Valentín de Vargas (*Firebrand,* 1962) and Jeffrey Huntera blue-eyed Murrieta in accordance with Latta's version titled simply *Murieta* (1965). The latter film was released in England, where the name Murrieta remains unknown, under the title *Vendetta.* In 1971 Mexican actor Ricardo Montalbán played Joaquín in a film made for television called *The Desperate Mission.* According to David Maciel, there are three or four Mexican films about the life of Murrieta. And they will continue to be produced, given the great interest in the Californian hero.

VIII
The *corrido* of Joaquín Murrieta

As the greatest popular hero of the Chicano in California, Joaquín Murrieta could not go unnoticed in the *corrido.* Given the reputation he has always enjoyed, however, the dearth of versions of the *Corrido de Joaquín Murrieta* is surprising as is the absence of a single study on this *corrido.*[35] By contrast, Gregorio Cortez, the popular Texan hero, has been immortalized by Américo Paredes in his well-known book *With His Pistol in His Hand.* Perhaps this is due to critics not regarding the song dedicated to Murrieta as a *true corrido.* By 1957 Professor Merle E. Simmons, in his book on the Mexican *corrido,* makes a passing observation regarding the fragments that Vicente S. Acosta collected in Arizona in 1947 and 1948:

Mention should also be made of two fragments of a *Corrido de Joaquín Murietta* (*sic*) (Acosta 46), which deal with an outlaw who terrorized the gold-rush settlements of California during the 1850s. Though one of the fragments is twenty-six lines long, it is written on a single note of boastfulness expressed by Murietta in the first person. Hence, though it is an interesting composition and important as a link in the history of the *corrido,* it does not show the close relationship with the modern *corrido* which we detect in *Leandro Rivera.* (1969: 487-8)[36]

In his *Mexican Ballads, Chicano Poems,* José Limón notes that the incomplete versions of the "song" of Joaquín Murrieta have unknown origins and that they are not true *corridos* (1992: 117). The only versions (simple fragments) that he mentions are the ones collected by Acosta, of which Limón says: "Murrieta's exploits in defense of his right and honor passed into legendry and balladry. We have only incomplete versions of the latter, and they are technically not true ballads but rather descriptive songs such as this one" (1992: 117). Here he includes his own translation of the second fragment (1948), and he continues to point out: "The origins of this song are unknown"; and adds: "Acosta collected this *corrido*-like song in southern Arizona in May 1948, but he provides no information concerning the song's origins or likely compositional history" (1992: 199).

The versions cited by Limón, found in Acosta's master's thesis, are two short fragments from the *Corrido de Joaquín Murrieta,* recorded in Los Angeles during the winter of 1934 by the Sánchez and Linares Brothers, and collected by Chris Strachwitz in the collection *Texas-Mexican Border Music,* volumes 2 and 3, *Corridos,* Parts 1 and 2 (1974), with the text, annotations, notes, and translation into English by Philip Sonnichsen *et al.* This version, the most complete known, consists of seventy-two verses divided into twelve sextains.

Corrido of Joaquín Murrieta

1
Yo no soy americano
pero comprendo el inglés.
Yo lo aprendí con mi hermano
al derecho y al revés.
A cualquier americano
lo hago temblar a mis pies.

1
I am not Anglo
but English I understand.
I learned it with my brother
forwards and backwards.
I make any Anglo
tremble at my feet.

2
Cuando apenas era un niño
huérfano a mí me dejaron.
Nadie me hizo ni un cariño,
a mi hermano lo mataron,
Y a mi esposa Carmelita,
cobardes la asesinaron.

2
When I was barely a child
I was left an orphan.
No one gave me a bit of affection,
killing my brother,
and some cowards
killed my wife Carmelita.

3
Yo me vine de Hermosillo
en busca de oro y riqueza.
Al indio pobre y sencillo
lo defendí con fiereza.
Y a buen precio los sherifes
pagaban por mi cabeza.

3
I came from Hermosillo
in search of gold and riches.
I defended the poor and simple
Indian with fierceness.
And the sheriffs put a good price
on my head.

4
A los ricos avarientos,
yo les quité su dinero.
Con los humildes y pobres
yo me quité mi sombrero.
Ay, que leyes tan injustas
fue llamarme bandolero.

4
From the greedy rich,
I took away their money.
With the humble and poor,
I took off my hat.
Oh, what unjust laws
to label me an outlaw.

5

A Murrieta no le gusta
lo que hace no es desmentir.
Vengo a vengar a mi esposa,
yo lo vuelvo a repetir,
Carmelita tan hermosa,
cómo la hicieron sufrir.

6

Por cantinas me metí,
castigando americanos.
"Tú serás el capitán
que mataste a mi hermano.
Lo agarraste indefenso,
orgulloso americano."

7

Mi carrera comenzó
por una escena terrible.
Cuando llegué a setecientos
ya mi nombre era temible.
Cuando llegué a mil doscientos
ya mi nombre era terrible.

8

Yo soy aquel que domina
hasta leones africanos.
Por eso salgo al camino
a matar americanos.
Ya no es otro mi destino.
¡Pon cuidado, parroquianos!

9

Las pistolas y las dagas
son juguetes para mí.
Balazos y puñaladas,
carcajadas para mí.
Ahora con medios cortados
ya se asustan por aquí.

5

Murrieta doesn't like
to be falsely accused.
I come to avenge my wife,
and I say again,
how they made my lovely Carmelita
suffer so much.

6

I entered many a saloon,
punishing Anglos.
"You must be the captain
who killed my brother.
You found him unarmed,
proud Anglo."

7

My career started
from a troubling circumstance.
When I reached seven hundred
  [deaths]
my name then was feared.
When I got to twelve hundred
my name terrified others.

8

I am the one who dominates
even African lions.
That's why I set out
to kill Anglos.
My destiny is no other.
Beware, countrymen!

9

Pistols and daggers
are mere toys for me.
Bullet and stab wounds,
hearty laughter for me.
Now with their means cut off
here they scatter in fear.

10
No soy chileno ni extraño
en este suelo que piso.
De México es California,
porque Dios así lo quiso
Y en mi sarape cosida
traigo mi fe de bautismo.

10
I'm neither Chilean nor a foreigner
to this land I tread.
California belongs to Mexico
because God wished it so.
And in my stitched sarape
I carry my baptismal certificate.

11
Qué bonito es California
con sus calles alineadas,
donde paseaba Murrieta
con su tropa bien formada,
con su pistola repleta,
y su montura plateada.

11
How beautiful California is
with its well-organized streets,
where Murrieta passed by
with his well-trained troops,
with his pistol loaded
and his silver-plated saddle.

12
Me he paseado en California
por el año de cincuenta,
con mi montura plateada,
y mi pistola repleta,
Yo soy ese mexicano
de nombre Joaquín Murrieta.

12
I have traveled in California
around the year '50 [1850]
with my silver-plated saddle
and my pistol loaded.
I am that Mexican
known as Joaquín Murrieta.
(1974)

The first of the two versions that Acosta cites, which has only two *sextillas* (six-verse stanzas), does not have in its title *Corrido de Joaquín Murrieta,* or *Song of Joaquín Murrieta*, but rather *Verses of Joaquín Murrieta*. They were compiled in Sásabe, Arizona, where they were recited by Isabel Urías in May 1947. Acosta does give the second version, which is a bit more complete (twenty-six verses), the title of *corrido*: *Corrido de Joaquín Murrieta*. Recited, sung and recorded by Lalo Guerrero, Tucson, Arizona, May 1948.

Although Limón considers that the content of Murrieta's *corrido* adheres to the traditional *corridos*, he finds its form irregular. He notes: "In meter, rhyme, and verse patterns, it is not a *corrido*, yet it does present the traditional heroic figure, pistol in hand, opposing the forces of oppression, the *americanos*" (1992: 117). Hence, he feels compelled to call the verses he translates, as we saw in the translated fragment on the first page, *descriptive songs* or simply *song*: "Whereas the *corridista* inserts occasional lines of boasting dialogue within a larger narrative of events, this song is spoken entirely by the figure of Joaquín Murrieta" (1992: 118). The *corridos* composed in stanzas of six lines are not rare, neither in Mexico nor on the Mexico-United States border, as we can observe in the cited examples by Daniel Castañeda in his *El corrido mexicano: Su técnica literaria y musical* (1943), in which he classifies the *corrido* by stanzas. Vicente T. Mendoza, in *El romance español y el corrido mexicano: Estudio comparativo* (1939), states: "The literary form of the *corrido* is always in stanzas, whether it be four verses, *six,* or eight. The stanzas of four octosyllabic verses are most common" (1939: 1932; my emphasis).

Corridos of six lines also exist on the border region, especially among those of recent origin, like those dealing with borderland topics. As examples we will mention the ones titled *El contrabando de Nogales*, the *Corrido de los mojados,* and *Pancha la contrabandista.* The first is a typical Chicano *corrido*:

> *Llegando casi a Tucsón*
> *los para el Highway Patrol*
> *Y se adelantó a decirle:*
> *Yo no conozco al señor;*
> *no sé si trae papeles,*
> *porque le di un aventón.*
> (Jaramillo, 1980: 173)

> [Almost arriving to Tucson
> and stopped by the Highway Patrol,
> he rushed forward to say:
> "I don't know that man;
> I don't know if he has papers,
> because I gave him a ride.]

In the second one the voice is that of an undocumented person:

> *Porque somos los mojados*
> *siempre nos busca la ley,*

porque somos ilegales
y no hablamos el inglés;
el gringo terco a sacarnos
nosotros a volver.
Si unos saca(n) por Laredo
Por Mexicali entran diez,
si otro sacan por Tijuana
por Nogales entran seis;
ai nomás saquen la cuenta,
cuantos entramos al mes.
(*El Foro* Sept. 1980: 6)

[The authorities always look for us
for being "wetbacks,"
because we're illegal
and don't speak English;
as the stubborn *gringo* throws us out
and we keep coming back.
If they throw some out through Laredo,
ten more enter through Mexicali,
if another is kicked out through Tijuana,
six more enter through Nogales;
so, go ahead and figure it out,
how many of us return each month.]

In the third one the character is a young woman, nineteen years old, as brave as any male hero:

Este es el corrido
de Pancha Machete
aquella mujer valiente,
que como era buena
también era mala
valor tenía suficiente.
(Anonymous; copy in my archive)

[This is the corrido
about Pancha Machete

that brave woman,
who was as good
as she was bad,
for courage she had plenty.]

Although it is true that in the *corridos* of the Mexican Revolution
the quatrain is the stanza that predominates, the sextain does appear
now and then. As an example, we can refer to the sextain of the
Zapatista *corrido*, "El Coyote," by Lalo Guerrero, compiled by
Celedonio Serrano Martínez. María Herrera-Sobek reproduces it in
The Mexican Corrido: A Feminist Analysis:

La Güera y su gente
improvisa(n) sus trincheras,
aunque es mujer, tiene el grado
de coronel, y sus trenzas
no han impedido que ostente
con orgullo sus estrellas.
(1993: 98)

[The blondie and her followers
improvise their trenches.
Although a woman, she has the rank
of a colonel, and her braids
have not hindered her from flaunting
her stripes with pride.]

Finally, we suggest that the frequency of the *corrido* in sextains
is confirmed by more than a dozen of that type we find in a single
anthology—that of Julián Calleja.

Taking into account these observations, it seems feasible to consider the compositions dedicated to Murrieta, in all their variants, as
corridos and not songs. Acosta and the publishers of the mentioned
recordings have done likewise, as well as Castañeda, Robbe, and others. But there is a more compelling reason that explains why the
Corrido de Joaquín Murrieta, in the versions collected up to now, is
composed in sextains. We claim that its origins can be found in a *corrido* from the north of Mexico that has the same form. Reading by
chance the book *El corrido zacatecano* (1976) by Cuauhtémoc

Esparza Sánchez, we came across the *corrido Mañanas de los cahiguas,* about which the author observes: "It is worth pointing out that the music of some *corridos,* probably originating in Zacatecas, later passed on to other places; in support of that, we can cite the musical text of the *Mañanas de los cahiguas,* which passed on to Sonora in the *Corrido de Joaquín Murrieta"* (1976: 8). This *corrido* from Zacatecas presents other similarities with the *Corrido de Joaquín Murrieta,* in content as well as form, which Esparza Sánchez fails to point out.

The *corrido* titled *Mañanas de los cahiguas* is composed in stanzas of six verses, a characteristic already noted by Esparza Sánchez (1976: 5–6), but he fails to point out that the *Corrido de Joaquín Murrieta* (in all its versions) is also a composition of stanzas in six verses.

It originates in Fresnillo, Zacatecas, as recited in that city by José Valdez, eighty-nine years old, on October 2, 1950.

1
Año de mil ochocientos,
año de cincuenta y tres,
ya los *apaches* llegaron
bufando como una res,
asaltando en el Estado
al derecho y al revés.

1
On the year eighteen hundred
and fifty-three,
the Apaches arrived
snorting like cattle,
attacking the state
right and left.

2
Cuando apenas era un niño,
huérfano a mí me dejaron
sin disfrutar un cariño;
a mi padre lo mataron
y a mi amiga Marianita,
¡cobardes!, la asesinaron.

2
When barely a child,
an orphan they left me
devoid of affection;
they killed my father
and those cowards assassinated
my friend Marianita.

3
Juré vengarme de todos
en esta tierra que piso,
pues yo soy zacatecano
porque Dios así lo quiso,
y en mi zarape, bordada,
traigo mi fe de bautizo.

3
I swore to take revenge of all
on this earth I tread on,
after all, God wished it so,
for I am from Zacatecas,
and on my sarape embroidered,
I carry my baptismal certificate.

4

Nos atacaron a todos	They attacked us all
en el cerro de Pardillo,	on a hill at Pardillo
porque un resorterazo echó	because Doña Isabel Hermosillo
doña Isabel Hermosillo,	flung a mighty slingshot
acabaron con cincuenta	wiping out fifty of our men,
aunque huímos a Fresnillo.	making us flee to Fresnillo.

5

Bonito pueblo de Nieves	The pretty town of Nieves
con sus calles alineadas,	with well-arranged streets,
donde me encontré a Pavón	is where I came across Pavón
en su llegua "La Plateada,"	on his mare "Silver-Plated",
con su pistola repleta	with his pistol loaded
y su gente uniformada.	and his people well-clad.

6

Francisco Pavón es hombre,	Francisco Pavón is a man,
se los digo, *compadraches*,	I affirm, fellow partners,
por eso sale a camino	that's why he sets out
a matar a los *apaches*,	to kill the Apaches,
ya no es otro su destino,	his destiny is no other,
achis, achis, achis.	*achis, achis, achis.*[37]

7

El cahigua más terrible	The most terrifying cahigua
es el mentado sargento,	is the said sergeant,
pues fama en todo el norte	his fame spreading throughout the
su salvajismo sangriento,	north from his bloody savagery,
ya que mutila a las gentes	mutilating people and later
y luego le grita al viento.	defying the wind.

8

Cuando *peliamos* con él	When we fought with him,
pronto vimos su *listeza*,	we soon noticed his cleverness,
y los jefes del Estado	and the bosses of the state,
al ver su grande fiereza,	upon seeing his great ferocity,
pusieron quinientos pesos	placed a price of five,
de valor a su cabeza.	hundred pesos on his head.

9
En los pueblos del Estado
mucho miedo le tenían
pues sabio es que el malvado,
De la sangre que vertia
a todos tenía azorados
y ya ni se defendían.

9
Among the towns of the state
much fear did he inspire;
it's well known the evildoer
alarmed all
to the point of numbness
from the blood he spilled.

10
Llegó el gobernador:
don Francisco G. Pavón,
y del Pardillo hasta Nieves
echamos persecución
de *apaches* y americanos
que huyeron hasta el *Tucsón.*

10
The governor arrived:
Don Francisco G. Pavón,
and from Pardillo to Nieves
we launched an assault on
Apaches and Anglos who fled
all the way to Tucson.

11
Recuerdos largos dejaron
cerca del *rial* de Fresnillo,
y a la gente revolcaron
en el cerro de Pardillo,
matando unos a balazos
o pasados a cuchillo.

11
Many memories they left behind
near the town of Fresnillo
with many people trampled
on the hill at Pardillo,
killing some with gunfire,
stabbing others with their knives.

12
Eran como mil quinientos,
con otros los combatí,
mas sólo a quince llegaron
la sangre que yo vertí;
compañeros me ayudaron
con valor que yo les di.

12
There were some fifteen hundred
and plus that I battled,
but only a total of fifteen
died from the blood that I spilled;
my fellow warriors helped me
with the courage I gave them.

13
Combatí con los *apaches*
y uno me dio una estocada,
—¡Con cuidado!—le decía—,
pues esto no vale nada
y en seguida le metí
veinticuatro puñaladas.

13
I fought against Apaches
and one stabbed me,
"Careful!" I told him,
for this is nothing
and then I stabbed him
twenty-four times.

14	14
Vuela, vuela, palomita,	Fly, fly, little dove,
del reino republicano.	from the republican kingdom.
Si no mata a los *apaches*	If the American government
el gobierno americano,	doesn't kill the Apaches,
les daremos *chicharrón*	we'll give them fried pork rinds
en el suelo zacatecano.	on Zacatecas soil.

(*El corrido zacatecano* 1976: 19–29)

This simple observation led us to compare both *corridos,* and with satisfaction we discovered that strong similarities also exist in content. In popular literature, intertexuality is not unusual, in form as well as in themes and content; and that is precisely what occurs with these two *corridos* whose parallelism in style and content is more than fortuitous. Below, we cite the stanzas that are most similar, underlining the similarities:

Cahiguas (A)	Murrieta (A)
1	1
Año de mil ochocientos,	Yo no soy americano
año de cincuenta y tres,	pero comprendo el inglés.
ya los *apaches* (sic) llegaron	Yo lo aprendí con mi hermano
bufando como una res	*al derecho y al revés.*
asaltando en el Estado	A cualquier americano
al derecho y al revés.	lo hago temblar a mis pies.
2	2
Cuando apenas era un niño	*Cuando apenas era un niño*
huérfano a mí me dejaron	*huérfano a mí me dejaron.*
sin disfrutar un cariño;	Nadie me hizo ni un *cariño,*
a mi padre lo *mataron*	*a mi* hermano *lo mataron*
y a mi amiga Marianita,	*y a mi* esposa Carmelita
¡cobardes!, *la asesinaron.*	*cobardes la asesinaron.*

3
Juré vengarme de todos
en esta tierra *que piso,*
pues soy zacatecano
porque Dios así lo quiso
y *en mi zarape* bordada,
traigo mi fe de bautizo.

5
Bonito pueblo de Nieves
con sus calles alineadas,
donde me encontré a Pavón
en su yegua *"La Plateada"*
con su pistola repleta
y su gente uniformada.

6
Francisco Pavón es hombre
se los digo compadraches,
por eso sale al camino
a matar a los apaches
ya no es otro su destino
achis, achis, achis.

10
No soy chileno ni extraño
en este suelo *que piso*
de México es California
porque Dios así lo quiso
y *en mi sarape* cosida
traigo mi fe de bautismo.

11
Qué *bonito* es California
con sus calles alineadas,
donde paseaba Murrieta
con su tropa bien formada
con su pistola repleta,
y su montura *plateada.*

8
Yo soy aquel que domina
hasta leones africanos,
por eso salgo al camino
a matar americanos.
ya no es otro mi destino
¡pon cuidado, parroquianos!

12
Me he paseado en California
por el año del cincuenta,
con mi montura *plateada,*
y mi pistola repleta,
y soy ese mexicano
de nombre Joaquín Murrieta.

Cahiguas (A)

1
On the year of eighteen hundred
and fifty-three,
the *Apaches* by then came
snorting like cows,
attacking right and left
anything in the state.

Murrieta (B)

1
I'm not Anglo
but I understand English.
I learned it with my brother
backwards and forwards.
I make any Anglo
tremble at my feet.

2
When barely a child
I was left an orphan
devoid of *affection;*
they killed my father
and those cowards assassinated
my friend Marianita.

3
I swore to take revenge
on this soil I tread on,
because God wished it so
since I am from Zacatecas
and in my embroidered *sarape*
I carry my baptismal certificate.

5
Pretty town of Nieves
with well-arranged streets,
is where I came across Pavón
on his mare *"Silver-Plated"*
with his pistol loaded
and his followers well-clad.

6
Francisco Pavón is a man,
I tell you, partners,
that's why he sets out
to kill the Apaches
now his destiny is no other
achis, achis, achis.

2
When barely a child
I was left an orphan
no one gave me *any affection,*
they killed my brother
and the cowards assassinated
my wife Carmelita.

10
I'm not Chilean nor a foreigner
on this soil I tread on,
California is Mexico's
because God wished it so
and in my stitched *sarape*
I carry my baptismal certificate.

11
How *pretty* California is
with well-arranged streets,
where Murrieta passed through
with his well-trained troops
with his pistol loaded
and his *silver-plated* saddle.

12
I have traveled through California
around the year fifty (1850)
with my *silver-plated* saddle,
and my *pistol loaded,*
and I am that Mexican
named Joaquín Murrieta.

8
I am that one who dominates
even African lions,
that's why I set out
to kill Anglos.
Now my destiny is no other
beware, countrymen!

Philip Sonnichsen, in his commentaries, discusses the recording of the *corrido* of Murrieta and points out: "There are many versions of the *Corrido* of Joaquín Murieta (*sic*), each contributing to the legend." The version here is no exception. It was recorded in 1934 by the Hermanos Sánchez y Linares. [....] In a 1975 interview with the surviving brother, Víctor Sánchez had this to say:

> The *corrido* was written before I was born; it is from the last century. I heard it as a child in Mexico, sung during the time of the Revolution. I also heard it in Arizona. We had many requests for this *corrido*, at parties, and then after we began to sing it on the radio, people would write us cards to the station and asked us to record it so they could have the disc. Felipe Valdéz (*sic*) Leal[38] added three or four verses to make it fit both sides of the record—I don't remember which ones but possibly the one about coming from Hermosillo.[39]

Without any knowledge of versions of the *corrido* of Murrieta before 1934, it is very difficult to identify the added stanzas by Valdez Leal, aside from the third mentioned by Víctor Sánchez, which begins with the verse "I came from Hermosillo." If other versions are discovered in the future, like the one used by the Sánchez y Linares Brothers to record their record, and the ones mentioned by Esparza Sánchez extant in Sonora, perhaps it will be possible to resolve such a mystery. Given the similarities, however, we can almost say that the *corrido* of Murrieta appears to be a radical adaptation of the *corrido Mañanas de los cahiguas.*

To prove the above, it would be necessary to establish the dates of both *corridos* since it can also be asserted that the *Mañanas* version was overlapped onto the *corrido* of Murrieta, possibly from a lost version. Although Esparza Sánchez does not mention the date of the *corrido* he transcribes, and that was collected in Fresnillo (Zacatecas), where José Valdez (eighty-nine years old) recited it on January 2, 1950, we find certain references in the text to historical characters and events that help to locate it in time, as well as the year of the narrated happenings—that is, 1853, which coincides with the date of Murrieta's death. In *Los cahiguas*, Doña Isabel Hermosillo is mentioned, who, according to Esparza Sánchez, was a Spanish lady living in Fresnillo who died in the city of Zacatecas in 1854—one year after the attack on Pardillo—at the age of forty years old. Another historical figure also appears, namely the brigadier general Francisco G. Pavón (1818–1861), governor and commander general of the department of Zacatecas from August 22, 1853, to August 17, 1855 (Esparza Sánchez, 114 n. 35). He was an acquaintance of the narrator of the *corrido*, whom he accompanied in the 1853 expedition against the Apaches. The text of the last stanza seems of greater importance relative to the incursions of the Apaches in Mexican territory after 1848. Article XI of the Treaty of Guadalupe Hidalgo makes reference to those incursions that seemed to continue in 1853, according to the *corrido*.

The date of composition of a historical *corrido*, whose content is generally contemporary, and is narrated in the third or first person by firsthand witnesses, can be determined by the date mentioned in the text and by the historical references. For that reason it is very possible that *Mañanas de los cahiguas* might have been composed in 1853 or a little afterward. This indicates that it is unlikely that a *corrido*: about Murrieta's deeds was composed prior to that year, the year of his death, although it is true that other versions have some stanzas with a verse that says "*Me he paseado en California/ por el año del cincuenta*" (I have traveled in California/ around the year '50).

Another circumstance that makes us believe that the Zacatecan *corrido* is of early origins is the use of "*mañanas*" in the title, a word that, according to Mendoza, appears in the oldest known *corrido*: "*De la época inicial del corrido y de los ejemplos que se refieren a hechos históricos se incluye (en su antología) por primera vez uno referido al Padre de la Patria: Mañanas de Hidalgo en Zacatecas, probablemente el más antiguo que se conoce*" (1964: 31-2). (From the beginnings of the *corrido* and from the examples which refer to *historical* events, one is included [in his anthology] for the first time that refers to the father of Mexico, [Father Miguel Hidalgo]: *Mañanas de Hidalgo en Zacatecas*, probably the oldest known *corrido*.) In his first book from 1939, Mendoza has observed: "*En el fenómeno histórico aparece claro que el corrido enraizó en el Sur y poco a poco, gradualmente, fue invadiendo con sus relatos la parte Norte del país; o transportado por los cancioneros y trovadores de las ferias o llevado por medio de la emigración de los braceros michoacanos que van al norte en busca de trabajo*" (1939: 153). (As to its historical quality, it seems clear that the *corrido* took root in the south and slowly and gradually began spreading to the northern part of the country with its stories, transported by singers and troubadours from popular fairs or transmitted via the emigration of laborers from Michoacán who went north in search of work.)

Esparza Sánchez rejects this theory because, as he stipulates, *"en Zacatecas hubo corridos anteriores a esa fecha (segundo tercio del siglo XIX); por ejemplo las* Mañanas de Hidalgo *que datan de 1811 y que, por ahora, son las más antiguas"* (1976: 5). (In Zacatecas there were *corridos* prior to that date [the second third of the nineteenth century]; for example, *Mañanas de Hidalgo* from 1811, which, for now, is the oldest.) The historical event recounted in *Mañanas de los cahiguas* occurred in 1853 and, according to the historian Elías Amador (*Bosquejo histórico de Zacatecas,* 1912: 2:517-8), is cited by Esparza Sánchez: "Como los pequeños centros de población [....] continuaban expuestos a las frecuentes depredaciones de los cahiguas [,] el gobernador Francisco G. Pavón [....] durante los meses de octubre y noviembre de 1853 [....] salió a su encuentro" (1976: 19). (Since the small centers of population [....] continued to be exposed to the frequent pillaging of the *cahiguas*[,] Governor Francisco G. Pavón [....] during the months of October and November of 1853 [....] set out to confront them.)

There are similarities and differences between *Mañanas de los cahiguas* and *Corrido de Joaquín Murrieta,* especially in the nature of the hero. Although in the Zacatecan *corrido* the narrator praises Pavón, calling him a brave man, the military man is not the hero of the *corrido,* but rather the narrator himself, a character similar to Murrieta, given that he also promises to avenge himself against those who harmed him: the Apaches, and those who killed his father and his friend Marianita. In this sense, the lives of the two heroes are similar except in ideology, because the main issue of *"Los cahiguas"* is the confrontation of the residents of a Zacatecan town with the Apaches. Meanwhile, in the *corrido* of Murrieta the theme is informed by the glorious deeds of the hero in his fight against the North American invaders in the California gold mines. The Indian is accused in the first and the Anglos in the second. It is interesting to note, however, that in *Los cahiguas* the Apache is identified with the Anglo:

echamos persecución
de apaches y americanos
que huyeron hasta *Tucson*.
(Esparza Sánchez 20)

[we set out to pursue
Apaches and Anglos
who fled all the way to Tucson.]

The transposition is obvious: in *Murrieta* the Anglo occupies the place of the Apache in *Mañanas*, which appears thus:

a mi padre lo mataron
y a mi amiga Marianita,
¡cobardes! la asesinaron.

[They killed my father
and those cowards killed
my friend Marianita.]

And Murrieta says of Anglos:

a mi hermano lo mataron,
y a mi esposa Carmelita
cobardes la asesinaron.

[They killed my brother
and those cowards assassinated
my wife Carmelita.]

Nevertheless, it is necessary to point out that in the Zacatecan *corrido* we discover a character, an Apache chief and unnamed sergeant, who bears some of the same characteristics as Joaquín Murrieta: He is brave, clever, and fierce. The government, as in the case of Murrieta, puts a price on his head:

Cuando peliamos con él
pronto vimos su listeza,
y los jefes del Estado

al ver su grande fiereza,
pusieron quinientos pesos
de valor en su cabeza.

[When we *fought* with him,
we soon noticed his cleverness,
and the bosses of the state,
upon seeing his great ferocity,
placed a price of five hundred pesos
on his head.]

We observed already that there are too few known versions of the *Corrido de Joaquín Murrieta* to allow us to trace its historical development. The only complete ones seem to be of recent origin, as the others are but mere fragments.[40] Other than the two collected by Acosta, we have knowledge of one that is found in the book *Hispanic Folk Music of New Mexico and the Southwest* (1980) by John Donald Robbe. Another fragment appeared in the journal *Revista Cultural de la U.A.C.J.* (Universidad Autónoma de Ciudad Juárez) in 1985. Manuel Rojas collected a version of the *corrido* called *Joaquín Murrieta* of nine sextains (1992: 65-6), and another two *corridos* related to Joaquín, *Las coplas de Juan Valenzuela* (p. 64) in quatrains, and one in sextains, *La cabeza de Murrieta* (p. 66), written by León Barraza G.

The influence of the *Mañanas de los cahiguas* on the composition of the *Corrido de Joaquín Murrieta* is obvious in form as well as content. However, it could be that a previous prototype might have existed and is unknown today from which both *corridos* derive. Until such is discovered, the similarities herein established between the Zacatecan and Californian *corridos* stand.

IX
This Edition

Any critic who attempts to clarify the history of a literary text must at times become a real detective. That occurs in the case of *Vida y aventuras del más célebre bandido sonorense, Joaquín Murrieta: Sus grandes proezas en California* (Life and Adventures of the Most

Celebrated Sonoran Bandit, Joaquín Murrieta: His Greatest Exploits
in California) in its various editions, all of them attributed to the
Mexican novelist Ireneo Paz. Upon consulting the *Biblografía de
novelistas mexicanos* (1926; Bibliography of Mexican Novelists) of
the meticulous bibliographer Juan B. Iguínez, we discovered that in
the list of novels by Paz, none devoted to Murrieta appears. This
stirred our suspicions, and we decided to investigate this omission
from such a prestigious bibliography. Upon examining the various
editions that exist of that work, we uncovered that none of them cite
Paz as the author; each states only that it was published in Mexico by
the Tipografía y Encuadernación de Ireneo Paz, 2a de Relox número
4 (Irineo Paz's Typography and Book Binding, second block of
Relox, [currently Argentina Avenue,] number 4). As explained in
Section III Paz's book, attributed to him as the author, appeared as a
translation into English in 1925 in Chicago. Without knowing the history of such a text, translator Frances P. Belle thought that the original
work was that of Ireneo Paz. And it is easy to believe it so, as Octavio
Paz himself (grandson of Don Ireneo) asserted.

The history of this edition is complicated. In 1939 historian
Joseph Henry Jackson, in a chapter dedicated to Murrieta (1977: 3-40)
in his book *Bad Company*, had already noted the similarities between
Belle's translation and John Rollin Ridge's original (p. 332). What it
doesn't explain is the complex history of the trajectory of such a text,
from Ridge to Belle, already detailed earlier and unnecessary to
repeat here. Let it be said that, more than the historical events themselves, Joaquín Murrieta's fame goes back in great part to the work of
John Rollin Ridge, or "Yellow Bird," whose translation is now made
available through the French version to the reader. Ireneo Paz's edition is the one to have Murrieta's life and deeds become best known
through the numerous Spanish editions published in the United
States, which are now out of print.

Bibliography or novel? The first critics and commentators classi-
fied Ridge's work as belonging to the genre of biography, and rightly
so, because the author himself tells us that what he tells about Murrieta
is literally true (1955: 4). Such an opinion is supported by the historians Hubert Howe Bancroft and Theodore H. Hittell, who resorted to
Ridge's work as a source of information in their scholarly historical
accounts of California. Nonetheless, it is not in history where

Murrieta's name has endured, but rather in literature, theater, film, the *corrido*, and poetry. This new edition is a tribute to Joaquín Murrieta, the only Californian hero at the level of art, history, and myth.

Luis Leal
University of California at Santa Barbara

[English translation: Francisco A. Lomelí,
University of California at Santa Barbara, and
Miguel R. López, Southern Methodist University]

Notes

I: The Historical Joaquín

[1]The name is written with a double r; however, many North American writers, as well as Chileans, spell it with one r, which in American English is pronounced as "rr." Examples of this tendency include the names Monterey and Carillo, instead of Monterrey and Carrillo. Sometimes Murrieta's name is misspelled with the addition of a t (Murrietta). We maintain the double r except in quotations, where we preserve the original spelling. See the comments of Albert Huerta and Manuel Rojas on this matter.

[2]It is curious that Latta does not mention this newspaper, which is undoubtedly an important source of documentary information regarding Murrieta. According to Latta, the name of Joaquín Murrieta does not appear until February of 1853.

II: Biography

[3]See Jay Monaghan, *Chile, Perú, and the California Gold Rush of 1849* (Berkeley: University of California, 1973).

[4]See Nadeau 1974:62, 65.

[5]The entire certificate is reproduced in Latta on p. 328.

III: Translation and Plagiarism of Ridge's Work

[6]See Franklin Walker, *San Francisco Literary Frontier* (New York: Knopf, 1939).

[7]See Walker, "Ridge's Life of Joaquín Murieta . . .".

[8]*Evangeline: Romance de la Arcadia.* Translated by Carlos Morla Vicuña (New York: Imprenta de Eduardo O. Jenkins, 1871). In royal octaves.

[9]Year 1, Number I, Santiago, Chile, August, 1936.

[10]Biblioteca Nacional, *Anuario de la prensa chilena, 1877–1885. I. Libros, folletos y hojas sueltas.* ([Santiago]: Imprenta Universitaria, 1952), p. 58, No. 411. The eighth edition was published in Santiago, at the Imprenta Valparaíso, in 1897.

[11]*Gaceta* de Santa Bárbara, núm. 106 (20 julio 1881), p.1.

[12]See the note by Charles W. Clough in Farquar (1969: xiii–xvii). Also, Luis Monguió, "*Lust for Riches:* A Spanish Nineteenth-Century Novel of the Gold Rush and Its Sources," *California Historical Society Quarterly* 27 (Sept. 1948): 237–248.

[13]Printed and bound by I. Paz. There are numerous reprintings. In 1908 Paz published the fourth edition; the fifth in Los Angeles, California: O[scar]. Paz y Cía., 1919, and another edition in Mexico City, Ediciones Don Quijote, in 1953.

[14]According to Jackson (1955: xliii), "This translation hardly seems to have been worth the trouble," since the Spanish translation is based on the English. This is true, but we must add that the Spanish translation was not made directly from the English, but by means of the French.

IV: Joaquín Murrieta as Myth

[15]See Richard Boyd Hauck, *Crockett Bibliography* (Westport, Conn.: Greenwood Press, 1982).

[16]See Leonard Pitt, *The Decline of the Californios; A Social History of the Spanish-Speaking Californians* (Berkeley: University of California, 1970).

[17]See Nadeau 1974: 115–116.

[18]The principal historians of Murrieta's life do not mention a Joe Lake.

[19]Over the last two decades there have been several exhaustive studies of Murrieta's family. The most important are those by Latta and Rojas, who have studied the matter in Sonora, interviewed numerous persons, and studied the archives.

V: Joaquín Murrieta in Narrative Fiction

[20]According to Nadeau (1974: 115), the whereabouts of first and only number of *Pacific Police Gazette* are unknown.

[21]Oddly, Jackson, though well-versed in the bibliography on Murrieta, does not comment on the second novel by Badger, only the first.

[22]Herbert Smith, *The Popular American Novel* (Boston: Twayne Publishers, 1980), p. 95. The film *Bonnie and Clyde*, directed by Arthur Penn and with leading roles by Warren Beatty and Faye Dunaway, appeared in 1967. The action takes place during the decade of the 1930s.

[23]According to Latta, all the Murrietas spoke English: "In the group of Joaquíns three members were blond, two were brunet, and all spoke English 'fluently' [. . . .] Murrieta spoke English so well that with no disguise he was able to pass either as a Gringo or an Englishman. In his own family he was known as Joaquín Murrieta, El Huero (The Blond One). In

c   Ireneo Paz

order to distinguish him from his three Joaquín Murrieta relatives, once in
California, he became known as Joaquín El Famoso, or simply as El
Famoso (The Famous One)" (1974, 12). Rojas rejects these notions as
absurd.

[24]We cite here the second edition, *Cuentos californianos,* with an introduction by Miguel López Rojo (Guadalajara: Secretaría de Cultura de Jalisco,
1993). "Joaquín Murrieta," pp. 89–97.

VI: Joaquín Murrieta in Poetry

[25]None of the writers interested in Joaquín mentions this character, who
might well not have any connection to Murrieta (in Miller's novel Joaquín
is an artist), but does make his presence felt in the creative work by Miller.
For analysis of the character, see Frost, pp. 75–80.

[26]The edition cited in this section is that published by Bantam Books (New
York: 1975).

[27]Translator's note: The reader will note that a few quotes, such as this one,
offer radical changes from the original edition of 1967. Prof. Leal quoted
the edition by the Grupo Mascarones (Coyoacán, México D.F.: *Casa de las
Américas* 82), but we have opted toward reproducing the lines as they
appear in the original with their corresponding pagination where indicated.
The Grupo Mascarones obviously exercised some poetic liberties in alter-
ing the actual order of verses.

VII: Joaquín Murrieta in Theater and Film

[28]A copy of this rare work can be found at the Bancroft Library at the
University of California, Berkeley. A contemporary edition exists, edited
by Glenn Loney (see Bibliography).

[29]Howe may have taken the name Ignacious from a news account published
on February 2, 1853, in the Stockton *San Joaquín Republican,* in which a
Mexican named Ignatius Moretto is mentioned. (See Latta 1980: 39)

[30]Wood explains (p. 60) that Owen perhaps did not know Gabutti's first
name, thus confusing the honorific title "Don," with the author's name.

[31]In the 1973 bilingual edition, translator Ben Belitt attempts to address the
language barriers faced by the miners. For example, the Ranger tells them:
"We no sello chicha in these parts. In California only sello weeskie" (65).

[32]According to Neruda, Juárez's speech asking Joaquín to defend the Indians
is "transcripción textual de un documento publicado en *The Last of the
California Rangers,* de Jill L. Cosley-Batt" (1973: 130) (a textual transcrip-
tion of a document published in *The Last of the California Rangers* by Jill
L. Cosley-Batt).

[33]*Plural*, second period, 17.2 Num. 193 (November 1987): 22–34.

[34]See Nicolás Kanellos, editor, *Mexican American Theater: Then and Now* in *Revista Chicano-Riqueña* 11.1 (Spring 1983): 32.

VIII: The *corrido* of Joaquín Murrieta

[35]For a more detailed analysis on the *corrido* of Murrieta, see our study *"El corrido de Joaquín Murrieta, origen y difusión"* in *Mexican Studies/ Estudios Mexicanos* 11.1 (Winter 1995).

[36]For further information on this *corrido*, see our study *"El corrido de Leandro Rivera"* in *La Comunidad* No. 199, Sunday Supplement of *La Opinión* (Los Angeles, May 13, 1984): 12.

[37]This represents a rhetorical device by the popular poet to maintain a rhyme; otherwise, the words contain no semantic meaning.

[38]Editor's note: "All that time Felipe Valdez Leal worked as a salesman for the Casa de Música, a music store in downtown Los Angeles."

[39]Editor's note: "Interview with Victor Sánchez, September–October, 1974."

[40]For these fragments and other versions, see our study cited in note #35.

Bibliography

Acevedo Hernández, A. *Joaquín Murieta. Drama en seis actos.* En *Excélsior, Revista Semanal de Literatura y Variedades.* Santiago de Chile, Año 1 (1936): [3]-30.

Acigar, El Profesor. *El caballero chileno bandido de California: única y verdadera historia de Joaquín Murieta.* Barcelona: Biblioteca Hércules, n.d.

Acosta, Vicente S. 1951. "Some Surviving Elements of Spanish Folklore in Arizona." M.A. Thesis, Arizona.

Aguirre Bernal, Celso. *Joaquín Murrieta. Raíz y razón del movimiento chicano.* México, 1985.

Alta California. San Francisco, 15 dic. 1852-23 agosto 1853.

Amador, Elías. *Bosquejo histórico de Zacatecas.* 2 vols. Guadalupe, Zac.: Tipografía del Hospital de Niños, 1912; reprinted in Zacatecas: Taller Tip. Pedroza, 1943.

Angel, Myron. *History of San Luis Obispo County.* Oakland, California, s.p. de i., 1883.

Anónimo. "A Pioneer's Story of the Notorious Bandit and Outlaw." *Call* (14 Oct. 1887).

———. [Joaquín....]. *Sunset Magazine,* 1927.

———. "Joaquín Murieta Lore." *Tribune.* Oakland, California, 20 Feb. 1949; reimpr. *Western Folklore* 8 (1949): 271–272 [Wade Wilson's speculations on Murrieta's death].

———. "'El Famoso' Conquers 8th Street Bridge." *The Tribune,* Oakland, California, 12 Sept. 1991, A12.

Ashbury, Herbert. *The Barbary Coast: An Informal History of San Francisco's Underworld.* New York: Alfred A. Knopf, 1933.

Badger, Joseph E. *Joaquín, the Saddle King.* New York: Beadle & Adams, 1881.

———. *Joaquín, The Terrible.* New York: Beadle & Adams, 1881; Reprinted. Brooklyn, New York: Dime Novel Club, 1947.

Bancroft, Hubert Howe. *California Pastoral 1769–1848.* San Francisco, 1888.

Beers, George. *The Hunted Bandit of the San Joaquín.* 1875; reprinted. *The California Outlaw: Tiburcio Vázquez.* Los Gatos, California: Talisman Press, 1960.

Belle, Frances P. *Life and Adventures of the Celebrated Bandit Joaquín Murrieta, His Exploits in the State of California.* Translated from the Spanish of Ireneo Paz by Frances P. Bell. Chicago: Regan Public Corp., 1925; Reimpr. Chicago: Charles T. Power, 1937.

Bell, Horace. 1881. *Reminiscences of a Ranger.* Los Angeles: Yarnell, Caystile & Mathes, 1885.

————. 1930. *On the Old West Coast.* New York: Morrow, 1930.

Bernaldo de Quirós, Constancio. *El bandolerismo en España y México.* México, 1959.

Block, Eugene. *Great Stagecoach Robbers,* 1962.

Boyce, Keith. "The Evolution of a Demon." *Pacific Monthly* 3–4 (April 1891): 143–51.

————. "The Fra Diavolo of El Dorado." *The Californian* 4.5 (Oct. 1893): 695–700.

Brewer, William Henry. *Up and Down California in 1860–1864. The Journal of William Henry Brewer.* Ed. Francis P. Farquhar. New Haven, Connecticut: Yale University Press, 1930.

Burns, Walter Noble. *The Robin Hood of El Dorado: The Saga of Joaquín Murrieta, Famous Outlaw of California's Age of Gold.* New York: Coward-McCann, 1932.

California Assembly Journal. 16 March 1853, 351.

California Police Gazette. "Life of Joaquín Murieta, the Brigand Chief of California." San Francisco, 1859.

————. *Idem.* San Francisco: Butler and Co., 1861.

————. *Joaquín Murieta, the Brigand Chief of California.* Ed. Francis P. Farquhar. San Francisco: Grabhorn Press, 1932.

————. *Idem.* Fresno, California: Fresno Valley Publishers, 1969. Supplement of Notes by Raymund F. Wood and Charles W. Clough.

California Senate Journal. 4 May 1853, 445.

Calleja, Julián. *Método de guitarra sin maestro. Con acompañamiento para corridos mexicanos.* México, D. F.: El Libro Español, 1972. On the cover: *Los mejores corridos mexicanos, con acompañamiento para guitarra.*

Callison, Charles M. "Searching for Murrieta's Home & Grove in El Canada Molino Vallejo." *California Historical Courier* (April/May 1987): 145–146. Summarized and translated in Rojas.

Campa, Arthur L. *Hispanic Folklore Studies of Arthur L. Campa.* With an Introduction by Carlos E. Cortés. New York: Arno Press, 1976. 102–103.

Caro, Brígido. *Joaquín Murrieta* [film].

Carrillo, Adolfo. *Cuentos californianos.* Los Angeles, 1922 2nd ed. Introduction by Miguel López Rojo. Guadalajara: Secretaría de Cultura de Jalisco, 1993.

Castañeda, Daniel. *El corrido mexicano: su técnica literaria y musical.* México: Editorial Surco, 1943.

Castañeda-Shular, Antonia, Tomás Ybarra-Frausto y Joseph Sommers. *Literatura chicana texto y contexto/Text and Context: Chicano Literature.* Englewood Cliffs, N.J.: Prentice-Hall, 1972.

Castillo, Pedro, and Albert Camarillo. *Furia y muerte: los bandidos chicanos.* Los Angeles: Chicano Studies Center, University of California, 1973. "Aztlán Publications," Monograph 4.

Cerecedo, Onofre. "Joaquín Murrieta."[Legend]. *El Regidor,* San Antonio, TX, 9. 359 (30 Apr. 1896): 3. Taken from *La Revista del Pacífico.*

Clough, Charles W. See *California Police Gazette,* 1969.

C.M. ver Morla Vicuña, Carlos.

Coolidge, Dane. *Gringo Gold. A Story of Joaquín Murieta the Bandit.* New York: Dutton, 1939; reprinted Boston: Gregg Press, 1980, 1981.

Corcoran, May S. "Robber Joaquín, As Seen in Statutes of California Legislature Journals and by One Living Ranger." *Grizzly Bear* (June 1921): 4.

Corle, Edwin. *The Royal Highway (El Camino Real).* Chapter 21: "Your Money or Your Life." Indianapolis/New York: Bobbs-Merrill, 1949.

Cortés, Carlos E. "El bandolerismo social chicano." *Aztlán, historia del pueblo chicano, 1848–1910.* Eds. David Maciel y Patricia Bueno. Trans. Roberto Gómez Ciriza. México: SepSetentas, 1975. 111–122.

Cossley-Batt, Jill L. *The Last of the California Rangers.* New York: Funk & Wagnalls, 1928.

Cunningham, John Charles. *The Truth about Murietta.* Los Angeles: Wetzel Publishing Co., 1938.

Daily Alta California. Ver *Alta California.*

Dale, Edward, and Gaston Litton. *Cherokee Cavaliers.* Norman: University of Oklahoma Press, 1939.

Duke, Thomas S. *Celebrated Criminal Cases of America.* San Francisco: The James H. Barry Company, 1910.

Elizondo, Sergio. "Murrieta en la loma". *Perros y antiperros: épica chicana.* English trans. Gustavo Segade. Berkeley: A Quinto Sol Publication, 1972. 62–64.

———. "Murrieta, dos." *Idem.* 64–67.

Esparza Sánchez, Cuauhtémoc *El corrido zacatecano.* México: Universidad Autónoma de Zacatecas, 1976, 8. "Colección Científica Histórica" 46, SEP.

Espinosa Domínguez, Carlos. See Grushkó.

Farquhar, Francis P. See *California Police Gazette,* 1932 and 1969.

Fitzgerald, John H. "Adventures with Joaquín, the Mountain Bandit." *Golden Era* 12 April 1857.

Foro, El. Sept. 1980.

Frost, O. W. *Joaquín Miller.* New York: Twayne Publishers, 1967.

Gabutti, Don. [A play on Murrieta presented in Hermosillo, Sonora, during the fall of 1872]. See Wood, "New Light" (Winter 1970).

Gaceta, La. "Vida y aventuras de Joaquín Murrieta." Capts. I–IV. Santa Bárbara, California, Año 2, números 98-106 (Junio 1–Julio 30 1881).

Gailard, Robert. *L'homme aux mains de cuir.* Paris: Presses Pocket, 1974.

————. *El hombre de las manos de cuero.* Barcelona: Editorial Picazo, 1986.

Girl Reporter, A. [Joaquín...]. *Call,* San Francisco, Dec. 1923–Feb. 1924.

Gollomb, Joseph. *Master Highwaymen.* New York: The Macaulay Company, 1927.

Gonzales, Rodolfo. *I Am Joaquín: An Epic Poem.*, 1967. Rpt. New York: Bantam, 1972.

————. *Yo soy Joaquín.* Coyoacán, D. F.: Grupo Mascarones, 1975.

Griswold del Castillo, Richard. *The Treaty of Guadalupe Hidalgo, A Legacy of Conflict.* Norman: University of Oklahoma Press, 1990.

Grushkó, Pável. "Estrella y muerte de Joaquín Murieta". *Plural* 2ª época, 17.2, Núm. 193 (nov. 1987): 22–34.

Gutierrez, Lalo. *Corrido de Joaquín Murieta.* Tucson, 1948 (recording).

Henshall, Joseph A. "A Bandit of the Golden Age." *Overland Monthly* 53 (April 1909): 313–319.

Hermanos Sánchez y Linares. *Corrido de Joaquín Murrieta.* 1934. *Texas-Mexican Border Music,* Vols. 2 & 3, *Corridos,* Parts 1 & 2 (1974).

Herrera-Sobek, María. *The Mexican Corrido: A Feminist Analysis.* Bloomington: Indiana University Press, 1993. First Midland Book Edition.

————. *Northward Bound: The Mexican Immigrant Experience in Ballad and Song.* Bloomington: Indiana University Press, 1993, 16–18.

Herrero, Ignacio (editor). *El bandido chileno en California.* San Antonio, Texas: Editorial Martínez, 1929 [c.1926].

Hittell, Theodore H. *History of California.* 4 vols. San Francisco: W. T. Stone, 1898.

Hobsbawm, Eric J. *Bandits.* New York: Delacorte Press, 1969.

Howard, William. [Article in] *Merced County Sun,* 3 May 2 1890.

Howe, Charles E. B. *A Dramatic Play Entitled Joaquín Murieta de Castillo, the Celebrated California Bandit.* San Francisco: Commercial Book and Job Steam Printing Establishment, 1858 2nd ed., Glenn Loney, 1983.

Huerta, S. J., Father Alberto. *Murieta y los californios.* Madrid, s. p. de i., 1983.

————. 1985. *Murieta el famoso.* Madrid, n.p. 1985.

————. "Joaquín Murieta: California's Literary Archetype." *The Californians; The Magazine of California History* 5.6 (Nov–Dec 1987): 47–50.

————. "California: el bandido y el vendido." *Religión y Cultura* 172 (enero–marzo 1990): 9–59.

Hyenne, Robert. *Un bandit californien (Joaquín Murieta).* Paris: Le'crivan et Toubon, 1862.

————. *El bandido chileno Joaquín Murieta en California.* Ed. Ilustrada. Barcelona: V. Acha, editor/México: Maucci Hnos., n. d.

————. *Idem.* Translated from French by C. M. [Carlos Morla]. Santiago [de Chile]: Centro Editorial "La Prensa", 1906.

————. *Idem.* 15th ed. Valparaiso, Chile: Sociedad Impresora y Litografía Universo, 1910.

————. *Joaquín Murrieta, el bandido chileno en California.* San Antonio, Texas: Editorial Martínez, 1926. 2nd ed., 1929.

————. *Vida y aventuras de Joaquín Murieta.* Prólogo de Ricardo Donoso. *Excélsior.* Santiago de Chile, año I (1936): 31–90.

Jackson, Joseph Henry. *Bad Company: The Story of California's Legendary and Actual Stage Robbers, Bandits, Highwaymen and Outlaws.* New York: Harcourt Brace, 1939. "Joaquín Murieta." Reprinted 1949. Lincoln: University of Nebraska Press, 1977. 3–40

————. *Anybody's Gold. The Story of California's Mining Towns.* New York: Appleton-Century, 1941; Rpt. San Francisco: Chronicle Books, 1970.

————. *The Creation of Joaquín Murieta.* Stanford, California: Stanford University Press, 1948.

————. "The Creation of Joaquín Murieta." *Pacific Spectator.* 2.2 (Spring 1948).

————. "Introduction" to the University of Oklahoma Press 1955 ed. of Ridge's novel, xi–l.

Jaramillo, Felipe. "Los corridos fronterizos de Agua Prieta, Sonora, México," *Borderlands* 3.2 (Spring 1980), 173.

Kennedy, Mary Jean. "The Gold Cap of Joaquín Murieta." *Western Folklore* 13 (1954): 98–101.

Klette, Ernest. *The Crimson Trail of Joaquín Murieta.* Los Angeles: Wetzel Publishing Co., 1928.

Klyn, Dianne C. *Joaquín Murrieta in California.* San Ramon, California: Publishing Place, 1989.

Kooistra, Paul. *Criminals as Heroes: Structure, Power and Identity.* Bowling Green, Ohio: Bowling Green State University, 1989.

Kyne, Peter B. "Robin Hood of El Dorado." *Chronicle,* San Francisco, Feb. 1936.

Latta, Frank F. *Joaquín Murieta and His Horse Gangs*. Santa Cruz, California: Bear State Books, 1980.

Leal, Luis. "El corrido de Joaquín Murrieta: origen y difusión." *Mexican History/Estudios Mexicanos* 11.1 (Winter 1995): 1–23.

———. "El corrido de Leandro Rivera". *La Comunidad* No. 199, Suplemento Dominical de *La Opinión* (Los Angeles, 13 May 1984), 12.

Lee, Hector H. *Heroes, Villains and Ghosts: Folklore of Old California*. Santa Barbara, California: Capra Press, 1984.

Limón, José E. *Mexican Ballads, Chicano Poems. History and Influence in Mexican American Social Poetry*. Berkeley: University of California Press, 1992.

Lock, Raymond Friday. *Joaquín Murieta. The Adventures of the Latino Robin Hood*. Los Angeles: Holloway House Publishing Co., 1980.

López, Jesse. *Joaquín Murrieta's Treasure*. Albuquerque, N.M.: Pajarito Publications, 1979.

Los Angeles Times. 9 April 9 1928.

———. March 16, 1969 (review of Neruda's book).

MacLean, Angus. *Legends of The California Bandidos*. Fresno, California: Pioneer Publishing, 1977. Reprint, Arroyo Grande. Bear Flag Books, 1989.

Mares, E. A. *El corrido de Joaquín Murieta*. Obra teatral presentada en la Compañía de Teatro de Alburquerque el 25 de mayo, 1984.

Martínez López, Enrique. *La variación en el corrido mexicano: interlocuciones del narrador y los personajes* Madrid: El Romancero Hoy: Poética, 1979.

Mason, J. D. *History of Santa Barbara County*. Oakland, California: Thompson & West, 1981.

———. *California. His California Diary Beginning in 1855 and Ending in 1857*. Ed. John S. Richards. Seattle, California: F. McCaffrey at his Dogwood Press, 1936.

McCarthy, Gary. *The Gringo Amigo*. New York: Doubleday, 1991.

McNeer, Mary. "Bandit!" *The California Gold Rush*. cap. 16. New York: Random House, 1950, 149–157.

Mendoza, Vicente T. *El romance español y el corrido mexicano: estudio comparativo*. México: Ediciones de la Universidad Nacional Autónoma, 1939.

———. *Lírica narrativa de México: el corrido*. México: UNAM, 1964.

Miller, Joaquín. *Joaquín, et al*. Portland, Oregon: S. J. McCormack, 1869.

———. "Californian." *Songs of the Sierras*. Boston: Roberts Brothers, 1872.

———. *Joaquín Miller's Poems* (in six volumes). Volume Two: *Songs of the Sierras*. San Francisco: Harr Wagner Publishing Company, 1920.

Mitchell, Richard Gerald. "Joaquín Murieta: A Study of Social Conditions in Early California", M.A. Thesis, Dept. of History, University of California, Berkeley, 1927, 39–69; reprinted in Castillo and Camarillo, 37–51.

Monaghan, Jay. *Chile, Peru and the California Gold Rush of 1849.* Berkeley: University of California Press, 1973.

Monguió, Luis. *"Lust for Riches: A Spanish Nineteenth Century Novel of the Gold Rush and Its Sources."* California Historical Society Quarterly 27 (Sept. 1948): 237–48.

Monroy Rivera, Oscar. *Joaquín Murrieta. Obra de teatro.* Ciudad Juárez, Chihuahua: Universidad Autónoma de Ciudad Juárez, 1989. "Cuadernos Universitarios," 7.

[Morla Vicuña, Carlos]. C. M. *El bandido chileno Joaquín Murrieta en California* [Santiago de Chile: Imprenta de la República, de Jacinto Núñez, 1867] (Translation from French by Hyenne).

————. [2nd ed., 1874].

————. 3rd ed. 1879.

————. 15th ed., ver Hyenne, Robert.

————. See Nombelay Tabares, Julio.

Murray, Walter. "Letters, 1857–1858." *San Francisco Bulletin,* 1858; Reprinted Angel Myron.

Nadeau, Remi. "Joaquín, Hero, Villain, or Myth?" *Westways,* Jan. 1963.

————. *The Real Joaquín Murieta. California's Gold Rush Bandit: Truth v. Myth.* Santa Barbara, California: Crest Publications, 1974.

Neruda, Pablo. *Fulgor y muerte de Joaquín Murieta, bandido chileno ajusticiado en California el 23 de julio de 1853.* Santiago de Chile: Empresa Editorial Zig Zag, 1966; Reprinted 1967. (drama).

————. *Splendeur et mort de Joaquín Murieta.* Paris: Gallimard, 1969.

————. *Splendor and Death of Joaquín Murieta.* Trans. by Ben Belitt. New York: Farrar, Straus, and Giroux, 1972; Reprinted 1973.

————. *Fulgor y muerte de Joaquín Murieta/Splendor and Death of Joaquín Murieta.* London: Alcove Press, 1973.

————. *Fulgor y muerte de Joaquín Murieta.* Buenos Aires: Losada, 1974.

Nicholson, Loren. *Romualdo Pacheco's California. The Mexican-American Who Won.* San Luis Obispo/San José: California Heritage Associates, 1990.

Nombela y Tabares, Julio. *La fiebre de riquezas; siete años en California.* 2 vols. Madrid, 1871-1872. Contains Hyenne's translation. See Monguió.

Pacific Police Gazette. "Joaquín the Mountain Robber or the Bandits of the Sierra Nevada." May 1954. "No copy of this 'biography' has ever come to light" (Nadeau 1974): 115.

Paredes, Américo. 1973. "José Mosqueda and the Folklorization of Actual Events." *Aztlán* 4.1, (1973).

Paredes, Américo. *With His Pistol in His Hand*. Austin: University of Texas Press, 1958.

―――. *A Texas-Mexican Cancionero: Folksongs of the Lower Border* (Urbana: University of Illinois Press, 1976), 23.

Paredes, Raymund A. 1973. "The Image of the Mexican in American Literature." Diss. University of Texas at Austin.

Park, Charles Caldwell ("Carl Gray"). *A Plaything of the Gods*. Boston: Sherman, French, 1912.

Paz, Ireneo ed. *Vida y aventuras del más célebre bandido sonorense Joaquín Murrieta; sus grandes proezas en California*. México: Tipografía y Encuadernación de Ireneo Paz, 1904. (A copy may be found at the Bancroft Library at UC Berkeley.)

―――. *Idem*. 4th ed. 1908.

―――. *Idem*. 5th ed. Los Angeles: Oscar? Paz y Cía, 1919.

―――. *Idem*. 5th ed. [*sic*] México: Editorial Don Quijote, 1953.

―――. See Bell, Frances P.

Peeples, Samuel Anthony. *The Dream Ends in Fury*. New York: Harper, 1949 [novel].

Ridge, John Rollin ("Yellow Bird"). *The Life and Adventures of Joaquín Murieta, the Celebrated California Bandit*. San Francisco, 1854.

―――. *The History of Joaquín Murieta, the King of California Outlaws, Whose Band Ravaged the State in the Early Fifties*. 3rd. [*sic*] ed., "with much and hereto unpublished material." San Francisco: Fred MacCrelish, 1871; revised ed. Hollister, California: Evening Press, 1927.

―――. *The Life and Adventures of Joaquín Murieta, the Celebrated California Bandit*. New edition with Introduction by Joseph Henry Jackson. Norman: University of Oklahoma Press, 1955; Reprinted 1969.

Robb, John Donald. *Hispanic Folk Music in New Mexico and the Southwest*. Norman: University of Oklahoma Press, 1980.

Robin Hood of El Dorado, The. Film directed by William Wellman. Hollywood, 1936.

Rodriguez, Richard. "The Head of Joaquín Murrieta." *California* 10.7 (July 1985): 55–62, 89.

Rojas, Arnold R. "Joaquín Murieta." *The Vaquero*. Charlotte, North Carolina: McNally and Loftin, 1964; Reprint in Luis Valdez and Stan Steiner, 107–109.

Rojas, Manuel. *"Joaquín Murrieta, el patrio." El "Far West" del México cercenado*. Mexicali, B.C.: Gobierno del Estado de Baja California, 1986.

―――. *Idem*. 2nd ed. amended. Mexicali, B.C.: Instituto de Cultura de Baja California, 1990.

————. *Idem.* 3rd ed. amended, 1992.

Romero, Michael. *Joaquín Murrieta: The Life of a Legend.* Soledad, California: Published by the author, 1979.

Rousseau, B.G. "Treasure of Joaquín Mureita [*sic*]" *Overland Monthly* 82 (Jan. 1934): 21–23, 39–40.

San Francisco Daily Herald. 1 March and 18 April 1853.

San Joaquín Republican. Stockton, California. 21, 23 Jan. 1853.

Scanlan, J. M. "Joaquín, a California Fra Diavolo." *Overland Monthly,* 26 Nov. 1895, 530–39.

Schroeter, Dr. O. V. "Joaquín Murrieta, Famous California Outlaw." *Los Angeles Times,* 4 Sept. 1915.

Secrest, William B. *Joaquín, Bloody Bandit of the Mother Lode.* Fresno, California: Saga-West Publishing Co., 1967: 40.

————. *The Return of Joaquín.* Fresno, California: Saga-West Publishing Co., 1973.

————. "Horrible History of a Highwayman's Head." *The Californians.* Nov./Dec. 1986.

Sherman, Edward A. "Recollections of Mayor Edward A. Sherman." *California Historical Society Quarterly* 23 (Dec. 1944): 349–377.

Silva Castro, Raúl. *Panorama literario de Chile.* Santiago: Editorial Universitaria, 1961.

Simmons, Merle E. *The Mexican Corrido as a Source of Interpretive Study of Modern Mexico (1870-1950).* Bloomington: The University of Indiana Press, 1957. Reimpreso en Nueva York en 1969.

Sonnichsen, Philip. See Hermanos Sánchez y Linares.

Statutes of California. 1893. Chapter 136, 194.

Steckmesser, Kent L. "Joaquín Murieta and Billy the Kid." *Western Folklore* 21.2 (April 1962): 77–82.

Steiner, Stan. "On the Trail of Joaquín Murrieta." *American West* 18.1 (1981). Publisher, 1906. Appendix: "Joaquín Murieta the Bandit," 181–200. (Extracted from Ridge's work).

Stewart, Marcus. *Rosita: A California Tale.* San Jose, California: Mercury Steam Press, 1882.

Strachwitch, Chris. See Hermanos Sánchez y Linares.

Valdez , Luis, and Stan Steiner, eds. "Love Secrets of Joaquín Murieta, from an Old Newspaper." In *Aztlán: An Anthology of Mexican American Literature.* New York: Knopf-Vintage Books, 1972.

Vasconcelos, José. *Breve historia de México.* 5th ed. México: Ediciones Botas. 1944.

Walker, Franklin. *San Francisco Literary Frontier.* New York: Knopf, 1939.

———. "Ridge's Life of Joaquín Murieta—The First and Revised Editions Compared." *California Historical Society Quarterly* 16 (1939): 256–262.

Weber, David J. "Joaquín Murrieta." *Foreigners in Their Native Land.* Albuquerque: University of New Mexico Press, 1973. 228–31.

Wells, Evelyn. "Story of California's Notorious Bandits of the Early Fifties." San Francisco, 1923–1924.

West, John O. *To Die Like a Man,* 1964.

Williams, Henry Llewellyn. *Joaquín, the Claude Duval of California, or the Marauder of the Mines.* New York: Pollard & Moss, 1888.

Wood, Dr. Raymund F. *Mariana La Loca: Prophetess of the Cantua & Alleged Spouse of Joaquín Murrieta.* Fresno, California: Fresno County Historical Society, 1970.

———. "New Light on Joaquín Murrieta." *Pacific Historian* 14.1 (Winter 1970): 54–65.

———. See *California Police Gazette,* 1969.

Chronology

1829   Joaquín Murrieta believed born in the Villa de San Rafael, "El Alamito," Altar District, in Sonora, Mexico.

1850   First evidence of "Joaquín" in California.

1852   First news (in the daily newspaper *Alta California*) concerning robberies committed by someone named Joaquín.

1853   May 17: The State Assembly in Sacramento approves a statute authorizing the creation of a company of twenty Rangers assigned to capture any one of five Joaquíns.
        July 24: Death of Joaquín in Arroyo Cantúa.

1854   John Rollin Ridge publishes his biography *The Life and Adventures of Joaquín Murieta the Renowned California Bandit*.

1858   Charles E. B. Howe publishes in San Francisco his drama *Joaquín Murrieta de Castillo, the Renowned California Bandit*.

1859   The magazine *California Police Gazette* publishes Ridge's work in a pirated version under the title *Life of Joaquín Murieta, the Brigand Chief of California*.

1862   The *California Police Gazette* version appears in Paris under the title *Un bandit californien (Joaquín Murieta)*, translated into French by Robert Hyenne.

1865   In New York, Henry Llewellyn Williams publishes the first popular novel on Murrieta: *Joaquín, the Claude Duval of California, or Marauder of the Mines*.

1867   C.M. [Carlos Morla] translates Hyenne's French translation into Spanish and publishes it under the title *El bandido chileno Joaquín Murieta en California*. Origin of the myth of Murrieta's Chilean origin.

1869   Joaquín Miller publishes his poem on Murrieta.

1871–72 Julio Nombela y Tabares includes the life of Joaquín in the second volume of his novel *La fiebre de riquezas, siete años en California*.

1881   In New York, Joseph E. Badger publishes the novel *Joaquín the Terrible*, also titled *Joaquín, the Saddle King*, as part of the Bell Dime Library collection.
        In Santa Barbara, California, *La Gaceta* publishes the first four chapters of *Vida y aventuras de Joaquín Murrieta*.

1882   In San José, California, Marcus Stewart publishes the poem *Rosita, a California Tale*.

1888   Historian Hubert Howe Bancroft narrates the life of Joaquín in his book *California Pastoral*.

1904   In Mexico, Ireneo Paz publishes the Spanish translation of Hyenne's French translation under the title *Vida y aventuras del más célebre bandido sonorense Joaquín Murrieta: sus grandes proezas en California*.

1932   Walter Noble Burns publishes his novel *The Robin Hood of El Dorado: The Saga of Joaquín Murrieta, Famous Outlaw of California's Age of Gold*.

1934   The Sánchez y Linares brothers record the ballad *Corrido de Joaquín Murrieta*.

1936   Burns's novel is made into a film. In Santiago, Chile, Antonio Acevedez Hernández publishes the play *Joaquín Murrieta: Drama en seis actos*.

1939   Dane Coolidge publishes the novel *Gringo Gold*, based on the adventures of Murrieta.

1955   A new edition of Ridge's work from 1854 is published, with an introduction by Joseph Henry Jackson.

1966   Pablo Neruda publishes the cantata *Fulgor y muerte de Joaquín Murieta, bandido chileno ajusticiado en California el 23 de julio de 1853*.

1974   Remi Nadeau publishes the biography *The Real Joaquín Murrieta*.

1980   Frank F. Latta publishes an exhaustive life of Murrieta.

1986   Manuel Rojas publishes the first edition of his book *Joaquín Murrieta, el Patrio*.

Life and adventures
of the celebrated bandit

Joaquin Murrieta

His exploits in the state of California

Joaquín Murrieta by Charles Christian Nahl,
California Police Gazette (1859).

Chapter I

Joaquin Murrieta was born in the Republic of the United States of Mexico. His family, highly respectable people of Sonora, brought him up in his native town, where he received a finished education.

During his childhood he was remarkable for his sweet and gentle disposition. There was nothing in him then to indicate that daring, unconquerable spirit which made him so celebrated later. All who knew him in his youth spoke affectionately of his good, noble and generous nature. They were hardly able to believe that the terrible adventurer of California whom we are going to portray could be the same kind, pleasant Joaquin Murrieta whom they knew.

In 1845 Joaquin left his native town in Sonora to seek his fortune in the capital. He was then sixteen years old, tall, well-formed, with a countenance not only agreeable but handsome, and in addition to these physical, qualities he had a great inclination for adventure of all kinds.

When he arrived in Mexico City he went to the home of Señor Estudillo, an old friend of his father, and presented a letter of introduction, by virtue of which he was very well received by that gentleman. Very soon his protector obtained employment for him as a groom in the stables of President Lopez de Santa-Anna.

This position, relatively mediocre, he was made to understand would lead him to the most elevated governmental posts; it was one of the steps of the ladder by which some, not all, began to rise and succeed in attaining power. Santa-Anna was very fond of horsemanship. Joaquin, whose deeds had given him renown in his native country, and who would often divert himself by taming the wildest horses of Texas, saw in the passion of the ruler of Mexico a means of becoming known to him and of winning his sympathy.

Nevertheless, his ambitious hopes were not realized as he would have wished, and he even had to give up some of his claims on account of the jealous suspicions of his comrades, the groomsmen of the presidential stables.

Among these was one named Cumplido, who had complained more than once of the aristocratic air which Joaquin had employed toward them. Joaquin pretended not to notice the jealousies of the companions; he tried, in fact, to overcome them by attending strictly to his own business, but this was not what the vain Cumplido wished. The occasion which he sought soon presented itself. One day he smiled sneeringly at the manner in which Joaquin mounted his horse. Joaquin was incensed and offered to have a contest with Cumplido, that they might prove to the satisfaction of both which of them was the more skilled in horsemanship. A date was set for the contest, and all of the inhabitants of the president's house waited expectantly for the appointed hour. When the time came the witnesses all stood about, secretly hoping to see the complete overthrow of the young Sonoran.

They commenced with some unimportant runs by way of diversion. Soon, however, came the final jump which must decide the question as to the merit of the horsemen. The test was to clear an adobe wall five feet in height and three in thickness without so much as a hoof touching it. Before the adversaries was a clearance of one hundred feet to prepare for the jump. Cumplido went first, clearing the wall easily and receiving enthusiastic applause from his comrades. Joaquin followed, and while still fifty feet from the wall, raised his horse by the reins and passed over the wall. Just at this moment, and while he was still in the air, a malicious lackey waved a white handkerchief before the horse's eyes, causing the noble animal to move, and thereby touch the wall with his hoofs. The spectators burst out laughing at the accident of which Joaquin was the victim. All but one joined in the ridicule. He was the son of General Canales and had passed through the same vexatious occurrence in his first days of service. Provoked by the shameful conduct of Cumplido, he hurled himself at him, dagger in hand, and had it not been for the quick intervention of Joaquin, in holding down the hand already raised for the blow, that malevolent rival Cumplido would have paid with his life for his cowardly act. Joaquin said that he would not suffer a single drop of blood to be shed on his account. Then, directing a smile of disdain at his adversary, he lightly mounted his horse, cleared the wall at a bound and left the city.

A short time afterward he arrived in his native town, determined to put aside all his ambitious desires, and to live happily and quietly among the delightful surroundings of his childhood. However, in January of 1848 Joaquin went to San Francisco in search of his brother Carlos, who had resided in California for many years past, and who had been given a grant of four leagues of land by a generous governor, as was often the case in those days. He did not find Carlos, nor obtain any news of him, and so returned to Sonora, where he soon married a beautiful young girl named Carmen Felix. A year after his marriage he received a letter from his brother asking him to meet him as soon as possible at the Mission of San Jose in California. Carlos added that he had discovered quantities of gold in the mountains, and that if Joaquin wished to make a fortune, he should lose no time in starting. Joaquin made all the necessary preparations for the journey, but family affairs and his father's illness delayed him ten months. Then he started on his journey accompanied by his beautiful little wife. He arrived in San Francisco and was so surprised at the change which had been made in that city since his last visit that he resolved to spend several days there. Two days after his arrival, walking into one of the rich gambling houses in the Plaza, he met his brother. After embracing him tenderly and entreating him for news of his family, Carlos informed him that the four leagues of land which had been granted him through the Mexican government had been taken away from him by means of false titles, and now he was on his way to the mines in search of a witness whom he needed. Then they would both set out for Mexico for the purpose of having an interview with the concessionary and, if possible, to recover the land in question.

Joaquin told his brother that he would like to accompany him to the mines so that he might see in what quantity the gold was being mined. Carlos agreed to this, but he advised Joaquin to leave his wife in the Mission of Dolores in care of an old friend whom he had there, Senor Manuel Sepulveda.

Joaquin accepted the proposition, and the following day he and his brother went to Sacramento, where they bought horses to carry them to Hangtown (Placerville). There they met the witness whom Carlos needed. He was a young Californian named Flores, who had just arrived from a distant mining camp to sell a quantity of gold dust. Carlos presented him to his brother, and the three went into a Mexican restaurant for dinner. While they were discussing the food which was served them, such as the tortillas and other dishes of that style, and also the robbery of which Carlos was the victim, two men entered the café, bought something to drink at the counter, and after directing a look of apparent indifference at Carlos' table, went out without saying a word. After dinner, Flores asked Joaquin if he might borrow his mule, so that he could ride around the town with Carlos. Joaquin was tired after his journey and remained in his room smoking.

During the war between Mexico and the United States, Joaquin had been thrown in contact with various North Americans, and although he did not agree with all of their ideas, nevertheless, disgusted with the weakness of his own people, he had sometimes regretted that he had not been born in the land of independence and liberty. He would frequently compare the slothfulness, the lassitude, the apathy and submissiveness of character of his own compatriots, with the energy, activity and progress of the Americans, and, above all, with relation to their eternal love of liberty. If his picturesque and pleasant little home, situated in one of the most beautiful valleys of Sonora, had not offered so many attractions, Joaquin would have given up his nationality permanently, converting himself into an American citizen, in fact as well as in preference. At heart he was one already, since the despotism and disloyalty of the Mexican government repelled him.

Soon Joaquin was interrupted in his meditations by the savage tumult of some hundreds of miners who were running through the streets shouting noisily "Hang them! Hang them! Put a rope on their necks and let these Mexicans be tried in eternity, the devilish thieves!" Joaquin rushed from his house and was confronted by the spectacle of his brother and Flores hung from the branch of a tree. They had been accused of stealing horses by the two men who had come from San Francisco, who appeared to be the owners of the stolen animals. Such was the rage of the crowd that the two victims had not had a chance to vindicate themselves, and all of their efforts to get themselves heard, and to prove that the horses were their legitimate property, had been unavailing against the imprecations and savage shouts of that blind multitude. Wondering and terrified at the same time, Joaquin only gathered courage by seeing the body of his brother Carlos swaying inanimately above the groups of demons who surrounded it, and by assuring himself that what he was seeing was not a dream, but the sad truth. Soon he burst into tears, and without losing any time, he procured a mule and returned to Sacramento, bearing in his heart the desire for vengeance.

At Sacramento he took the boat for San Francisco. On his arrival he went to the mission, and from there to the home of Sepulveda, where he told his wife all of the details of the murder of his brother. Joaquin's story made poor Carmen tremble, but with that accent which warmth of sentiment gives to a woman, she admonished him to abandon his project of vengeance, which would be fatal to him, and wait for the consciences of the culprits themselves to punish them sooner or later. She assured him that not all Americans were so depraved and bloodthirsty as those who had taken part in the murder of his brother Carlos. With all the passion of a truly loving heart, she entreated him not to drag himself into their criminal designs.

Her tears and supplications, her kisses of love and of counsel, produced a remarkable change in the intentions of Joaquin and disposed his spirit toward forgetfulness of the evil.

"I will do as you say," he said, arising. "All this has now passed. We will forget and be happy. When we have gathered a quantity of gold dust, we will return to our own country and we will never go away from there again."

Some days afterward, Joaquin, accompanied by his wife, went to the mines situated on the Stanislaus River. There he built a little wooden house, and began to wash the dirt to collect the golden particles which were found in it. In those days the country was invaded by a number of individuals without faith or law to govern them; they were an evil lot and professed a hatred of all Mexicans, seeing in them only a conquered race without any right or privilege, and useful only under domestic bondage or the yoke of slavery. These people could not or would not overcome the prejudice of color and the inborn antipathy of race, two elements which are always more violent, more bitter and more intense among ignorant people. But for those original causes, what is there to excuse their inhuman oppression?

One band of those mad people who delegated to themselves the brutal privilege of doing everything at their caprice, presented itself to Joaquin, and advised him to abandon his claim, since no man of his race was allowed to work in the mines of that region. When Joaquin refused to leave a place which promised him the hope of working out a fortune for himself, the fiercest ones of the gang left him prostrated from the force of blows with the butts of their revolvers. While he lay senseless on the ground, they over-powered his sweet and beloved wife, Carmen, and after subjecting her to the worst indignities imaginable, they took her life.

Carmen, Joaquín's wife, is killed after she is raped.

Chapter II

It is easy to imagine the desperation and the thirst for vengeance which agitated the heart of Joaquin when he came to himself and saw what had happened. But while that grief was torturing his soul, he felt himself incapable of fighting alone against the murderers of his wife and brother. One imprudence might cost him very dearly. He resolved, therefore, to wait and to suffer with composure until an opportunity to put his plans into execution should present itself.

With that object, in April of 1850, he went to Calaveras County and worked hard in Murphy's mines. Presently, he rested from his work in the mines and tried to make a fortune playing cards. "Monte" was a game very much in vogue in Mexico, and furthermore it was considered by some classes of society as one of the most honorable occupations.

At first fortune smiled on him, but very soon the tyrant luck declared itself against him in an abrupt and thorough manner. Joaquin then threw himself into the murky depths of crime.

One day he went to see one of his friends named Valenzuela, not far from his camp, and at night returned to Murphy's mounted on a horse which his friend had loaned him. Suddenly, he found himself surrounded by a furious crowd, which accused him of stealing. Several persons said that the horse which he rode had been stolen some weeks before. Joaquin declared that the animal had been loaned to him, at the same time trying to convince his accusers of Valenzuela's honesty. But they would not listen. They took the despised Mexican youth, tied him to a tree and gave him a shameful beating before all the crowd. Following this, the savage mob went to the house of Valenzuela and he was hanged without giving him any time to prove his innocence.

This was sufficient to provoke a sudden change in Joaquin's character: one of those terrible changes, both implacable and sordid. His impassioned soul did not recognize any limit: the perception of honor lost all its worth in that heart, ruined by adversity. He swore that from that time on he would live only for revenge, and that he would not leave in his pathway a single place that was not sprinkled with the blood of his enemies.

A short time after this affair, on a beautiful night, an American was following a foot-path a short distance from the village. On going down through a ravine which the narrow path crossed, he found himself suddenly face to face with Joaquin, whose eyes were sparkling with rage, like those of a tiger thirsting for blood. All his body shook with a nervous trembling. For a moment the two men looked fixedly at each other. At last Joaquin threw himself upon the traveler, giving a ferocious shout, and buried his dagger in his breast.

"What have I done to you?" murmured the American, falling to the ground. "Mercy! Have pity on me!"

"Did you have it for me when you helped them to give me a beating before a great multitude of people, when, with the consciousness of your strength and protected by the brutality of your friends, you overpowered an innocent man—a man like you, a man made in the image of God and possessing a soul and a heart like all others, a man who in himself alone has more honesty than all of you together? And did you have pity when you overcame that man and horsewhipped him and made him suffer a thousand tortures? When they hanged my brother by the neck like a dog, was he given any grace? When they killed the most beloved treasure which my heart possessed and when she sought mercy of those wretches, throwing herself at their feet, did they have compassion on that unhappy creature? Oh! Just to think of it, my heart is set on fire," continued Joaquin fired with passion, raising a hand toward his heart, while with the other he struck another dagger thrust at his victim.

"Murderer!" exclaimed the American, leaning upon an elbow on the ground and directing his dying gaze at the terrible Joaquin. "Pity! Oh, pity!" But before he finished the phrase, the sword of Joaquin pierced his heart, leaving him a corpse.

Beside himself with the thirst for vengeance with which he was possessed, the Mexican continued to stab his victim, until the body of the unfortunate American was practically reduced to bits.

"Now," said Joaquin, "my work of extermination has begun. Forward!" His teeth chattered convulsively; his body twitched; his eyes were raised to the blue sky overhead; his hand, convulsed and trembling, grasped the dagger which dripped with the blood of his victim. He continued speaking: "I have here one of my offenders, extended at my feet. Now that I have taught my heart and my hand what it is their duty to perform, I swear not to rest nor to live in peace until I have destroyed the last one. And you, Carmen, whose spirit waits to keep watch over me and to protect me, you, too, will be avenged, and in a terrible manner. My arm is strong now to accomplish its work of destruction. Hereafter, the blood of my enemies will flow in abundance, and as clear as our mountain torrents."

The next day the body of the American was found by some miners, and although he was horribly mutilated, they recognized him as one of the men who had done most to maltreat Joaquin at the time of his whipping.

A short time afterward, a doctor happened to pass near the place where the murder had been committed and met two persons, mounted on horses, who fired their revolvers at him. Thanks to the agility of his legs and the unevenness of the land, the doctor succeeded in escaping without any other damage than that his hat was pierced by a bullet. If the bullet had been directed an inch lower, he would have been a dead man.

These deeds terrorized all those who had taken part in the conspiracy against Joaquin. They did not dare to go outside of the town. They would hardly go a short distance into the country, or move to go out upon the highway, where they would be mysteriously murdered. Each time news was received of a murdered man having been found on the roads or bypaths, it always developed that the victim was one of Joaquin's enemies.

A committee selected on account of these frequent murders declared Joaquin to be an outlaw, and there remained for him no other recourse than to follow the criminal career which he had begun in such a bloody manner. He considered it necessary for the best accomplishment of his enterprise to have horses and money, which he was unable to obtain in any other way except by robbing his victims. In this manner he was converted into a bandit before he was twenty years old.

In 1851 everybody knew that a band of highwaymen was committing excesses throughout all of California, and their chief was no other than the youth, Joaquin Murrieta. Caravans were surprised on the highways. They were obliged to stop and give up whatever they had with them. Those who traveled through wild and solitary regions were violently pulled from their saddles with lassoes and killed in the thickets. Horses disappeared from the ranches. In a word, the whole state was disturbed by the exhibition of pillage and destruction caused by Joaquin's party of bandits.

Joaquin's superior intelligence and education sufficed to make him respected by his comrades. He was soon surrounded by a crowd of his compatriots, whose number increased day by day with the fame of his exploits. Among those who joined Joaquin, a youth by the name of Reinaldo Felix stood out above all the others. He was a brother of Joaquin's wife, and had the same desire of avenging the murder of his sister as Joaquin himself. Felix was named second lieutenant of the gang, and more than once he distinguished himself at the front of a detachment, or at the side of "Jack Three Fingers," a chieftain who had affiliated under Joaquin's standard, attracted by the fame of his bravery.

Jack was a wild beast disguised as a man, and was known in Mexico under the name of Manuel Garcia. During the Mexican war he lost a finger in a skirmish. From this he received the name by which he was known in California. This was the fellow who surprised two Americans on the road between Sonora and Bodega, undressed them, and tortured them cruelly, stabbing them repeatedly. He cut their tongues out and plucked out their eyes and then burned their quivering bodies.

Of Joaquin's satellites may be cited Pedro Gonzalez, Luis Guerra, Juan Cardoza and Joaquin Valenzuela, all daring men, crafty, accustomed to fatigue and burning with desires of vengeance. Gonzalez, who had the merit of knowing horses very well (he had stolen so many!) was commissioned to provide them for the company. He also served as a spy and wherever the band was directed, he would give exact details of the situation of the neighboring towns. Valenzuela was a brother of the man who was hanged the same day that they gave Joaquin a beating. He had served much time in Mexico in Guerra's company at the orders of a very well-known bandit, a guerrilla and a monk at the same time, called Father Jarauta. At the time when the events which we are narrating took place, Joaquin's band was composed of forty-five men, more or less, and reinforcements were continually arriving from lower California and Sonora.

At the head of this powerful group of bullies, Joaquin plundered the state in the year 1851, without the many people who were friendly with him even imagining, when they saw him frequently in the towns, that that man had the least part in the affairs which everyone was discussing, and which had terrified the inhabitants of California. Sometimes he would remain several weeks in the same village, gambling, without anyone suspecting his true character.

In the summer of 1851 Joaquin was living in a remote part of the town of San Jose. One night he was arrested because he was implicated in a brawl, which occurred in one of the "fandango" dance halls. The judge fined him twelve dollars. As soon as he was free, he asked Sheriff Clark to accompany him to his house. He said that he would pay him the twelve dollars and a fee for his trouble. Joaquin and the sheriff began the walk, talking in a friendly manner, but when they reached the edge of a grove, the bandit drew out his dagger. He told Clark that he had brought him there to kill him and before he was able to make use of his revolver, Joaquin stabbed him in the heart. Clark had incurred the animosity of Joaquin's gang because of the vigilance which he exercised over their members. Several times he had tried to arrest some of them, and on account of that, their chief had taken the opportunity of disposing of him.

Some months afterward, Joaquin established himself near a group of tents and shacks known as Sonora Camp, situated four or five miles from Marysville. Very soon nothing else was talked of in that locality except the frequent and diabolical murders which occurred there. From the seventh to the twelfth of November, no less than twelve people were killed, and in a territory which was only about twelve miles long. All of these crimes were committed by Joaquin's band. Some of the citizens of Marysville were alarmed at the knowledge of what was taking place almost at the gates of the city. They quickly organized a company to go out to meet the authors of such nefarious crimes, with the hope of capturing them and delivering them over to justice. The company made all the investigations which they believed necessary, and the only thing which they accomplished was the discovery of six more corpses not far from Honcut Creek, which showed visible signs that death had been caused by strangulation with the lasso. After they had scoured all of Yuba County without having found any of the murderers, the investigators returned to Marysville, regretting very much their inability to accomplish their mission satisfactorily. The following day it became known that several persons had been killed near Bidwell's Bar, which terrified the whole town. The fear was general, and none dared to travel the public highways. Finally, their suspicions fell upon Sonora Camp, occupied exclusively by Mexicans, many of whom possessed splendid horses, magnificent serapes, a great quantity of jewelry and much gold, without the appearance of working at anything. One night when the moon was shining in all of its beauty, the sheriff of Yuba County, Mr. Buchanan, accompanied by Elke Bowen, went out to Sonora Camp to inspect the place and to arrest three individuals who were suspected of being hidden there. When they crossed a palisade, four Mexicans attacked them, and the sheriff was badly wounded by a revolver bullet, which penetrated his body from one side to the other. The Mexicans fled. Buchanan was taken to Marysville, where his life was in danger for some time. He finally recovered from his wound.

Then the bandits tried to leave the vicinity of Marysville as soon as possible. They retired toward the western edge of the Shasta Mountains, continuing for several months in a savage manner and only appearing in the valleys at intervals to secure food for their horses. In that solitary region, visited principally by miners, there were found some human skeletons. Some of them had no signs to indicate the manner of their death, but in others could be plainly distinguished the marks of revolver shots which had conducted them to another world in a mysterious manner.

Chapter III

In the first days of the spring of 1852, Joaquin and his party went down from the mountains, taking with them about three hundred horses, stolen during the winter. They took them to the state of Sonora, crossing the southern part of California, and taking great care to travel only at night. There in Mexico they sold the horses.

Some weeks later the men returned to California, establishing their headquarters in a splendid place covered with forage and known as Arroyo Cantova. It was a valley seven or eight miles long, fertile, with water in abundance, and protected by a range of hills which had only one narrow pass in which a few determined men would be able to defend themselves against a colossal army. This rich and delightful valley was situated between the Tejon and Pacheco Passes east of the great range of mountains and west of Tulare Lake. From its topographical position the place was suitable for a retreat inasmuch as there was not a single habitation for fifty miles around it. Game was very abundant there; bear, elk, antelope, deer, quail, wild turkey and many small animals seemed to be placed there for the express purpose of feeding mankind. The location which Joaquin and his gang selected for making their camp could not have been more suitable.

In the center of a group of dense oak trees, always green, Joaquin fixed his dwelling. The bandit chief was often seen reclining in the fine grass with which nature had adorned that pleasant valley, at his side a beautiful and winsome young girl whom he had won in Sonora, when he and his band of outlaws went there to sell their stolen horses.

Clarita, as the graceful girl was called, was a daughter of Don Sebastian Valero, a Spanish grandee, who after having lost his fortune extravagantly, had retired to Mexico with a small capital and had bought a piece of land adjoining the ranch of Joaquin's father. The first time that Joaquin and Clarita saw each other, she was only ten years old, and Joaquin was thirteen. Nevertheless, with her feminine instinct she did not fail to notice the perfect manners and hand-some face of the boy, as well as his martial air in mounting a horse. As the years passed, each time they met Clarita cast tender and impassioned glances at the youth. But Joaquin only answered these demonstrations of affection with indifference. Clarita was really in love with the youth, and in her lively imagination many romantic ideas took shape, which were not dispelled by the observation of Joaquin's matter-of-fact conduct.

Some years later, when Joaquin went away from his paternal home with the woman whom he had chosen for a wife, and when he said good-bye to all of his relatives and friends, Clarita put on one of his fingers a gold ring, hiding herself away immediately to weep in silence and to try to relieve herself of the weight which oppressed her heart. Joaquin only saw in the gift a proof of friendliness toward his wife, and hastened to give it to her, but Carmen saw in it anoth-er idea very different, and begged her husband to wear it always, as evidence of her love. Carmen supposed that the Spanish girl had given the ring to her husband as a token of friendship and that she would be offended if he should not fulfill her wish. Carmen imag-ined, too, that the ring would be of use in time of danger. Her simplicity still retained certain remnants of old Spanish superstition.

"It would not be strange," she said to her husband, "if this ring should have some secret, and perhaps it might be necessary to you in the hour of danger." Joaquin smiled ironically, but from that time on until his death he never failed to carry with him the pretended tal-isman. There was just one time when he forgot to put it on; the day when he was treated so shamefully at Murphy's camp. The ring had been forgotten in his room, among other jewelry. After that, he never failed to carry it with him.

When Joaquin returned to Sonora, Clarita observed that the ring was always to be seen on his hand. She believed that it was because he loved her, and told him of her affection. During his stay in California, Joaquin had sent the news regularly to his family of all of the events which formed a part of his history. Clarita knew, more-over, that his wife had died and that he was a notorious bandit. But in spite of all, she loved him with tenderness and with all the warmth of young Spanish girls.

At first, Joaquin contented himself with admiring the innocence and candor which the young girl displayed in proving her feeling for him. But soon he succumbed to the influence of Clarita's beautiful eyes and decided to throw himself at her feet, declaring that his first love had been nothing more than the whim of a youthful heart, and that for the first time he found himself bewitched by a feeling as pure as it was violent. In this manner he soon became the possessor of a faithful friend, and when the two young people seated themselves under the verdant foliage, in the shade of the live oaks of the Arroyo Cantova, the name of poor Carmen, and all of her tenderness, faithfulness and love had already been forgotten.

The bandits remained some weeks at headquarters, and Joaquin then divided them into detachments. At this time his band was composed of seventy-five persons. He gave the command of the detachments to Valenzuela, to Luis Guerra and to Jack Three Fingers, sending them to different places with the order to occupy themselves only in stealing horses and mules, for he had a plan under consideration for which he needed from one thousand to twenty-five hundred of those animals.

Joaquin went in another direction, accompanied by Reinaldo Felix, Juan Cardoza and Pedro Gonzalez. They went with three women disguised as men, and armed to the teeth. One of them was Joaquin's sweetheart, the other two the wives of Gonzalez and Felix. All who formed a part of this expedition were very well mounted, but only the chief knew its object.

When they arrived at Mokelumme Hill, in Calaveras County, they mingled with the Americans who lived there, and who were friends of theirs. When they visited the gambling houses or passed through the town, no one would have been able to distinguish them from the other inhabitants of their race. This was in April 1852. The women had returned to the dress of their own sex and everyone admired their modesty and their irreproachable conduct.

The men would go away from time to time, mounted on their horses, and would travel a distance of several miles, after which they would return to their houses, where they would be awaited with impatience by their faithful companions. Joaquin had all the appearance of an elegant and fortunate gambler and the life he lived confirmed the public's opinion.

In the meantime, the other detachments performed with zeal the mission which Joaquin had committed to them, each one taking its own direction. Joaquin saw in the papers each day that most of the ranches of the South had been despoiled of their horses and mules. The papers blamed him for all of these thefts.

In all of the murders and robberies in which Joaquin had figured personally, he always appeared in a different suit. In that way no one was able to recognize him. If anyone should have met him on the road, and by chance should again see him in some town, it would hardly have been imagined that it was the same man, such was the change which was made in him by means of his disguise. Various times he had mingled with the loungers and heard conversations which referred to him, laughing to himself on hearing the suppositions of which he was the object, with reference to his gang and the kind of life which he and his companions were accustomed to lead.

After he had been on Mokelumme Hill as long as he considered it necessary, he prepared to leave. It was the first of May. In the middle of the night all was ready for the departure. Before starting out, Joaquin, as was his custom, visited the gambling houses and saloons, establishments which figured most prominently in the towns of California at this time.

He was seated at a table of monte, upon which he had carelessly piled a small quantity of silver, playing to kill time, when suddenly he was distracted from the game by a person who pronounced his name, directly in front of the place where he was seated. He looked toward four or five Americans who were discussing him heatedly, although in low voices. One of them, a tall and robust man, who had a dagger and a revolver in his belt, declared that his greatest desire would be to find himself face to face with Joaquin, that if this should happen he would kill him with the same speed which he would be dealt with by a snake.

On hearing these words, the audacious bandit leaped over the card table, and before the whole crowd, drew from his belt a six-shooter, and with manifest bravery, without any defense except his extended arm, he spoke to the crowd which surrounded him:

"I am Joaquin Murrieta! If any of you wishes to kill me, now is his chance. I wager that you do not fire a shot."

The movement of the youth had been so sudden, so unexpected, that all remained in silence, as if petrified. Profiting by the consternation and the confusion by which all were possessed, Joaquin wrapped himself in his mantle and went out of the saloon like lightning, mounting his horse and fleeing at full speed. A few moments were enough for the players to arouse from their stupor and recover their natural courage. Joaquin heard the revolver shots ring out, which they sent him from the saloon, but, fortunately, none made any impression on him, and the shooters received in exchange for the powder and spent bullets some words of contempt which Joaquin flung at them as he calmly withdrew from the town.

Chapter IV

When Joaquin returned to the Arroyo Cantova, decided upon beforehand for a meeting place, he found three or four hundred horses and mules brought by his companions, who were encamped, awaiting new orders. The chieftain dispatched some of them to take the animals to Sonora for better security. At the same time he sent the sum of five thousand dollars to be delivered to one of his secret agents, a resident of that state.

At the end of May he began to be bored. The inactivity was irksome. He began again his excursions along the highways, accompanied always by Gonzalez, Felix, Cardoza and the three women, who, mounted on magnificent horses, formed the handsomest trio of horsemen that any young man would ever imagine.

In the first ten days they met only some poor travelers who were going to the mines on foot. Joaquin's purse was about empty, so that he resolved to fall upon the first person whom he should meet with the appearance of having any money. At nightfall there appeared a young man named Allen Ruddel, who was conducting a convoy of provisions. Joaquin left his friends behind, made his horse gallop toward Ruddel, and cutting across a field, he confronted him, and asked him to lend him all the money which he carried with him. Deceived perhaps by the youthful face of his questioner, the driver believed that he was accosted by a highwayman who was a novice at the work. He therefore responded to his request with a sneering smile, and urged his horses forward. Joaquin advanced toward him, and drawing his revolver, in a brusque and peremptory tone he ordered him to stop. Ruddel began to tremble and obeyed him.

"Now, friend," said Joaquin in a very mild voice, "I only desire that you should lend me your money, for although I am a robber, I do not enjoy robbing a poor working man, and I swear to you, by my name of Joaquin, that I will return all that you lend me."

Ruddel, instead of answering, made a sudden movement to draw his revolver. Joaquin continued:

"Come, I tell you, don't do anything crazy. I am seldom without money, and you may count upon my word. I do not wish to kill you, but if you threaten me with your revolver, I will most certainly take your life."

Ruddel did not take Joaquin's advice. It may have been the effect of fear, or because his revolver caught on some obstacle as he drew it out, but it is certain that he was not able to arm himself in time. In that instant Reinaldo Felix came up at a trot, to advise his chief to leave soon, as two well mounted men were coming toward him.

Joaquin replaced his revolver in his holster, swearing, pulled from his belt a great dagger, and gave a thrust at the driver, who fell from his seat dead. Ruddel was carrying with him four hundred dollars. Joaquin left the body in the road, joined his companions, and they resumed their journey. Hardly five minutes after this affair, the two horsemen whom Felix had reported, appeared on the highway. Then Joaquin said: "We shall see now how much money these travelers carry, and I swear that this time they will not laugh at me."

He spurred his horse a little in advance of the others. Revolver in hand, and pointed toward the travelers, the young bandit ordered them to stop. The horses, pulled up violently by the bridle, rose up on their hind feet, and one of the horsemen answered, laughing, "What! Joaquin, don't you know me? Have you forgotten Bill Miller?"

"The devil! It is true," said Joaquin, smiling. "Now I remember. It seems to me that you travel very well mounted."

"Oh, yes, well enough. You know I select my animals in the Sacramento Valley. At present I am in the wool growing business in this beautiful country. My funds are very low, so that I have to make some money as soon as possible."

"Is that so, Bill? Well, you are an American, but you have always been a good friend to me. If a hundred dollars will help you any, here they are, take them."

"Thanks," said Bill, taking the money, "this is a real fortune. Now I must leave you. Good luck until we meet again."

"Good-bye friend!" responded Joaquin, "and may you have as good luck as you always do."

After that, the two parties went off, each one in its own direction.

At that time there lived a captain named Harry Love, who had the idea of organizing at his expense and upon his own responsibility, a small company to pursue the daring Joaquin. From his youth Captain Love had traveled and withstood all kinds of fatigue. He had performed very good service in the war with Mexico as a dispatch bearer, when, in exchanging messages between military groups, he had penetrated into the wildest and most dangerous places of the enemy country. Cool-blooded in any trial in the hour of danger, and with an exceptional ability in handling a dagger, a revolver, or a rifle, Captain Love was the man most suitable to face an adversary as formidable as Joaquin.

After the death of Allen Ruddel, Captain Love followed the trail of the bandit, pursuing him to the ranch of San Luis Gonzaga, which he knew served as a shelter for the company of outlaws. He arrived there at night, and was informed by a spy whom he had posted in the place, that those whom he sought were in a tent at the other side of the ranch. He went cautiously to that side, at the front of his men. Before he arrived at the door, a woman who lived in a cabin close by gave the alarm, and, alert as a greyhound, Felix, Gonzalez, and Cardoza cut the cloth at the back of their tent and escaped, protected by the darkness of the night.

When Captain Love arrived there, he found himself in front of four or five women, three of whom were the sweethearts of the desperadoes. He did not know this or he would have overpowered them in some way, and would have compelled his adversaries to appear. He had other matters to which to attend, on account of which he did not consider it expedient to continue the pursuit. For one more time the bandits escaped with only a scare.

After they left the tent, the robbers went in a direct line to the place called Orris Timbers, situated some eight miles from the ranch of San Luis. There they stole about thirty beautiful horses, which they took to the neighboring mountains. The following night they returned to their companions, who were hastily disguised and all rushed out on a gallop toward the mountains, where they stopped until the next day. They then went on to Los Angeles, across the plain of Tulare, driving the stolen animals before them.

When they reached the country of the Tejon Indians, the bandits camped on the edge of a small stream about five miles away from the principal encampment of the tribe. All appearances indicated that there was nothing to fear from those inoffensive people, so they laid aside their arms and resolved to rest and enjoy themselves a few days. Nevertheless, an Indian had approached the camp of the Mexicans, and observing their elegant equipment, their jewels, their beautiful horses which were grazing all about them, he hurried to the Indian capital to tell the old chief Sappatara.

Excited by his avarice, Sappatara saw in this a favor of the Great Spirit, who was sending those riches to his territory for the good of his tribe, and he determined to appropriate them himself. One night Murrieta, Gonzalez and Felix were reposing peacefully in the shelter of some oaks, without dreaming that any sign of danger menaced them. Cardoza, extended lazily upon the grass, was watching the horses who were grazing a short distance away. Suddenly, they found themselves surrounded by a formidable number of Indians, who bound them firmly with great leather thongs. The Indians were overjoyed at the success of their enterprise. As a matter of fact, if the outlaws had offered the slightest resistance, if the Indians had only seen a dagger or revolver, they would have fled like antelopes. They led the Mexicans to the place which served as the residence of the Indian chief, where they were relieved of their jewels and their clothing, being permitted to retain only some pieces of blankets.

The outlaws left with the robber Indians four thousand dollars in gold and two thousand dollars in jewelry, to say nothing of the danger of losing their lives at any moment. For eight days the old chief held them as prisoners of war, racking his brain to decide whether to shoot them, to hang them, to drown them, or to burn them. At last, believing that they had already paid with interest for their temerity in invading his territory, old Sapparata gave them a long lecture, to enlarge upon the enormity and the number of crimes which they must have committed to have in their possession so much gold and silver. Then he had them escorted to the edge of his domain by a detachment of Indians armed with the daggers and revolvers stolen from the Mexicans, who had no other recourse than to leave that region, completely routed.

Chapter V

Joaquin had endured his captivity with the greatest resignation, hardly able to keep from laughing at his ridiculous plight. He admired the Tejon Indians, who were not warriors by nature, because they had sufficient courage to carry out their enterprise with such good success.

After traveling two days, the little band arrived at the entrance of the Tejon Pass, situated several miles from the San Francisco Ranch. There, by chance, appeared one of their friends named Jim Mountain or Mountain Jim. Learning of their adventure, he returned immediately to the ranch and soon fitted them out with the necessary clothing. He also provided three horses. One of these, a black one, very beautiful and well harnessed, was presented to the chieftain, together with a Colt revolver and a dagger. Joaquin, who a few moments before had been a defenseless fugitive, found himself unexpectedly dressed, spurred, well mounted and armed—in short, transformed into a powerful and terrible bandit, thanks to the resources of the association formed and directed by his genius as an organizer.

When all were ready, Joaquin, Felix and Gonzalez mounted horses, each one with his sweetheart, and rushed off at a gallop in the direction of San Gabriel. Cardoza followed them on foot. When they arrived at San Gabriel, it was already late at night. They went to the place where they usually met, and were surprised to find Guerra, Valenzuela and their gangs. These outlaws had returned from Sonora earlier than they had expected, and, not finding the chief in the Arroyo Cantova, they prepared to start out on an expedition of robbery rather than to be idle. Since their return, they had committed numerous depredations in the vicinity of San Gabriel. But they had been pursued by General Dean, who was employing all his forces to capture them.

"That man will have to die," said Joaquin. "He has made it dangerous for us and we ought to rid ourselves of him before leaving this place." All agreed with the words of their captain.

Then the conversation turned to the journey to Sonora, the bandits informing their chief that the horses had been put on the ranch which he had indicated.

The band had been well provided with food, blankets, liquor, and cigars, and so they decided to remain two or three weeks in the encampment near San Gabriel. During that time Gonzalez and Cardoza had been sent by their leader with a special mission to the ranch of San Buenaventura. It is known that Joaquin was accustomed to hiding himself on this ranch when he judged it necessary.

Some days later, Captain Harry Love, then deputy sheriff of Los Angeles County, who knew Gonzalez personally, saw him with Cardoza on the outskirts of San Buenaventura and directly he undertook to take them prisoners and to deliver them to justice. After he had spied upon their movements with the greatest patience, he saw them enter a small saloon situated on a road which led into the mountains. The captain hid behind a rock and waited for them to come out of the saloon. At the end of twenty minutes Captain Love emerged from his hiding place and went toward the saloon. He was near it when Cardoza came out, but alone, and took the road toward the mountain.

Harry Love threw himself upon him, but the daring bandit escaped from his hands and ran like a deer. The captain fired two pistol shots. One of the bullets grazed Cardoza's head, the other struck a rock behind which the fugitive was hiding. The captain did not particularly desire to catch Cardoza, but rather preferred to capture Gonzalez, whom he knew as a great rascal, and directed all of his attention toward him. He entered the bar-room, pistol in hand, expecting a ferocious resistance. He was very much astonished to find the bandit very drunk, which enabled Love to disarm him at his pleasure. A half hour later the two started on to Los Angeles. Cardoza saw them from a distance and hurried to give the news of the arrest to his chief.

Joaquin, accompanied by Jim Mountain and Valenzuela's gang, left hurriedly with the object of surrounding Love and saving the life of their valiant comrade. They proceeded, or rather ran, all night, and at dawn they perceived the prisoner and his guardian Gonzalez, seeing the help which had arrived, waved his handkerchief in the air. Love realized then the danger which menaced him traveling alone with such a dangerous companion, and seeing the sign he made, he drew his revolver and fired a shot at his prisoner. The bullet penetrated Gonzalez' heart. Love cast one look behind him, and saw, in the midst of a cloud of dust, a party of horsemen coming like the wind in his direction. He considered it prudent then to move on very speedily, which he proceeded to do without delay.

A few minutes later the bandits stopped at the place where Gonzalez had fallen, and at the sight of his dead body a shout of rage and desperation arose from all. But there was no remedy. The body was abandoned and the gang returned to San Gabriel. Joaquin supposed that Jack Three Fingers and his detachment would be found in Los Angeles. He also had notice that Captain Wilson, deputy sheriff of Santa Barbara County, had been in San Gabriel the night before seeking the chief of the outlaws, whom he had sworn to take, dead or alive.

Desirous of seeing Jack Three Fingers, Joaquin took two of his strongest men and went with them to Los Angeles, where he met his sub-lieutenant. He told him that ten miles from San Gabriel he had burned a house, whose inhabitants had been murdered, one after the other, as they fled to escape from the flames.

Joaquin remained several days in Los Angeles awaiting the unknown. One night he had gone out for a little walk, and had found out that Captain Wilson was lodging at the best hotel in Los Angeles, and that he was talking openly of his intention of doing away with the chief of the outlaws so famous in that locality. The following night there was a quarrel in front of the hotel, and the people gathered around the spot to witness a deadly combat between two Indian miners. Wilson mingled with the other people as a spectator of this scene. Suddenly, there appeared before him a well mounted man who murmured in his ear, "I am Joaquin Murrieta!"

Surprised, the Captain raised his head; but hardly had he done this when he received a bullet which left him extended on the ground. Immediately, the reckless outlaw spurred his horse and disappeared. The battle of the two Indians was a ruse invented by Jack Three Fingers so that Wilson would go out of the hotel and Joaquin would be able to rid himself of that enemy.

After a short conference with his sub-lieutenants, the young bandit sent Valenzuela and his gang, and Jim Mountain and Cardoza to San Diego County. He gave them orders to seize all of the horses which they found and take them to the headquarters at Arroyo Cantova. Meanwhile, Joaquin would return to San Gabriel with Jack Three Fingers and some others.

A week later, Luis Guerra, who had been commissioned to spy upon the movements of General Bean, saw him go out one night from his residence in San Gabriel and direct his horse toward a private estate situated several miles from there. Joaquin, Guerra and Jack Three Fingers rushed out in that direction, lying in ambush along the road about a mile from the house. When the general appeared, the outlaws surprised him, without giving him time to make use of the arms which he carried with him. Guerra and Jack Three Fingers pulled him down from his saddle, while Joaquin twice buried his dagger in his heart, leaving him extended at his feet.

Jack Three Fingers wished to satisfy his brutal instincts further on the corpse of the ill-fated General Bean. He drew his revolver and fired three shots into his head.

This terrible deed concluded, Joaquin rejoined his gang and advanced toward the north, to Calaveras County, leaving traces of his passage by means of innumerable robberies which he committed.

One night when he was traveling along the highway alone, he met a man named Joseph Lake, whom he had known before he became an outlaw. They had worked together in the mines on the Stanislaus River, and had lived a long time in the greatest intimacy. After he had greeted him in a friendly way, Joaquin took the same direction and for several minutes proceeded at Lake's side, mute and silent. After a short time he struck his companion lightly on the shoulder and said to him in a disturbed voice:

"Joe, you know what I was before and what I am now. But I swear before heaven that only injustice and tyranny have led me to the place where I am now. I do not ask today either your regard or your good opinion; but I seek a favor of you, and it is that you will not betray me before those who do not know my name and my character."

"Joaquin," answered the other, "it is true that in another time we were bound by ties of friendship so strong that anyone would have

General Bean's assassination.

thought us brothers. Indeed, to this day we would have continued to be the same if you had not left the good road. But now there is between us an immense abyss of dishonor, and the tie which united us has been broken forever."

"What you have just said is right, Joe," answered Joaquin, "but you ought not to betray me for that. In spite of all, I like you and I remember the past, and it would grieve me very much to have to kill you. Nevertheless, if you speak a word of this encounter, which we have had here tonight, it will not leave me any other recourse than to send you to another world."

"Do not be afraid," said Lake, "No one shall know that I have seen you." And courteously bidding each other good-bye, they separated. Joaquin took a winding road for returning to his headquarters, and the American followed the road which led to village of Hornitos, where he lived.

The following day Lake informed several of his townsmen of the encounter which he had had. He told them that he had seen the famous Joaquin Murrieta, and that he was near there. A short distance from the American, a Mexican was standing, wrapped in his serape and smoking without seeming to pay any attention to what was going on around him. Lake asked him for a light, and the Mexican gave it to him with all of the usual courtesy of a Spaniard or a Spanish American. Three hours later a horseman whose face was hidden under a thick black beard slowly approached a store in front of which Lake was loafing with some of his friends. With the greatest politeness, the horseman asked the American to come to him.

"You know me, Joe," said the man on the horse.

"Oh!" exclaimed Lake, retreating one or two steps, "I recognize your accent; yes, you are—"

"Yes, sir, I am Joaquin. You have betrayed me." And saying these words, Joaquin blew out Lake's brains with a pistol shot. Thanks to the swiftness of his horse, Joaquin departed unhurt by the volley which the friends of Lake sent after him. Some minutes afterward he was to be found on the top of a hill, accompanied by forty or fifty men who were proceeding quietly at his orders.

Chapter VI

Joaquin felt uneasy about the luck of Valenzuela, Cardoza, and Jim Mountain. Anxious to know the result of their mission, he started out with his gang toward the general meeting place. The next night the bandits camped above a ravine, and after lighting an enormous bonfire they began to refresh themselves with Nantes sardines and crackers, which they always carried with them. In the middle of the supper, Jack Three Fingers called the attention of his comrades to a ray of light which seemed to come from the depth of the ravine.

"It is probably the glare of a campfire of some Indian vagabonds," said Joaquin, casting an indifferent glance toward the place where it originated. Soon, addressing himself to Jack Three Fingers, he said smiling, "Since you are the discoverer, Jack, and since it is possible that there may be something better than is commonly found in miners' cabins, I will ask you to go reconnoitering toward that place."

"With the greatest pleasure, Captain," replied the other, and immediately he set out on foot. Wiping his mouth on his shirt sleeve, he added, "I am always ready for this kind of an enterprise."

"That is good," said Joaquin, "but finish your supper."

"Certainly not! I am going at once. There is no danger of the sardines getting cold." And Jack Three Fingers, after putting a dagger and a revolver in his belt, started out quickly to the place which had been indicated.

"Jack is a valiant companion," said Felix. "Unfortunately, he is too bloodthirsty."

"Oh!" answered Guerra, "he is much less so than old Father Jarauta, who was the chieftain of several of us in Mexico."

"That's right," a half dozen of the outlaws exclaimed in chorus.

"That fellow was a regular demon!" continued Guerra. "What a monster! If you had seen him one night when he surprised a company. But we will not speak of that. My heart bleeds and I feel bad when I remember those good times."

At that moment, Jack Three Fingers appeared, driving in front of him eight Chinamen who trembled like quick-silver. When they saw themselves in the presence of so many armed men, they fell on their knees and began to beg for mercy in a most pitiful manner. Their dismal entreaties, their pleading looks and their grimaces and gestures excited the hilarity of the bandits, who could not contain their laughter. Jack ordered the unfortunate prisoners, half with words and half with signs, to change their position and to seat themselves on a rock a short distance from the bonfire. This order was obeyed with the greatest promptness, after which Jack brandished his dagger over their heads and warned them that if they moved he would carve them all. Then he began again with a very good appetite the interrupted supper of sardines and crackers.

"Well, friend Jack," Joaquin asked him, "what does that fresh blood mean which I see on the blade of your dagger ?"

"It means," replied the bloody outlaw, "that I was obliged to kill one of those animals in order to subdue the others. When they saw their comrade stretched out, one of them, more reasonable than the others, put himself in front of them, and the rest followed him like a flock of sheep. That is the way I succeeded in bringing them with me."

"And now that you have them here, what are you going to do with them?" asked Antonio.

"By the life of * * * I like that question—to bleed them as if they were sheep."

"Then it would have been more of a kindness to have done it at once," remarked Felix. "They are half dead with fear."

"Oh, they can be quiet," answered Jack, looking ferociously at his prisoners. "I have brought them here to entertain our people a little. But it is fair to finish eating before commencing the party. It is a strange thing, but I have adopted the American maxim 'business before pleasure.'

A quarter of an hour later, during which time Jack continued to eat while the other bandits smoked, Jack went over to the Chinamen, and after tying seven of them together by their queues, he took the eighth one near to the fire. Those present had withdrawn a little to leave a free field.

"Stop! Stop! Jack," exclaimed Guerra, "I hope that you are not going to harm them. Such a thing could only occur to a man full of sardines."

"No, I have brought them near the fire so that you will be able to witness the scene more clearly."

Jack then drew out his dagger and buried it to the hilt in the heart of the unlucky Chinaman, who had been trembling, almost dead of fear. The murderer drew out his weapon covered with blood, and raised in his arms the body of his victim. A stream of blood issued from the wound and put out a little of the fire.

"Caramba!" said one of the bullies, "you have spattered me all over."

"And the fire!" said another. "Don't put it out."

"Come, Jack, come here," said Joaquin impatiently. "Stop that spectacle. Such cruelty is unbearable. Finish with them all at once, and let us talk no more of this business."

"Very well, Captain, I will do as you wish. I believed that the company needed to be entertained, but now I am going to entertain myself only."

Saying this, he threw the dead body to one side carelessly. Then he went toward the other prisoners and without giving ear to their shouts, entreaties and sobs, he began to cut their throats and stab them in the most cold-blooded manner. Before the execution of the first Chinaman, the three women had covered their faces with their serapes in order not to see that savage act. The unhappy women trembled, horrified to think that involuntarily they were accomplices to those crimes committed against inoffensive persons. Clarita, who was seated at the side of the chief, had heard the order which he gave, to finish at one time with the prisoners. Moved by the fortune which awaited them, she tried to use her influence to secure mercy for those wretches. Without uncovering her face, she let her head drop on her lover's shoulder and said to him in a tender and emotional voice, "Oh, Joaquin! Why do you not forbid this horrible carnage, this useless destruction of so many human beings? Have compassion on their cries of desperation, on their vain supplications. You who have the command over him, will you not stop the arm of the murderer?"

"Oh, my sweetheart, I am not able to do anything. Garcia is violent, cruel; he has only joined us to satisfy his insatiable thirst for blood. But he is daring and he does not know danger. It would be a calamity if he were to withdraw from me."

"Then they are condemned irrevocably?" murmured Clarita.

"Oh, yes, and I am sorry from the bottom of my heart. Listen! Even now only two voices are heard. Now one—now it has stopped. The fatal work is done; they will suffer no more."

"Oh, Murrieta," exclaimed Jack Three Fingers, seating himself near the fire, "by the life of all the saints, this is a pleasant night for me! What delightful moments I have passed with these scoundrels. They did not offer the least resistance. By San Miguel! What a gift of blood!"

At dawn the following day the outlaws again resumed the march. Notwithstanding the tragedy of the night before, they were all very cheerful, cherishing the idea of remaining at headquarters for some time. The women above all were very contented in spite of the impression made on them by the terrible scene of the preceding night. They rode peacefully at the side of Joaquin and Felix, a little ahead of the rest of the company, and talked animatedly on matters of amusement. From time to time a peal of laughter escaped from their womanly lips, which gave new expression to the faces of the girls, whose eyes shone with the greatest brilliancy.

After several stops the party arrived at last at Arroyo Cantova. Great was the surprise and pleasure in store for Joaquin as they entered the immense valley. More than a thousand horses were there, grazing contentedly, making graceful turns through the meadows. Then his sight was delighted by groups of tents, white as snow, set up in the middle of a grove of live-oaks, which indicated that after having accomplished the mission faithfully, the bandits had come to await new orders from their chief.

Joaquin gave the short call with which he used to make himself known to his friends, and they all advanced toward the tents at a trot. On arriving there, they dismounted from their horses. Immediately, Valenzuela, Cardoza and some of their gang surrounded them. The others had gone hunting. After exchanging compliments and passing back and forth many felicitations, they sent the horses to be relieved of their saddles and other trappings, and turned loose to graze with the others. As for the horsemen, they extended themselves indolently over the grass to recuperate from the fatigues of the journey, which was a much-needed rest.

They slept for about five hours, when they were awakened for supper. The hunters had returned at nightfall, laden with game. A huge bonfire was kindled and now there was a savory odor of roasted rabbits and hares, bear meat and the flesh of other animals which the hunters had killed. Quails and wild turkeys, suspended from the branches of trees fixed in the ground, revolved in the midst of the flames. On the edge of the immense bonfire were placed several iron pots full of coffee, whose aroma invited one to try it. A little farther away, and over a hundred or more little Indian mats, there were some tin plates full of frijoles and tortillas, canned oysters and squids, fruits and jellies. At the side of each mat was a tin cup, a package of cigarettes and a bottle of wine. It all made a banquet most delicious as well as abundant, which would have captivated more than one disciple of Epicurus. At a sign from the cooks, the bandits seated themselves on the grass, each in front of his mat, and prepared to satisfy their appetites. The head place was occupied by Joaquin and Clarita; at the right of the chief sat Felix and his beloved, the merry Margarita, and at his left Juan Cardoza and the beautiful Mariquita.

The latter had dressed in mourning for a long time on account of the death of her first lover, Gonzalez, who had been killed by Captain Harry Love. Later she had become the sweetheart of Juan Cardoza. At intervals a joyous laugh was heard, which served as testimony to the brave and chivalrous attention with which Cardoza entertained his sweetheart.

Supper was finished, and the conversation began to be animated, when the call of recognition was heard. A company of twenty men approached at a trot, Mountain Jim traveling at the front of them. The circle was enlarged; the cooks returned to their work, and the newcomers began to eat while they received the greatest congratulations from their comrades.

These new recruits were natives of Chile, Peru and Sonora. One of Joaquin's best friends, named Fernando Fuentes, had joined them and accompanied them to the general headquarters. They brought with them as a tribute of their good will seventy-five horses, and Mountain Jim informed Joaquin that in a few days two hundred more horses he had left on the San Francisco ranch would arrive.

The conversation, interrupted for some moments, took its regular course. Each one of the old bandits tried to get acquainted with some of those who had just arrived; they told a thousand stories, innumerable tales of incredible deeds, and who knows what else. From time to time some of the youths sang a melody, ballad or legend, which caused great merriment among those iron-hearted men.

Suddenly the merry-making was disturbed by a very violent quarrel which arose between Jack Three Fingers and Mountain Jim. This affair, as it will be seen in the following chapter, was very serious.

Chapter VII

"I will never allow one the these d---- Americans to even put his foot in our headquarters, or to be initiated into the secrets of our company!" From this declaration had arisen the quarrel between Jack Three Fingers and Mountain Jim. The latter, who alone represented the American element in the gang, replied sourly that although a Yankee by birth, he was Mexican in the depth of his heart, and the interest which he showed on all occasions for the safety of the band was the more sincere because he had not joined it merely to satisfy his lust for blood, but that he had higher aims.

"If you meant that for me," bawled Garcia, "what you have just said is a lie, and I say that you are a coward." At the same time the bandit drew his revolver. Seeing his tiger eyes sparkle, and his brow wrinkle, and seeing above all that face of a demon protected by the limbs of a giant, the most valiant man would have hesitated before declaring himself his enemy.

At the word coward Mountain Jim also had drawn his pistol. He was about to shoot when Joaquin got up suddenly and in a very grave and imperious tone ordered the two adversaries to put down their arms and end the controversy.

"With pleasure," said the mountaineer, "I obey my chief's orders."

"One moment," yelled Jack. "That is not the way I understand the thing." At the same time a shot was heard, and one of the new arrivals, who was seated at the side of Joaquin, fell to the ground, mortally wounded. Immediately, a shout of indignation arose. All the band jumped up, all revolvers were pointed toward the murderer, and the bandits awaited only the order of their chief for discharging them.

"No!" said Joaquin, extending his hand. "Down with the arms! Down with the arms!"

The order of the leader was executed instantly and all eyes were turned toward Garcia, who, on foot and revolver in hand, looked at the chief with an air of indifference. Joaquin then drew out his pistol, whose mountings of silver shone in the firelight like burnished gold, and pointing it at Jack Three Fingers, he said in a tone which displayed the greatest rage: "Jack, you have disobeyed your leader; not only have you committed an act of rebellion, but you have killed one of your comrades. And the one whom you have just murdered is not an enemy with whom you quarreled, but a man whom you have only seen tonight, and with whom you have never had the least dispute. Jack, you have earned death, and I am going to prove to you that I have as good aim as you."

"Joaquin," said Garcia, throwing down his revolver and opening the woolen shirt which covered his heart, "I do not fear death. You may shoot me. I am ready. Fire!"

After these words were spoken, a beautiful hand was placed on Joaquin's shoulder, and the sweet voice of Clarita murmured in his ear. "Pardon him, Joaquin. I beg it of you."

Murrieta was undecided for some moments, and at last he lowered his revolver. "Jack, I am not able to kill you" he said. You are too brave to die in this way and in spite of the fact that your daring impels you to barbarism and the most savage cruelty, I pardon you for it because in you that failing is inborn and you are not able to repress your ferocious instincts."

"Yes, yes, it is his nature. Pardon! Pardon!" exclaimed several bandits at once, who, admiring Jack's cool blood, had already forgotten his crime.

The body of the victim was taken out of the encampment; peace was proclaimed and the fiesta began again with more jollity and animation than ever. After a night of rural pleasure Joaquin dispatched Antonio and Guerra, the latter at the head of his gang, to the state of Sonora with fifteen horses. He left for San Luis Obispo with Valenzuela, Felix, Cardoza, Mountain Jim, Jack Three Fingers and the three girls.

The next day, while they were traveling along a sloping path, they saw two French miners who had taken refuge in one of the cavities in the rocks in order to eat lunch without being bothered by the mid-day sun.

"It would be a good idea," said Jack, drawing out his dagger, "to learn whether those friends carry money."

"Run along," said Joaquin, "but remember that I do not wish blood-shed."

Hardly a minute passed before Jack appeared in front of the miners and in a thunderous voice ordered them; "Empty your purses, if you do not wish to be knocked into smithereens!" The blood-thirsty eyes of the outlaw and his ferocious attitude made them realize very clearly that the threat would be carried out at once. So, the poor Frenchmen hastened to pull out their pocket-books and turn them over to Jack, who emptied them. He had hardly counted the contents when, exasperated because there was only forty dollars, he threw himself upon the miners and cut their throats, leaving them bathed in their own blood. Joaquin had seen all of this from afar, but he contented himself with murmuring a few words and looked away.

At sunset the small company had just gained a dense woods at the edge of which three Chinamen were stretched out. Pierced from side to side with sharp sticks, two were already dead. The third, although his wound was not mortal, certainly would have succumbed a few days later, deprived as he was of all medical assistance. Seeing the bandits passing on their horses, the wretch raised his head and, with a pleading voice and a look worthy of compassion, tried to utter some words which would serve as an entreaty.

"It is useless for us to stop," said Joaquin. "In the state in which that man is found, there is no human succor which could save him."

A few moments later, Joaquin, looking back, saw Jack, who, bent over the unfortunate Chinaman, was putting out his eyes with the same stick which he had just pulled out of his shoulder.

"Garcia! Garcia!" shouted Joaquin.

Jack, seeing that his chief was looking at him, and divining his intentions, hastened to draw out his dagger and bury it in the heart of his victim. Then he mounted his horse and started off at a gallop to where Joaquin was.

"Garcia," the young bandit said to him, "you are too cruel. This man would have lived perhaps two or three days."

"Then," answered Jack, while he cleaned his bloody dagger on his horse's mane, "what evil have I done in killing him? My only desire was to shorten his suffering."

"Torturing him until he was dead, eh? Ah, Jack, not another word. Your soul, down to its secret recesses, is as black as Satan."

When they reached the Mission of San Luis Obispo, Joaquin sent Reinaldo Felix to Los Angeles, and Mountain Jim and Jack Three Fingers, who were now the best friends in the world, to San Diego, with express orders to steal as many horses as they could, and to find out what was said about the death of Captain Wilson and General Bean.

Hardly a week had passed after the departure of the three companions when Texas Jack, another member of the company, arrived at the camp with the news that Felix had been hanged by the residents of Los Angeles. While he was resting in a dance hall he was recognized by an American whom he had robbed, in company with other outlaws, at Mokulumme Hill. Arrested unexpectedly, he was accused of complicity in the murder of General Bean; and although there was not sufficient evidence to implicate him in that matter, his character as a robber and a member of Joaquin's band was made to serve as proof of his complicity. A few minutes sufficed to put a rope around his neck, and he had hardly kissed the crucifix which a priest put to his lips, when the fatal platform went down. This was the end of Reinaldo Felix.

His sweetheart, the young and pretty Margarita, at first did not wish to believe this terrible news; but Valenzuela went to Los Angeles and a few days later he confirmed it officially. As soon as Margarita was persuaded that the fatal news was true, she drew out from her belt a stiletto which she always carried with her, and buried it in her bosom before anyone could stop her. The unhappy one died murmuring the name of her lover.

This unpleasant matter had not been forgotten when Jack Three Fingers arrived in his turn, bringing news of the death of Mountain Jim. Jack and his comrade went into a tavern situated on the road some miles distant from San Diego, and while they were drinking two or three glasses of bad liquor, a party of Americans suddenly appeared. The party commenced to watch them in a manner so suspicious that Jack confided his fears to his companion, asking him to come away immediately. Jim, who was under the influence of the liquor which he had just inbibed, laughed at Jack's advice and far from observing it, advanced to the counter to order another glass of liquor. Some moments later another company of Americans arrived. As soon as he saw them, Jack Three Fingers jumped on his horse and made signs to Jim to do the same. Jim merely answered with a drunken oath, and remained near the counter. The Americans went into the tavern, and drawing their revolvers, suggested to Jim that he surrender. A quarrel was started. Jack, realizing what was going to happen, and knowing perfectly well that it was useless to make resistance before such a superior force, contented himself with sending two bullets into the midst of the group, and riding away as fast as the wind.

Some of the Americans rushed out in pursuit, but with the horse that Jack rode, he feared no one. In fact, it was the same as if they had wished to overtake a locomotive under full steam. It took much less work for them to overpower Mountain Jim, who was taken to San Diego and hanged without any more delay than the time strictly necessary to put a knot at the end of a rope.

A month after these disastrous losses, Joaquin, although he did not mention it except to five companions, including the two women, began a pleasure trip to Tuolumne County. His only object was to distract his sweetheart Clarita, who had fallen into the most profound melancholy since the death of her friend Margarita. The bandit traveled slowly, in a pleasant manner, and at the end of two weeks they reached the Merced River. At the bank of the river, and in the shade of some leafy trees, the leader of the bandits set up his tent, with the intention of remaining some time in such a peaceful place, where no one seemed to disturb the calm. Nevertheless, (that is the way things are) this plan was very soon spoiled.

The next day, in the morning, Joaquin was awakened by Jack Three Fingers, who told him that a group of four miners was coming on the opposite side of the river.

"If they do not seek us," said the chief, "let them pass." And while he spoke, he cast a look across the river, through the narrow opening of the tent. "Ah! But no! By the life of all the saints!" he exclaimed, his face distorted with rage. "Come, Jack, Cardoza, Valenzuela, get up and follow me!"

And immediately, without heeding the pleading or disturbing himself over the tears which the women shed, he took his revolver and rushed out of the tent followed by his three companions.

The travelers by this time were not more than a few meters' distant, walking peacefully along without thinking that their existence

Four miners are assassinated on the Merced bank.

was in danger when a volley was heard, and three of them dropped to the earth, dead, in the middle of the road. The fourth, who had only received a light wound, looked over to see the class of enemy with which he had to deal.

"Ah! D'you!" exclaimed the leader. "Do you know me now? I am Joaquin." And at once he fired three times at the American, and seeing him fall dead at the side of his companions, the bandit gave a shout of joy.

"Jack," he said, pointing to the bodies, "for this time I am not only going to give you permission, but I command you to exercise your bloody instincts. Some of the men may perhaps not be completely dead. You finish killing them."

At the first words of his chief, Jack had thrown himself into the river, and with water up to shoulders, he fought against the current. In two minutes he gained the bank and quickly put his hand to the work. With what infernal joy the ruffian perceived that two of the unlucky miners were not yet dead, but that they were not able to escape from him! Excited by their shouts, and to stop at once all resistance, that demon in human form pulled out their entrails, ending that abominable scene by tearing out their hearts.

When Jack reached Joaquin's tent, after performing his horrible commission, he wished to know the motives of hatred and vengeance of his chief toward those men.

"Jack," responded Murrieta, "three of them belong to the band of murders who killed Carmen, the ones who drove me from the house I had at the mines. As for the fourth one, I do not know him; but he deserves the same fate as the others for being found in such bad company."

"Wretches!" shouted Jack, making an atrocious grimace. "Well, Captain, I believe that we shall have the good fortune to meet some of those gentlemen on our way."

"If that happens, you may be sure that your knife shall not rust for lack of blood. But let us go from this place, and tonight we shall camp in some other spot.

A half hour later Joaquin and his gang were proceeding in the direction of Mariposa. The chief had resolved to rest not far from there on the ranch of his friends.

Chapter VIII

After having remained about thirty days in the vicinity of Mariposa, employed by the insatiable Jack Three Fingers in the perpetration of a dozen robberies and almost as many murders, the party set out on the march. The bandits crossed the Merced, fording the river at a place where it was not very deep, and continued their journey, sometimes in the middle of forests, at others climbing hills and mountains, until they found a road to lead them in the direction of Tuolumne County.

After traveling for some time, they arrived at a place called Shaw's Flat. On all sides sounded the picks, shovels and all the instruments which miners use to separate the gold from the earth. A great number of Chinamen had set up their cabins at various points nearby, and united in companies, they worked energetically, realizing reasonable profits from the claims which the Americans had abandoned as too poor for them. Throughout this whole place, animated by assiduous labor, an atmosphere of peace, prosperity and contentment prevailed.

The laborers saw Joaquin and his party, but no one had any idea of suspecting them. There was no apparent reason for doing so. It was very common among drivers, cattle dealers, cowboys, hunters and all classes of travelers, to camp days, and even whole weeks, sometimes at the edge of a spring of crystalline water, others in the shade of a tree in a solitary place. On the other hand, the arms which they carried did not cause the miners the least alarm, because the custom of those days to go fully armed favored Joaquin and his band, until someone should happen to discover what they really were, through some of their misdeeds.

As Joaquin had some money at that time, he decided that he would rest near Shaw's Flat for some weeks. His intention was, while he took some rest and enjoyed life, to put into circulation some hundreds of dollars in the gambling houses, restaurants and fandango dance halls in the neighboring towns and villages. Luck favored his plans. He met some miners who, before leaving for their native land, sold the cabin in which they lived, with all the utensils which it contained, situated on dry and arid land which the miners had worked a thousand and one times to extract the last particle of the gold which it held. This cabin had a double value for the bandits because of its solitary position and of being free from the view of the gold seekers, who did not venture to explore in a place as solitary as that.

Every night, Joaquin, accompanied by Cardoza and the two women, went to the little towns and adjacent camps for the purpose of entertaining themselves. During his absence the headquarters were in charge of Valenzuela and Garcia. The latter had received a formal order to keep quiet and not compromise the safety of the whole gang by committing some robbery or murder. Jack Three Fingers, for the first time in his life, seemed not to have any pleasure in bloodshed, and for the space of three weeks he was contented in the domicile of the outlaws, dividing his time between cards and drinking. But at last his instinct conquered his reason. One night while Valenzuela was in Sonora with Joaquin and the others, the wretch sharpened his knife and started out in search of his victim. Some Chinamen, grouped in front of their cabins, were occupied in examining the result of the day's work. At the sight of them the eyes of the ferocious Jack shone with joy, but with a savage brilliance. It might have been said that he was a hunter who had just discovered his favorite game. But as the Americans had occupied some cabins near those of the Chinamen, and as the desperado only had the intention of cutting the heads off of two or three people, but without noise, he continued his way toward Sonora, with the hope of finding a more convenient or less dangerous place for doing his favorite work. Several times he met on the highway companies of miners armed to the teeth. A little farther, on chance, presented a solitary Chinaman. But as the miners were always in sight, he restrained himself and prudently remained wrapped in his serape.

At a point where the Sonora road forked, and formed an angle, he went toward Columbia, and drawing near the city, he seated himself at the side of the road to smoke a cigarette. The night was most beautiful; the sky was covered with stars. Jack Three Fingers decided not to go farther then, resting until two or three in the morning, enveloped in cigarette smoke. Then, he told himself, when he returned to Joaquin's cabin, he would be able to fall upon some Chinamen stupefied by opium, and kill a half dozen with the greatest ease in the world.

While he was enjoying in anticipation the pleasure the terrible carnage offered him, he was disturbed in his reflections by the noise of approaching footsteps, mingled with the sound of a human voice which essayed to sing some melodious fragments in the manner of African Negroes. Anyone hearing the tones of the singer would understand perfectly that this singing was the result of numerous libations. His lung power increased with the energy from the drinking. The traveler, after having sung "Jim Crow," jumped without stopping into "Possum up a Gum Tree." Then he sang "Coal Black Rose." Soon he tried to whistle "Yankee Doodle" and the famous song "Auld Lang Syn," but not being able to keep in tune, he delivered himself with energy of a music composed of singing, shouts, prolonged screeches and shrill whistling.

This new kind of song, although not translatable into any language, sounded something like this: "Oh, Su (hic) sannah! Don't you cry (hic) for me; I'm goin' to Cal(hic)fornia with....Horro!...I don't care a cuss for nothing....Ki yi! Yow! Hooraw for Jackson! Hoop hey!"

"Hello, old comrade!" added the traveler, stopping suddenly, or rather, trying to stop in front of the Mexican, "Hello! Hello! What are you doing here, eh? Come take a drink. What? What does this mean, you don't want to? Then go to blazes." And shouting so that he could be heard five miles around, he continued on his way making ridiculous curves and again singing his interrupted song. He was some yards away from Jack when the latter threw himself upon him, and before he could utter a word, he gave him several blows in the neck, breaking it and killing him instantly. Then the assassin hastily began to search the body of his victim. After possessing himself of a leather belt whose contents in gold dust and silver money amounted to some three thousand dollars, Jack Three Fingers quickly took the road back to headquarters. The first thing he did on his arrival there was to throw himself on his bed "to sleep or perchance to dream" of some new deed.

Four or five hours later, Joaquin and Valenzuela entered, or rather dashed into the cabin. The former rushed over to Jack, and shaking him violently, awakened him.

"What's new?" he asked, sleepily getting up.

"The body of a man has just been found on the highway," said Joaquin, "and from the nature of his wounds, I have deducted that only you could be the murderer."

"You are sure of it?"

"Oh! very sure. You are excused from denying it to us. But do you know whom you have killed?"

"Certainly not," answered Garcia in a very humble manner, "and I confess that I have not troubled myself to investigate. I thought that you might need some money and I went in search of that prize. I have the honor of presenting to you the result of it; take what you wish."

"Well, Jack," said the leader, testing the weight of the leather belt which Garcia offered, "it is true that here is a pretty sum which comes just in time, for lack of money is beginning to be felt. The unfortunate part is that the owner of it, as I think, was no other than one of the two miners of whom we bought this cabin, and as his partner is at present in Sonora, it may very well happen that he may tell the details of the acquisition of this hut, and cause suspicion to fall upon us."

"In such a case, what do you expect to do?"

"To remain in this vicinity one or two days at most, while you and Valenzuela go quickly to Stockton. Clarita and Mariquita have gone already and probably you will overtake them before they reach the city."

"The best thing to do," said Valenzuela, "is to go altogether. Forward, then!"

In a few minutes they were mounted on horses. Jack Three Fingers and Valenzuela dashed off at a gallop toward Stockton. Joaquin traveled slowly toward Sonora. Morning was beginning to dawn, and all the gambling houses were full of miners and professional gamblers. They were all talking heatedly over the latest murder, showing their firm determination to lynch the murderer as soon as they found him.

Joaquin got down from his horse and quietly entered a gambling house, with his cape thrown over his shoulder, in the Mexican style. First, he saluted some of his compatriots with a light inclination of his head; then he took a chair and went to seat himself in a corner of the room near the door.

Much was said among the groups of the brutality of the drunken man's murderer, who had taken delight in inflicting innumerable wounds on his victim, when only one would have been enough to finish him. In this fashion they repeated their vows, protesting that the assassin would not escape popular vengeance.

"It would not surprise me in the least," suddenly said a man of savage countenance, striking with his massive hand upon the counter, "if those Mexicans had a part in the murder of our friend."

"What Mexicans?" asked one of the gamblers.

"There is a question! Who bought the claim on the bank of the river? Why did they buy it? I do not know, and I have no interest in knowing it. But it is certain that they have never worked, not even an hour. They have passed the time since they lived there, riding around the city on horseback, playing monte, singing and laughing with their pockets always full of gold."

"The devil take me! It is very certain," said a third speaker whose thinness and smallness formed a contrast to the stature and weight of the other. "It is very certain, yes, very certain. And there is no way of knowing where those satanic Mexicans fish for so much gold. But the thing is that their purses are never empty."

"By George!" exclaimed the one who had spoken first. "Look over there, John. I'll be hanged if that fellow over there isn't one of them." He pointed at Joaquin with his finger.

"That is so; it is as sure as that you are here. I swear to you that if he understood Yankee, he would have the cold shivers. It seems to me that his skin belongs to me."

Joaquin had not lost a word of this conversation, but he remained quiet and passive until the end of it. The American threw himself upon him and the other shook his shoulder with his thick hand, saying, "I think I have you, all right, comrade!"

Joaquin contented himself with smiling and got up, in appearance with the best will in the world. Before the smile had left his lips he had already given the American a violent blow with the butt of his revolver, which left him extended on the floor.

With a leap, Joaquin went outside of the saloon and a second later, he was fleeing rapidly toward Stockton, mounted on his horse.

Chapter IX

One day later Joaquin went down to meet his companions, whom he found installed in a tavern situated six miles from Stockton. In a few words he told them what had just happened, after which all the company set out. At the end of an hour they arrived at the end of their journey. The next day when the sun was setting, Joaquin, Valenzuela and Jack Three Fingers saw in the distance three German miners, dressed in green. They were walking slowly along the highway, apparently without any other ostensible object than to show their new clothes, whose elegance was enhanced with trimmings of gold nuggets in the form of pins, taken from the mines.

"Here are some people," said Joaquin "who seem well pleased with their appearance."

"Yes," responded Valenzuela, "and if their vanity is based on what they are worth, they must be possessors of a great quantity of gold."

"It is my opinion," declared Jack, laying hold of his dagger, "that it would be a good thing to investigate this matter."

He had hardly finished pronouncing these words when the miners entered a restaurant. Joaquin, seeing that they had disappeared, advanced in their pursuit, charging his companions to await him. He entered the restaurant and seated himself at a table not far from the one which the Germans occupied. In less than ten minutes, while he was drinking a cup of coffee, he secured all the information necessary. Then he went to join his companions, and all took the road to the house where they had stopped temporarily in the Mexican part of the city. After harnessing their horses, they began the journey to San Andreas.

Four miles from Stockton they stopped. The horses were hidden behind the shrubbery and the men themselves penetrated into it a short distance from the road.

"Our men will be here within a short while," said Joaquin, "ready to return to their country with a fortune which they have accumulated in California, and they expect to embark for San Francisco. Another companion should join the three today. Seeing that he does not come, they are going to seek him in San Andres."

"It is a stroke of fortune for us," added Valenzuela, "and makes the business easy, remarkably easy."

"I believe that I hear them," murmured Jack Three Fingers, looking out again through the shrubbery. The three individuals drew near, jogging along peacefully without any fear. They spoke openly of their country, or their plans for marriage; each one told the others the results which he had obtained in the mines, while all were laughing and joking about the envy which their sudden departure had caused their comrades. They had hardly arrived in front of the place where the bandits were hidden when the latter came out suddenly from their hiding places, seized the horses' bridles, and before the unhappy miners could recover from their surprise, broke the top of their skulls with their revolvers, and threw them down from their saddles. The bodies were searched at some length. The three Germans carried with them nearly eight thousand dollars' worth of gold dust.

Valenzuela and Cardoza went to Stockton with the two women, while Joaquin and his band crossed a part of Sacramento County and went into camp on the south bank of the American River. A few days later Fernando Fuentes joined them with his gang. One of his men had seen Joaquin and his companions and he arrived hastily to inform his chief. Fuentes had been commissioned to gather together all the horses which he could steal, and he had already taken to headquarters about four hundred, taken from different counties. Fuentes informed the chief that Antonio and Guerra had returned to the Arroyo from Sonora, each one bringing a sweetheart.

Joaquin was very pleased by all of this news. For a moment he was tempted to start out with all of his men for the headquarters, such was his impatience to know the details of the journey of his sub-lieutenant to Sonora, and to see the new girls who had come with them. But special matters of the highest importance decided him to defer for some days the pleasure which he promised himself beforehand from that meeting. Nevertheless, improving the occasion which was offered, he sent Clarita and Mariquita to the Arroyo, confiding them to Cardoza, Fernando and two other Mexicans. In this way they would be able to travel undisturbed over the highway, and they were less exposed to the dangers which threatened them until the moment of entering the headquarters.

The two girls had hardly left the camp with their companions when a dispute was begun between Mariposa and her lover. The girl claimed that he was very far from being as amiable as Gonzalez, her first love, and declared that she did not wish to live with him anymore. Cardoza believed that all of this was idle talk; he pulled off a little branch of brambles, and used it to give the rebel what he called a wholesome corrective, Mariquita submitted to the punishment apparently with the greatest resignation, but in the depth of her heart she swore to avenge herself in a bloody manner. On the following day they were both climbing slowly by a path which lost itself in the crags of a mountain, surrounded by precipices. Cardoza was on the edge of one of these, which was about a hundred and twenty feet deep, when the vengeful Mariquita suddenly drew her dagger out of her belt and buried it in the bosom of her lover. Cardoza called out and tried to turn towards his sweetheart; but with the movement which he made, his horse reared, and both went rolling to the depths of the abyss.

Mariquita executed her sinister design with such speed that no one could be a witness to it. When her companions joined her, she had returned the dagger to her belt and no one would have thought that she had just committed a crime. She shed abundant and apparently very bitter tears for the loss of the horseman and his mount. Were her shrieks and moans perhaps the work of remorse? At any rate her sorrow did not last long. As soon as the band arrived at headquarters, where all was joy, the crazy girl accepted the advances of a young and daring bandit called Manuel Sevalio, who took the title of her third husband.

Two days afterward, Joaquin learned of the catastrophe which had deprived him of one of his men, Fernando having immediately detached one of his own men to carry the news to the chief. The thing seemed very strange to Joaquin. Cardoza was really one of the best horsemen of the band, and he could not understand how he could have allowed his horse to get so close to the chasm; the accident must have resulted from some other cause and not through a lack of precaution on the part of the horseman. Thinking thus, Joaquin took a dozen of his bandits and all set out toward the place

Juan Cardoza's assassination.

where the accident occurred, with the object of burying their beloved companion.

The outlaws took a different road from the one which Cardoza had followed, but at last they arrived at the place where the man and his horse were lying together. The body of Cardoza was examined carefully; but he had been mangled in such a manner in his fall against the rocks that it was impossible to distinguish the stab which Mariquita had given him. The bandits, after having stripped the body of the fire-arms and the money in his clothes, buried him in the sand and returned to headquarters very sad.

A week later Joaquin, Jack Three Fingers, Valenzuela and Fernando's company, which made a total of twenty-six men, started out again to resume their depredations in El Dorado County and in the neighborhood of Calaveras. Not far from Mud Springs they discovered a cabin on the slope of a hill. Believing it unoccupied and thinking that it would be an excellent place to spend the night, Jack spurred his horse, and a few moments later found himself in front of it. He opened the door and entered. Contrary to what the bandits had thought, it developed that the cabin was occupied. A German lived in it. A serious illness held him prisoner in his house and this gave to the outside of it that appearance of abandonment and of solitude which had attracted Joaquin's men.

The highwaymen arrived in front of the cabin. Joaquin made a sign to Jack Three Fingers, who drew his dagger, and approaching the bed, cut the throat of the poor sick man. Then, aided by two of his comrades, he carried the body outside of the cabin and threw it into a hole in the ground at the foot of the hill. The company then took possession of the house, in which there were provisions of all kinds, blankets, mining utensils and instruments, pipes and tobacco. A quantity of tobacco was used in the manufacture of cigarettes; the bandits smoked for two hours and then each one spread out his serape on the floor, wrapped himself in it as best he could, and slept.

At the beginning of daybreak, the leader dispatched three men to the camp of Mud Springs with the commission of bringing coffee, butter—in a word, everything necessary to satisfy the appetites of the men who formed the gang. Two hours later one of the emissaries returned alone, with empty hands and a very altered countenance.

"Where are your companions?" asked Joaquin.

"They are dead!" answered the man.

"Why, is it possible? Dead!"

"Oh, yes, Captain. Hung by the neck like dogs. As soon as they arrived at the camp, they entered a store to get the provisions, while I was in a saloon taking a glass of brandy. I was speaking with the proprietor of the house, who is a Mexican, when I heard a commotion outside. I looked toward the camp and saw that my comrades were surrounded by five or six Americans, who made them wait at attention. One of them affirmed that he recognized Sebastian as a horse thief—that in 1850 a party of them had robbed him in the Sacramento Valley, and that having been imprisoned, he escaped from the jail; finally, that his companion must be a robber or they would not have been traveling together. This was enough to excite the people to riot; our two comrades were dragged to a tree and hanged without ceremony, while I, assisted by the Mexican of the saloon, climbed out of a window and fled with the greatest speed."

"This is a very ugly story," said Joaquin. "We must leave here at once. If it were not that I need to assemble all the men that I know, in order to carry out an important project, we would go to that miserable camp and leave not a single man with his head. But they may rest assured; some day they will receive their payment. Come, friends, to your horses and let us depart."

In a twinkling of an eye they were mounted and on their way. The bandits were careful not to follow a direct line. After having made a number of detours and stopping in several places, now to despoil some traveler, now to cool the throats of the horsemen, now to appease the thirst of the horses, the troop came to a summit, sad and dreary looking, situated about a mile from Salmon Falls. Joaquin gave orders to pass the night there. Nature seemed to have disposed this place especially for the purpose it was now serving. Encircled by two enormous rocks, covered on all sides by underbrush, with a clear space in the middle about twenty feet in diameter, the spot seemed most appropriate for a retreat.

Chapter X

After having placed their horses in a safe spot, the bandits attacked the provisions which they had stolen that day, and then the cigarette took its place.

"Fellows," said Valenzuela, "the only thing they talk about here is hanging. It is tiresome."

"That's so," said Carillo. "Hanging is a poor topic. But it is a mania with these Americans. They are taught it in the cradle. They must hang someone or they may be hanged; it is in their blood. The mania is there and no one can reform them."

"That is all very well," said Jack Three Fingers, "but since we cannot keep them from hanging our comrades, at least we can pay them in their own coin by hanging all the Americans who fall into our hands. But no! That is a poor system. When I kill anyone I have to see what color his blood is. Oh, well, Caramba! Let them hang if they like to, and in return, we can handle them with the dagger and revolver."

"Comrades," replied Joaquin in his turn, "I have suffered more than any of you from that mania which the Americans have for hanging, since I have seen my own poor brother strangled before my very eyes—he who never harmed a soul, and at a time when it was impossible for me to save him, or punish the assassins. But since then, I have taken and am still taking revenge. Let us lay aside this sad topic of conversation and let me tell you about an adventure that happened to me sometime ago in Tuolumne County."

"Bravo! Bravo! That's right," they all cried.

"Listen!" added others.

"I was beginning the career in which you now accompany me," said the chief. "I had just entered Tuolumne County with my companions, only numbering six, and I encountered in the little encampment of San Diego, about a half mile from Columbia, a headquarters which was exactly suited to our needs. Immediately, we set our hands to work, beginning by killing and despoiling the miners during the day, whether we met them alone or in crowds in search of amusement, or whether they were working in solitary places. When nightfall came, we would go to deposit in the gambling houses part of the gold we had acquired in this way."

"In order to visit the monte tables, I had to take great care to disguise myself so that those who had seen me other places might not recognize me, and would take me for a foreigner. Among those who had seen me so many times that my face and carriage were not unknown to him, was a constable by the name of Leary, whose presence annoyed me. I tried to avoid him whenever it was possible, so that he would not recognize me beneath my disguise and force me to put myself on guard. Moreover, he was the only man in the whole state whom I would have regretted having to draw my revolver on, for he had always treated me with the greatest courtesy and kindness. I knew that if he should ever recognize me, as a civil official and above all as a man of honor, he would feel obliged to use every means of obtaining my arrest, and for this reason I tried to avoid his presence.

"However, one night I forgot a part of my disguise which I was accustomed to wear; my false beard seemed to me to be superfluous and I believed that it would be enough to cover part of my face with my cap. In fact, I took great care to muffle myself well as I left the gambling house about midnight. As I went out, Leary entered, giving me a very searching look. I acted as if I had not seen him, and when I was in the street, I sped toward the camp, keeping in the darkest of places. Dawn was scarcely breaking on the following day when I saw a number of men, guided by Leary, making their way toward our camp. I awakened my companions, who were still sleeping, and realizing that our only hope was to flee, we did so with the greatest speed. They aimed their shots at us and succeeded in capturing three of our men. At first I must confess that I believed that we were lost; but our comrades were very brave. After a desperate struggle, they recovered their liberty. I alone was wounded in the shoulder by Leary, while the others escaped. Neither those who pursued us nor ourselves were mounted, which favored us greatly in our flight, as we were more accustomed than the Americans to travel in the mountains, and we could skirt the narrow paths, the high rocks and whatever difficulties beset our path, more quickly than they. Thus, very soon we left

Leary's company far behind, and we found a place which would hide us from our persecutors. It was the first time that I ever saw myself pursued and routed, as you might say, by the Americans. But if I had had the good fortune to have possessed more men, by God! I would not have given up one inch of ground to them."

"Bravo! Bravo!" cried all the outlaws in a voice, drinking then to the health of their chief.

On the following day Joaquin and his men met one of their countrymen who was leading forty or fifty mules, laden with sacks full of provisions. Joaquin bought from him a quantity of wheat, coffee, sugar, beans, etc. The bandits kept on until they came to the edge of a vast prairie, so fertile that they decided to camp in the shade of a tree. It was decided that they should remain there a week or ten days if necessary, so that the animals could graze and rest and the men could also enjoy a bit of recreation and repose.

In the place where one of the branches of the southern end of the Mokelumne river begins, in a very deserted spot not far from the boundary line of Calaveras and El Dorado counties, there was established a colony of miners consisting of about twenty-five men. One day they set out well armed in search of placer, and upon arriving at this point, they encountered incomparable riches. Immediately, they set up their tents in that place, which had no other inconvenience than that of being separated from all habitation.

One morning the miners were breakfasting tranquilly in front of their cabins, armed with their revolvers, according to the custom, when a young horseman, with eyes and hair black as jet, advanced toward them and saluted them. The youth spoke such good English that it was impossible for the miners to make out whether he was a Mexican or an American. They invited him to eat with them, but he politely refused. He crossed one leg indifferently over his horse and finding himself at ease in this position, he began to converse lightly on different subjects, until a miner by the name of Jim Boyce appeared, coming up from the stream where he had been to carry water. At the miner's first glance at the young horseman, the latter took his natural position, straightened himself in his saddle and spurred his horse.

Boyce was raving. "Comrades! That is no other than Joaquin! Shoot at him! Quick! Fire!" And while he was shouting, he discharged a pistol full of shots at Joaquin. They all missed.

The young chief had started his horse at random and was suddenly confronted by some steep rocks. There was no way left but a narrow path which wound around an immense mountain to the edge of a ledge of rocks some hundred yards long. These rocks, situated above the river, were in a direct line with the hill on which the miners had their tents, and were only thirty yards from them. To venture by that road would be very dangerous for any man who found himself in Joaquin's position. He not only faced the danger of falling from a height of more than one hundred feet, but he also had to follow a line of more than two hundred yards within reach of the enemy's shot. Joaquin saw that all of the miners had their hands on their guns. As if he were mounted on a phantom horse, Joaquin hurled himself upon the dangerous path, shouting to his enemies: "I am Joaquin Murrieta! Kill me if you can."

At that instant, twenty-five shots were heard, and the bullets, passing over Joaquin's head, crashed against the nearby rocks. In this first discharge, one bullet knocked off his hat, leaving his long black hair flying. The moments were too precious for him to think of using his revolver. He was not unmindful of the fact that his only salvation lay in the fleetness of his horse. And so he contented himself with drawing a dagger from his belt, which he raised above his head disdainfully. A few minutes afterwards a prolonged whistle was heard from the depths of the woods about a quarter of a mile away. The fearless horseman was safe.

Joaquin well knew the character of Jim Boyce, too well to rest while being pursued by him. Moreover, it was very probable that the miner had heard of the great reward offered for capturing or killing the Mexican chief. It was very probable then that all of the miners of those parts would unite and attack them soon. In view of that, it would be dangerous to remain there any longer, since the bandits' camp was only three miles from the cabins of the miners. However, his enemies could not assemble the horses necessary for the attack, nor the arms and ammunition which they would have to have before early morning. Joaquin conceived the most brilliant and ingenious plan that had ever come out of a human brain—a plan which would destroy all of the projects of his enemies and permit the Mexican youth to possess all of the riches that the miners had been able to collect.

Knowing that he could make a trail by night perfectly, but that it would be impossible to follow it until daylight, he ordered his men to mount their horses and hasten on a journey. All obeyed immediately without questioning their leader, and soon they were ready to leave. Joaquin rode at their head, and silently moved in and out among the tall rows of pines. All night they tramped over roads almost impassable, and they found that they had come twenty miles. Joaquin wished to go still farther away from the camp which he had just left. Only a short time later he gave orders to halt.

They picked up some dry branches to which they set fire, tied the horses near them and then spread out their blankets and lay down to rest. The sentinels charged with watching the safety of the camp were relieved every half hour during the night. At daybreak the entire company arose and in a few moments started to take up their journey. The desperadoes had slept but five hours. Until noon our men went on with the same speed as of the night before. They found themselves in a beautiful valley, covered with vegetation, irrigated by a stream that flowed though a row of tall oaks. This place was some twenty miles from the spot where the bandits had bivouacked the preceding night. There, they remained two hours so that their horses could rest and that they themselves might cool off. They did not leave until they had left signs to make the Americans believe that they had passed the night in that place. Then, galloping until nightfall, they were safe from their enemies by another twenty miles. They rested some minutes, built a fire as on the preceding night, ate hastily and then mounted their horses, and described in their route a circle of five miles, suddenly turning east, and about three o'clock in the morning, they encamped one day's journey from the last encampment.

Some days after all that starting and stopping, the train found itself in a place where it had been before.

Jim Boyce and the miners had set out in pursuit of the bandits the day after chance had led Joaquin their way. Each night they stopped in the place that the bandits had just abandoned, and boldly hoped that finally they would meet the Mexicans face to face, although it might be at the other end of the world. A smile of satisfaction escaped from Joaquin's lips when he saw by infallible signs that Jim Boyce, that man whom he considered his worst enemy, was

Moments later, Joaquin calmly visited the campsite.

following him so near.

Nightfall had come, after a march of a whole day over mountains and plains. Jim Boyce and his men, seated tranquilly around one of the bon-fires which Joaquin had lately abandoned, and which they had rebuilt, were smoking and laughing with gusto, and without the least presentiment of any harm, when suddenly the air was rent by the report of twenty revolvers discharged at one time. The fire shone more brightly and the miners who had been honored by the shots saw twenty of their comrades stretched out about them, and at the same time heard another discharge similar to the first, directed at them.

Horrified, trembling, frantic, the only two whom the second discharge had left standing, one of whom was no other than Jim Boyce, hurled themselves into the darkness and without thinking what road they were taking, fled far from that terrible scene. A few minutes afterwards Joaquin coolly visited the encampment, to find if Jim Boyce was among the dead. As for Jack Three Fingers, he was satisfying his sanguinary appetite in finding which of the miners were still breathing and finishing them with dagger thrusts.

It is known that death produced by a bullet spreads an extreme and sudden pallor over the face of the victim. In the light of the bon-fire, the corpses scattered over the ground presented such a repulsive sight that even Joaquin himself was horrified.

"Come!" he said. "Let us leave this place. We can camp until morning in a more agreeable spot."

Chapter XI

Two or three days afterward, the company went to visit the cabins of their victims. After taking possession of the horses and mules which were there, the bandits commenced to search for the precious metal, and they found around fourteen thousand dollars' worth of gold and gold dust. Joaquin took possession of this sum, and then they turned towards Yaqui Camp, situated a short distance from San Andreas, where the chief had an engagement. The day following their arrival in this place, he ordered six of his men to Arroyo Cantova, led by Valenzuela, with all the animals which were not useful to the company, and part of the gold which they had found in the camp of the Americans. From this time on, the chief began, with the men who were left, a series of expeditions against their common enemy, killing and robbing as many as came into their hands. For many miles around San Andreas, Calaveritas and Yaqui Camp, one heard of nothing but the bold robberies, and no one knew how they had been committed nor what became of the victims. Various individuals had been beheaded without so much as knowing whom the assassin was. All that the miners knew was that some robbers and murderers, like so many phantoms, were in their midst without their being able to recognize them. Thus, one only saw frightened faces and wild eyes, since each one feared an assault on his way.

Captain Ellis, deputy sheriff of the county, succeeded in organizing a company of the bravest citizens of San Andreas, and immediately set out in search of the outlaws. Having ascertained by means of a spy that Joaquin was to be found in Yaqui Camp, and that one of his men was accustomed to frequenting the monte tables, he lost no time in going there, recognizing the man whose description he had, and took his prisoner.

Carillo, for it was none other than he, was condemned to be hanged at once for robbery and murder. But they offered to pardon him if he would reveal the hiding place of his companions. The bandit refused the offer disdainfully. Nevertheless, he begged them not to kill him, and he promised to help them in their enterprise, but in a way that would not excite the suspicions of Joaquin's gang. Seeing that his proposition was not heeded, he changed his tone, and said with brava-do, "Then hands to the work!" After which he added: "If you decide to visit our hiding places, you will find in my trunk a sword which is still covered with the blood of one of your men. With that sword I have killed at least twenty of your friends, while you can only kill me once."

This speech, as our readers may well suppose, was received with great indignation. The ruffian without further formality was dragged to a tree and hanged from one of its boughs.

The companions of Captain Ellis, thinking of nothing but their vengeance, continued the work which they had begun, destroying and burning all the places that might serve as a refuge for the bandits. The flames illuminated the neighboring mountains for miles around. Joaquin, who, with his men, was on a hill a short distance away, saw and heard all that happened.

"I think," said the chief, laughing heartily, "that really if they got us in their power, they would be tempted to kill us. Poor Carillo! They have hanged him. He has undoubtedly gone to join his old friend Father Jarauta; but Caramba! I swear that the first twenty enemies that we meet shall follow him on the road at least to inferno, and not without having first satisfied my desires for them."

Our hero, convinced that Captain Ellis's company would traverse the whole country in search of his band, hid his men in the mountains, so situated that they could go quickly into headquarters, where they would defend themselves from all who dared pursue them. On passing near the mill of the Phoenix Company, some individuals hidden behind a parapet on the building shot at them, only slightly wounding two or three of them. Immediately, Joaquin made his men stand by and return fire. As the enemy did not present itself, he went into the building with five or six of his men, including Jack Three Fingers. They found but two men who were rash enough to defend themselves hand to hand with the bandits. As can easily be imagined, one minute was enough to overpower them and send them to another world. After this, Jack Three Fingers dragged them out and mutilated them horri-bly with his dagger. Meanwhile, Joaquin and his companions fired some shots within the mill and then again they took up the march, which had been interrupted by the foregoing episode.

On the other side of Bear Mountain, where they arrived by a road which follows the bank of Santo Domingo Creek, the Mexicans encountered a Chinese camp from where they took five or six hundred dollars, which was all these sons of the Celestial Empire possessed. Jack Three Fingers could not keep from showing his anxiety on seeing them so weak and miserable. He would have liked to free them from such a sad existence, but Joaquin ordered him to curb his sanguinary desires. Jack conformed with his chief's orders, but not with a good grace. Our man was anti-Chinese by nature and nothing would have been more pleasant than to skin a number of those inoffensive beings. Nevertheless, knowing his obligations, he obeyed Joaquin's command without a murmur.

Our men crossed the river on Forman's Ranch; then they followed the main highway which skirts the woods, until coming to the one which leads to San Andres. About a mile from the town they began to climb a mountain in the vicinity of Greaserville. On the road they met two men who were traveling on foot. They shot them and once dead, they handed them over to the fury of Jack Three Fingers.

Near Angel Camp the bandits found a cabin in which four Germans were sleeping. They awakened them, made them give up their daggers and all the money they had, which scarcely amounted to two hundred dollars. Jack Three Fingers let his comrades go on, and when they were a short distance away, he returned to the poor Germans, who were still stupefied. With a wicked curse, he told them that he was going to cut off their heads because they had so little money. The action would have followed close upon the words if Joaquin had not arrived at that moment and interrupted him. The terrible Jack renounced for this time the pleasure which he was expecting. More than once on the road he tried to leave his comrades to go to fulfill his threat, but Joaquin, who never lost sight of him, knew how to prevent it.

Some days afterward, one of the men of the company named Florencio, told Joaquin he would not be able to accompany him any more since he had to return to Jacqui to settle some particular matter.

"What is that matter?" asked the chief.

"Ah!" said the other in a tone which seemed very natural, "it is a small matter that concerns only myself."

"I do not doubt it," replied Joaquin, "but I need you at this time. I intend to assemble all the members of the company at the head-quarters, and since you do not give me a plausible reason, I cannot grant you the permission that you solicit."

"But I am not soliciting, I am demanding."

"Then, Senor Florencio, what you demand is inopportune."

These words were followed by a fleeting smile of disdain.

"Any time seems good to me," replied Florencio. "It is enough that I find it opportune. I suppose it happens that I have found you in a bad humor today, but I must add that I must do as I wish," and say-ing this, the bandit turned his horse and was about to leave, when Joaquin drew his revolver and ordered him to stop.

"Oh, well," said the rebel, pulling up his horse, "what do you propose?"

"I think," said Joaquin, furious at seeing that he was treated this way by one of his subalterns and before his company, some of whose number were novices, "I believe and repeat that you are a traitor. Without doubt you are trying to find the road which we follow, and discover our headquarters."

"Think what you wish of me," answered the wretch, drawing his revolver and looking at his chief insolently.

"Ah!" exclaimed Joaquin, angry and cursing, "you are going to die, if for nothing else than your insolence."

Almost instantly two shots were heard, and Florencio, mortally wounded, fell from his saddle. His horse, freed from the weight of the rider, set out on a gallop. All the bandits censured Florencio's insub-ordination and congratulated their chief for his timely punishment.

"He asked me for some time, and I gave him eternity."

Two hours afterwards the bandits were riding over a road which was concealed in a mountain canyon when they suddenly came upon a camp occupied by five Chinamen. In spite of the fact that each one was armed with a revolver and a sword, they did not offer the least resistance to the men, begging them on their knees to spare their lives. Florencio's rebellion had put Joaquin in a bad humor. He gave the sign to Jack Three Fingers, who hurled himself upon the unfor-tunate Chinamen, and one by one he buried his sword in their hearts. His eyes shone with pleasure as he did it, making him appear more like a wild beast who was satisfying himself with the blood of his victims, than a human being endowed with reason.

Chapter XII

When they arrived at Arroyo Cantova, Joaquin was convinced that his ruffians had not been without something to do. Some hundreds of horses, many of them broncos, were grazing peacefully in the fields. In the camp, good-looking tents were set up, which, all together, resembled a small city. Seated all about, the bandits were peacefully killing time, some playing cards, others smoking cigarettes. A short distance away, seated on the short grass were eight beautiful black-eyed girls with their sweethearts, talking, laughing and singing with all the joy and natural vivacity of their sex and age.

Joaquin was greeted on all sides by his comrades. At the same time two lovely arms encircled his neck, and the beautiful eyes of Clarita gave him a loving welcome. She was so overcome by her emotion that she could not speak. After having thanked his companions for their warm reception, Joaquin retired with his sweetheart to a favorite tree, under whose boughs he had chosen to spend his leisure moments. When they were seated away from the eyes and ears of others, Clarita said, "Joaquin, you have been gone so long! Oh, so long! And I have been very sad in your absence as I was lonely in the midst of so many people."

"Is it possible, Clarita? Lonely and sad among all these pretty, happy girls?"

"Ah, that is just the reason I was sad."

"Really? Tell me then, sweetheart. I want to know the cause of that sudden change. What! Are you crying? Is it as serious as that?"

"Yes, Joaquin, I am crying," she said, laying her head upon her lover's breast. "I am crying because I cannot hold in my tears. I feel as if my heart is almost breaking. Do you remember your promise to me? Oh! When will you abandon this dangerous and unhappy life to go to our own beautiful and peaceful country?"

"Our country! If only I had never left it, I would not have been what I am today. But come, Clarita dear, do not lose heart. A few more months and we shall see the beautiful skies where we were born, where we passed our childhood, where all our suffering will be forgotten in the joy that we shall find there."

The girl's face reflected the memories that Joaquin's words brought to her, for in spite of the life that he led, Clarita truly loved him. She would have given her life gladly for him. She knew all of his secrets, read in his eyes his sorrows, his troubles, his pleasure and happiness. With one searching look, she read the secrets buried in the furthest depths of his heart. Joaquin had told her that he would end his career on the day when he had completed his vengeance and when he had accumulated a sum equal to what they had taken from him. He added that they would return to the state of Sonora and build a home filling it only with their love. She listened with entire confidence, since his intentions were sincere, and in spite of all that people said to her about Joaquin, Clarita loved him and considered him the noblest, bravest, most generous of men.

"Will this be our last parting?" said Clarita tenderly.

"Yes! My dear. My vengeance is almost complete, and as for my fortune, a few more thousand dollars will be enough."

He had scarcely finished saying these words when the young chief was suddenly interrupted in his lovemaking by one of the sentinels who came running towards him with a message. About a mile above Cantova Creek, the sentinel had just discovered a trail which was lost in the high grass and from all appearances they could make out a party of twelve or fifteen men not far away. It was very important that the camp should be well guarded, and that no one else should be allowed to leave the valley, lest he should reveal the secret of the headquarters of Joaquin's company. An occurrence of that nature would have completely spoiled the Mexican chief's project, forcing him to seek another hiding place. Without delay he took one of his best horses and sped from the valley, accompanied by twenty of his best men, among whom were his faithful assistants Jack Three Fingers and Valenzuela and the no less valiant and faithful Guerra, Antonio and Fernando. The little company followed the trail indicated by the sentinel, and at the end of two hours of fast riding they perceived before them a company of fourteen Americans, who were awaiting them abreast.

When the bandits were some few paces from the Americans, Joaquin ordered them to stop. The Mexican chief had observed with surprise that the leader of these intruders was no other than a big husky individual who had tried to arrest him in a dance hall in Sonora.

"What are you looking for in this valley?" Joaquin asked him, advancing his horse a few steps in order to observe more closely the face of the person in question, to make sure that he was not mistaken.

The American hesitated. Irritated by the chagrin which Joaquin had caused him in the gambling house, the American, having to endure the jests of his friends each time they met him, asking how Joaquin was, had decided to organize a company and go out in search of the bandit to bring him back to Sonora, dead or alive, and end the criticism of which he was the victim. For such a laudable purpose, he easily assembled a dozen experienced men who undertook the enterprise. We must observe that when the American decided to pursue the bandit chief, he supposed that the gang was composed of men of little valor, and for this reason he believed that his undertaking would be very simple. He was not ignorant of Joaquin's bravery, but not being aided by his men, he would soon have to give himself up.

The sudden appearance of Joaquin at the head of twenty men, well equipped, well mounted, well armed and very lusty and with an appearance anything but agreeable, surprised Arkansaw (that was the name by which the American was known in California) to an extent that for the moment he could not even answer Joaquin. Arkansaw did not lack decision or valor, but he was very egotistical, vain and cautious. Upon seeing himself confronted by a company of men greater than his own in number and in quality of arms, he understood that he would gain nothing by fighting them, but would only antagonize them and still not gain his end. The American, therefore, remained silent and perplexed.

Joaquin impatiently said to him, "Did you understand me, or will it be necessary for me to explain myself more clearly?"

"Oh! A little bit, more or less," said Arkansaw, biting off an enormous quantity of tobacco which he had just taken from his bag, while with one look, he tried to search the faces of his companions.

"Well, what have you to say? Speak quickly! Who are you? And what are you going to do in this valley?"

"Do not be angry. You can easily guess that I am a stranger. You scarcely give me time to reply. To put it briefly, the purpose of our presence in these parts is this; we are a company of hunters who are traveling in search of grizzly bears and other wild animals. Since you have no reason to seek any argument with us, neither have we any for becoming vexed. There is the truth, pure and simple."

At these words, surprise appeared on the faces of the Americans who were accompanying Arkansaw. Some uttered indistinct sounds of discontent. One of them stepped toward Joaquin and said to him very emphatically, "I am convinced that I know you. You are Joaquin Murrieta."

Chapter XIII

Scarcely had the American uttered the name of Joaquin when all drew their revolvers. Firing started on both sides with great confusion. Five of Joaquin's men had fallen from their horses and two of the Americans had been killed when, at a signal from their chief, the bandits threw themselves on the enemy and began a hand to hand fight in which strength and valor must be the winners. In the midst of shouts and curses were heard the voices of the leaders who were encouraging their men, while at the same time fighting with the ferocity of tigers. Wounded, bloody, but always brave and never discouraged, Murrieta ran from one side to the other, in the midst of the tumult, and was seen everywhere. When one of his men began to lose heart, he encouraged him; as a result, he was victor over his adversary. Nevertheless, the Americans fought desperately. For a moment they had the advantage over their opponents, and would have been victorious if the invisible spirit which accompanied the Mexican chief everywhere had not come to his rescue. After having discharged the contents of his revolver upon the enemy, Jack Three Fingers had laid aside his weapon and begun using his dagger, with his usual ferocity. He struck pell-mell, and sometimes, blinded by the sight of blood, he did not even see where he struck, wounding some of his comrades and their horses.

After Joaquin had shot down one of the most obstinate Americans and he could calmly survey the battlefield, he saw that nine of his men had met death. Of the enemies, but one remained alive, and he was the gigantic and robust Arkansaw, who was fighting desperately with Jack Three Fingers. The American, who was a sturdy fellow, was giving more blows than he received, which increased the wrath of Jack. Joaquin and the others of his band, wounded and blood-soaked, weak with fatigue, remained quiet spectators of the fight, confident in the strength and dexterity of their comrade. Lurching from side to side, with their horses covered with foam, the combatants tried to end the struggle by one mortal blow; it could be seen that they were resolved not to abandon the battle until one of them was conquered. Suddenly, Arkansaw, enraged by the pain of a terrific leg wound, which he had just received, hurled himself and his horse on the left side of his adversary, and brandishing his dagger, cut Jack's cheek so deeply that the Mexican fell from his saddle. His astonished companions tried to assist him, but Jack, suddenly regaining consciousness, emphatically ordered them to retreat. Resolved to prevent a useless sacrifice, they did not heed him, and were about to put an end to the American. The latter, aware that with all of his courage he could not for long resist enemies more powerful than himself, turned his horse quickly and like a flash, shot down the road, pursued at a distance by his avid enemy, who had been joined by Joaquin. For five miles the Mexicans pursued him. Joaquin remained a little behind, but Jack almost caught him. Joaquin was convinced that it was impossible to capture Arkansaw, and so called to Jack, and together they rode back to headquarters.

The Mexicans who had been wounded during the combat were also there. Some of the most experienced were trying the best they could to render first aid. Fernando and some others were so badly wounded that they died the following day, increasing the total loss to eleven. Joaquin, for his part, had not been seriously wounded, but due to the loss of much blood, was forced to remain in his bed for several days; during this time Clarita cared for him most attentively. Antonio and Guerra, no less fortunate, found ease for their pain in the tender care of their sweethearts. Thus it was that those three were fully recovered before the others, less fortunate than they, were even convalescing. Joaquin was ill at ease, as he remembered the intrepid Arkansaw, who alone had survived the combat. He reproached himself for having let the American escape when he could have killed him easily with a shot during his struggle with Jack Three Fingers. Fifteen days had passed since that bloody battle, and if the American had not succumbed to his wound, there was the danger of his organizing another company of adventurers, who were never lacking for such an expedition. Who would prevent him from assembling the different bands which he had organized throughout the country to punish the bandits, and starting out in search of our men?

Fearing this, Joaquin resolved to abandon, at least temporarily, the headquarters. "By means of this strategy," said the chief to himself, "I shall deceive my pursuers, who, meeting a deserted valley, will believe that we have returned to our country, or better still, will begin looking for us in different directions." This would have allowed Joaquin to hide in the mountains, there to kill them one by one without exposing his own men. With this in mind, the bandit prepared to leave the valley. The horses, of which he had several hundred, were assembled in groups and sent to Mexico under the supervision of four of the bravest and most intelligent men of the company. The company tents were strapped on the beasts of burden, as well as everything else that might be useful to them. The women were dressed for traveling, gaily making themselves ready for the trip through the mountains, plains, deep canyons and trails. It was to be a series of fatiguing experiences in which not only would they suffer privation and weariness, but would even have to defend themselves against the wild bears and mountain lions of California.

The convalescents, who had not fully recovered their strength, were mounted on the gentlest horses, which ordinarily were ridden by women.

Preparations concluded, the entire band set out little by little from the valley, one hundred and six men and nine women. All were loath to leave the spot and were sad, but as the distance between them and the old home increased, they took heart and became reconciled.

Joaquin marched at the head of the column, surrounded by his assistants. The handsome features of the chief had taken on an expression of sadness and gravity while he explained to his men the reason for abandoning Arroyo Cantova.

Chapter XIV

The journey did not distract Joaquin from his constant preoccupation. The memory of the last encounter with the Americans tormented him. Although he had completely routed them, he had paid dearly for his victory, and he realized the necessity of admitting the weakness of his own men before a strong enemy. He felt certain that their band was not composed of such skillful men as Jack Three Fingers, Valenzuela, Antonio and Guerra. Disturbed at letting Arkansaw escape, he also had to admit that Jack Three Fingers was not always invincible. Nevertheless, he was the strongest in the whole company, the most astute, the cruelest, the most audacious of all the bullies. Formerly, he had been a favorite and a right-hand man of Father Jarauta, that most famous bandit chief. Moreover, his service record was increased by his many wounds which he had received during his career, the scars of which could still be seen. This exalted him in Joaquin's eyes. If this great champion had such great difficulty in escaping the clutches of the great intrepid Arkansaw, it was more than probable that any of the other bandits who had figured in that affair would have equal difficulty. Joaquin understood from this that it was to his interest to avoid a formal combat with the Americans. Such an encounter, even though he happened to be victorious, could deprive him of a great number of men whom it would be difficult to replace, which would greatly impede his original purpose.

This and other similar reflections kept Joaquin morose and silent. It was the first time that he felt a keen and sincere desire to renounce as soon as possible that criminal existence, and to retire and return to his mother country with his dear Clarita. That young girl was marching behind the company with her friends, who were far from sad. She did not feel the same misgivings as her lover and was in a very different humor. She was making an effort to distract and entertain her pretty companions, who liked above all things to be entertained. Upon hearing the jokes and songs which were falling from the lips of the young Mexican girls and their echo from the mountains, one would have said that an entertainment was being held in that vicinity, such was the shouting one heard.

After having crossed the rich valleys which extend to the north of Tulare Lake, the Mexicans crossed the San Joaquin River about twelve miles from Fort Miller, and continued north as far as the cascades of Yosemite. There, they again crossed the river and climbed the Sierra Nevadas, passing through the fertile valleys which they found on the other side. Finally, they came to the summit of the mountains to the east of Lake Mono. Joaquin had found refuge in these mountains in the early days of his career, when some Americans followed him and his company from Hangtown to Castle Peake, some distance from Sonora Pass. Ever since that time he considered it the safest hiding place in the United States.

The young chieftain penetrated into the interior where he came upon a pass where no one would be able to find him, it was so hidden by rocks and undergrowth. And when they arrived at their destination, they beheld one of the most picturesque and isolated spots that one could imagine. It was a clear space situated about twenty five miles southwest of Lake Mono between two sloping mountains crowned with rocks which seem about to tumble down, and in the midst of which a man could easily avoid pursuit. If he should venture to climb the neighboring mountains, at a single glance he would command a view of all the country for many miles around. In this isolated and uncivilized spot, a few miles from which wolves, mountain lions, grizzly bears and many other wild beasts had their dens, the bandits pitched their tents. Already the shadows of night were scattering little by little over the earth. Nature seemed to invite these fearless adventurers to rest. They spread their heavy blankets over the ground, and covering themselves comfortably, they abandoned themselves to sleep. They slept until dawn, to all appearances no less tranquilly than one who had never felt the touch of blood upon his hands, or who had no remorse on his conscience.

On the following day Joaquin assembled his comrades and explained his ideas and plans for the future.

"You know already that we have actually a hundred men in active service. Our spies, our friends, our allies, scattered though almost all the cities and districts of the state, amount to four hundred. These allies, to be sure, can only assist through the information which they furnish us. They can supply no active cooperation for reasons which it is unnecessary for me to explain. I have in a safe place a considerable sum of money and it is my intention to enlist in Sonora and Lower California a certain number of helpers who will increase our number of active soldiers to three hundred. I will equip the new recruits, arm them, and then we shall be able to clean up all of the southern countries, all this so rapidly that there will be no time to organize in companies and offer resistance. They will scarcely know my plans when I will have finished my work, retiring to the mountains of Sonora. When I come to that point, I will abandon this life of adventure which we have endured together for so long. We will divide the spoils acquired in our expeditions and go to live in peace the rest of our days."

The chief's speech was greeted with prolonged applause. Enthusiasm shone in the eyes of the bandits; the splendid picture which Joaquin had just unfolded before their eyes seemed to them so brilliant, the revelation was so unexpected, that they could scarcely contain their joy. In spite of their love and admiration for their chieftain, in the many phases of their dangerous career, they had never suspected so much talent. His words gave them new zeal, and they were more determined than ever to follow him, to obey him at all costs, whatever might be the fate that fickle fortune was reserving for them.

That same day Joaquin ordered eight companies, each composed of ten men, to different parts of the state, south, east, extreme north, with express orders to do everything possible to procure money and horses. He remained at headquarters with twenty-five men whose sole occupation was to hunt, care for the horses and keep the arms in good order.

It was already ten days since the eight companies had set out from headquarters. In this time the men who were wounded in the last battle had just recovered. Joaquin, seeing that they were ready to begin their service once more, set out on a campaign with Valenzuela and Jack Three Fingers to see what they could accomplish. Antonio Guerra had to stand guard for the safety of the women and protect the camp against invasions of wild animals, who did not cease to pass by, in spite of the continual hunting which the men did.

Upon his arrival at Fiddletown, Joaquin met the captain of one of his companies who handed him a sack full of gold coins and informed him that his men, divided in pairs, were operating with great success in the vicinity of Jackson. The captain had come to Fiddletown for an important engagement over a transaction which he was making. The conversation between Joaquin and his assistant lasted for a few minutes longer, after which they said good-bye. The Mexican chief called Jack Three Fingers, who was calmly passing before a cabin of Chinamen, whom he was eagerly watching. The bloodthirsty Jack abandoned the spot with a look of displeasure and then the bandits took the road to Indian Creek.

Chapter XV

Upon arriving at Diamond Springs some days later, Joaquin learned through one of his associates who owned a dance hall there, that on the following day the post which operated between Hangtown and Sacramento would carry very few passengers, and a great quantity of gold dust destined for eastern states.

In the early days of his career Joaquin had the opportunity of holding up a stage coach which came and went from Mokelumne Hill, but the disastrous result of that enterprise had filled him with an aversion to that sort of work. Ever since, he had tried to obtain money in a less dangerous way. Nevertheless, he judged it prudent not to throw away the opportunity which was offered him, and resolved to take possession of the valuable contents of the coach at any cost. Indeed, the sum of forty thousand dollars was not to be thrown away. It was as much as it would take to go to Mexico, enlist the men whom he needed, and put into action the plan which he had laid out to plunder the southern counties.

Joaquin held a secret interview with Valenzuela and Jack Three Fingers and disclosed his plan of holding up the post. Their approval was immediate and enthusiastic. That night they went to examine the road, to find a hiding place. After riding almost all night, the three Mexicans decided on a deserted spot covered with undergrowth and surrounded by trees, situated halfway between Mississippi Bar and White Rock House. Joaquin placed his two companions at the left side of the road behind a thicket, very near where the post would pass, and he hid on the right side, in a similar position. The bandits were hidden for two hours, consumed with anxiety. Dawn was beginning to break and the coach did not appear. Joaquin knew for a fact that it was the custom to leave Hangtown between one and two o'clock in the morning. Now it was six-thirty. The chief began to wonder if he had been deceived. He started down the road where Garcia and Valenzuela were stationed, almost deciding to return to

Diamond Springs and take the chance of meeting the coach at any point, even though less advantageous.

The two bandits, seated comfortably in their saddles and puffing at their inseparable cigarettes, were awaiting the stage with all of the patience imaginable. Murrieta, seeing them so well disposed, decided to wait another hour. Fifteen minutes afterwards, Jack Three Fingers drew his revolver and said, "Here comes the post!"

"Oh! yes," said Joaquin. "I hear the creaking of the wheels. A few words before it arrives. I was so engrossed in other things that I did not think to tell you what to do."

"Caramba!" said Garcia, "I did not know that there were two ways of doing a thing like this!"

"Silence!" said Joaquin, "Listen; at the first signal I give, rush out and stand one on each side of the coach, while I hold the horses. I do not want you to fire a single shot unless I order it. Don't forget that, Jack! And now, friends, do you understand everything?"

"Perfectly, sir," replied Valenzuela, saluting his chief courteously.

"Well, all right," murmured Jack, "but I must confess that I don't like that plan."

"Attention!" replied Joaquin. "Not another word, and remember my orders."

And then, as the squeaking noise of the wheels sounded nearer each moment, the chieftain hastened back to his hiding place. Five minutes later the stage appeared at a turn in the road; it was drawn by four galloping horses, fired with the brisk morning air. In the twinkling of an eye it was opposite the bandits' hiding place. Suddenly a terrible whoop was heard, Joaquin rushed out in front of the horses, pistol in hand; with a threatening expression and shouting in a thunderous voice, he ordered the postillion to stop. At the same time Valenzuela and Jack Three Fingers placed themselves at the doors. Jack thrust his pistol in the faces of the unfortunate travelers, and with such gestures and shouts that the passengers were more dead than alive, he commanded them to hand over all of the gold and other valuables which they carried with them.

When he saw Joaquin, the post-man had drawn up the reins with all his strength; he understood perfectly that it was useless to try to escape, as he saw painted on Joaquin's face the firm resolution to die rather than to give up. When the driver succeeded in stopping his horses, Joaquin changed places with Valenzuela to attend to the most delicate part of the proceedings himself.

"Now, gentlemen," said the chief, turning to the dismayed passengers, "hand over the precious coffer, and do it quickly, because I have no time to lose. Come! Hurry!"

"Quick! Caramba! Pass it over, or off with your heads," said Jack.

"Hello! Hello! Sir highwaymen, sir Mexicans, don't be in such a hurry," spoke an English Hercules from one of the back seats, as he tried to evade Jack's revolver placed near one ear, "I swear to you upon my soul that there is no coffer here; if there were, it would be given to you immediately."

"No, there is no coffer here of any kind," agreed the other travelers, crowding together like sardines in a can to avoid the dangerous proximity of the revolvers.

"Driver," shouted Joaquin furiously, "where is the gold you are taking to Sacramento?"

"We have no gold here, sir, none, I assure you. Yesterday we took a large iron chest full, which we left in Sacramento. But today we do not carry anything."

"That's all right," said the chief. "We are going to make sure of that." Opening one door while Jack opened the other, he continued, "If you have deceived me, you will pay with your heads. Come, get out one at a time!"

As readers can imagine, the order was obeyed immediately. Two of the travelers who were on the side Jack was guarding hurried to go out by the door, but the bandit grabbed them by the neck. In the midst of this scene Joaquin noticed in a corner of the coach a woman who appeared to be Mexican, who up to this time had escaped his view. When Jack entered the coach, she opened her shawl and drew from underneath it a gold crucifix set with precious stones, which was handed over to the bandit. He took it, examined it and returned it to the owner, to whom he gave a very expressive glance, murmuring some words which the woman probably did not hear.

After having carefully searched every seat without finding anything, Joaquin left the coach and examined the driver's seat, but his explorations were all in vain. Cursing his bad luck, he ordered the travelers to take their seats and the driver to continue on his way.

When Jack Three Fingers heard the order, and the noise of the horses who set out at a great pace, goaded by the driver's whip, he could not restrain a movement of disgust, and drawing his revolver, shot two bullets at the driver, which fortunately did not hit the mark. At the first shot Joaquin threw himself on his unruly assistant and with an angry look he ordered him in the midst of his act to put his revolver in its holster under pain of death. The Mexican obeyed unwillingly and grumbling. The three bandits returned to Diamond Springs by forced marches. The chief went immediately to see his friend who was also his ally, told him the details of his expedition and rewarded him with one of the well-filled purses which they had taken from one of the travelers. The bandits were hidden for a week in the house of their confederate, and when the robbery had been forgotten, they secured their horses from their hiding place and turned toward Sonora Pass.

Chapter XVI

A short time after his departure from Diamond Springs, the chief and his companions established their provisional camp on the northern branch of the Stanislaus River. That place seemed to them at night to be far from all habitation; but when the rays of dawn appeared, they were disagreeably surprised to find that a short distance away there was a camp, evidently occupied by Frenchmen. It seemed they had not noticed the proximity of that danger. They were completely ignorant as to the kind of neighbors they had. When the bandits asked them why they were living in such a secluded place, the Frenchmen replied without the slightest suspicion of fear that they were miners and were looking for gold.

"We are also miners," said Joaquin, "and we want to find plenty of ore if it is possible."

"Oh, it is indeed possible. The place is excellent, and ore abundant. But," said the miner with an accent which proclaimed his origin, "you have no implements with which to work."

"Yes, we have everything necessary; are you sure this is a good place?"

"Perfectly. Do you think that four or five men would amuse themselves by working for nothing? No, we have found what we consider a good claim, and have decided to remain in the great republic as long as we can."

"You will live in it a shorter time than you imagine," said Joaquin, drawing his revolver, his companions doing likewise, "unless you hand over to us immediately the last particle of gold you have."

Seeing the threatening attitude and the firm resolution of the Mexicans, the five Frenchmen had no illusions concerning the danger they were in. Four of them rushed into their cabins and reappeared armed with pistols. But before they could aim them, Jack and Valenzuela had taken off the tops of their heads. The fifth miner begged them to save his life; but when he had surrendered to them a number of pounds of gold dust, the fruit of long hard labor, he was pitilessly assaulted as had been his companions. After which the three Mexicans calmly sat down to eat the dinner which their victims had ready.

While they were thus occupied, they were suddenly interrupted by a loud exclamation. Looking up, they saw on the other side of the arroyo, ten Americans, perfectly mounted, armed with rifles and revolvers, led by the intrepid Arkansaw.

"And still that Yankee!" said Joaquin, arising. "Come, quickly to your horses." Already, the bullets the Americans had discharged from the other side of the river had grazed their heads. The bandits advanced, cursing Arkansaw with all their hearts.

"Caramba!" exploded Jack Three Fingers. "Here is a chance to attack those confounded men from the front."

"Indeed! When they are three to one, when they are better armed than we are? No, no! I know too well the kind of rifle they carry. We will be lucky if we escape their fatal shots."

"Hush! They have already crossed the river," said Valenzuela. "They are coming. Attention!"

Just at that moment he drew up his horse at the side of his chief, while Garcia, who remained a few paces behind, was raving with anger at the idea of abandoning the camp without fighting.

The bandits had scarcely attained the summit of the nearby mountain when they perceived two Chinamen, who were carrying on their shoulders their mining tools, with no other weapon than a saber, curved like a half moon, similar to a Turkish scimitar. Jack Three Fingers jumped on them, stabbed them without loss of time, cutting off their heads and threw them in the direction of the Americans. Five miles farther he repeated the scene; this time seven victims were sacrificed before the Americans could prevent it.

For four days the Mexicans fled westward from Sonora Pass, and on the morning of the fifth they arrived in the vicinity of the headquarters. They dismounted from their horses without announcing their return with the usual sign, and while Jack Three Fingers led the horses to the lake to drink, Joaquin and Valenzuela went to the camp. At the first tent they saw three of their men playing cards. They were so absorbed in their game that they did not see the two chiefs standing there.

"Here is a game in which a few Yankees would soon beat you," said Joaquin in a severe tone.

Immediately, the players, as if awakened from a dream, jumped up and drew their revolvers, but seeing their comrades, began to laugh at the joke and welcome Joaquin.

"Caramba!" said one of them. "The devil take me if I didn't think the Americans had invaded our camp."

"They would not have the least difficulty in doing that," said Joaquin, looking around at the camp, which was completely deserted. "Where are the rest of the men?"

"Out hunting grizzly bears!"

"And the women, are they also hunting?"

"No, captain, I'm sure they must be somewhere nearby, probably resting in the shade. Perhaps they have gone to bathe in the cool lake on account of the heat."

"All right," said Joaquin, "I shall look for them."

"Stay here, Valenzuela, and if they return before I do, station some sentinels around in the places that you think most need them. These confounded Yankees are so dangerous that they would be guilty of disturbing our peace even up here."

"Indeed, sir, that is something to be feared and prevented, above all on account of the women: your orders will be obeyed to the letter. In case the rest of the company should not return within an hour, I shall place three of these men on the west side of the mountain, and I shall remain outside near the entrance to the pass."

Joaquin approved of these plans, and confident of his officer, he set out to look for the women. He arrived at the lake and hid behind a heavy thicket. From there he saw that they were quietly bathing without the least suspicion that they were being watched. The young Mexican was thinking of the surprise that he was going to give them by appearing suddenly on the scene, when a sharp cry, followed by several others, aroused him from his reverie. The cry was scarcely uttered—it sounded like his own sweetheart—when Joaquin appeared at the edge of the lake. But the danger was all over before that. Jack Three Fingers was seen thrusting his dagger into a huge grizzly bear. Jack had been resting in the shade near the lake, somewhat more quiet than usual, due to the heat. He was dreaming, half asleep, about the happy days of his youth and the woman whom he had loved with all his heart. Suddenly he was aroused from the sweet memories by a deep growl. He jumped up quickly and arrived at the lake in time to save the sweetheart of his chief from the clutches of a grizzly bear. Seeing the fierce beast, he threw his coat over its head to keep it from fighting him. Then he thrust his dagger deep into its heart several times. When he was giving the death blow, Joaquin arrived.

Clarita was following her companions, who were fleeing from the horrible scene, but seeing her lover, she stopped still, trembling, and threw herself into his arms. In a few words she related what had happened. Joaquin, without stopping to ask Jack how he had arrived at the lake so quickly, gave him a hearty handshake and thanked him for the rescue.

"Garcia," said his chief, "you have just saved my dear Clarita's life. You have made me deeply indebted to you by this deed, and from now on you have in me a loyal friend."

For the first time in many years a smile spread over Jack's usually fierce and unfeeling face—poor Jack, who had committed such crimes to avenge the death of his own sweetheart.

"It's a great thing to kill a bear!" said Jack. "What does that amount to? Anyway, if I have saved the life of one of my compatriots, it is because I was just thinking of another woman."

"What!" exclaimed Joaquin.

"My word of honor! What would you say if I should tell you that my presence in this place is due to a sentimental thought?"

He had scarcely spoken these words when he turned his back to Joaquin and Clarita in a very ungallant manner, and walked away.

"Garcia in love!" exclaimed Joaquin involuntarily. "Really, if he had not just rendered me such an important service, I would be tempted to laugh at him before the whole camp."

"He must have referred to something in the past," said Clarita, "You remember that he told us that he was thinking of a woman."

"In that case," added Joaquin, "there is something queer about it. But come, we must return to camp. Perhaps you may wish to visit a certain tree . . ."

"A tree, Joaquin?"

"Yes, dear Clarita. Ah! do you not believe that I have seen the

Battle between Jack Three Fingers and a grizzly bear.

beautiful place in which you have chosen to comfort yourself during my absence? I know that place very well, for I hadn't been here more than twenty minutes before I had seen it all."

"Then there is no use in thinking of the surprise which I had prepared," said the young girl. "Oh, Joaquin! What is that?"

A muffled sound as of a man falling in a thicket came from somewhere about. In a second, another bear, smaller than the first, ran past Joaquin and Clarita and fled into the brush where Jack Three Fingers had lain hidden. A few minutes later, half a dozen bandits appeared, each with a revolver and dagger, led by Manuel Guerra.

"Stop," said their chief as soon as he saw them. The bandits obeyed, and filled with admiration and pleasure at his return, grouped themselves about him, giving him a hearty greeting.

"I see you have accounted for our hunt very quickly, Captain," said Guerra glancing at the dead bear lying on the ground.

"Oh, no," replied Joaquin. "This is not your bear; this is the result of Jack Three Fingers's hunting."

"Caramba!" exclaimed the officer. "Then ours has escaped and his funeral will have to take place tomorrow."

Just then twenty or thirty shots were heard echoing through the mountains. Joaquin and his men started for camp; in less than five minutes the company was assembled at headquarters. It was no little surprise to Guerra to see the second grizzly bear lying before his companions. They had killed it in the act of invading the camp.

Chapter XVII

Toward nightfall of that day, so memorable for the killing of two bears, Valenzuela and the three men who had assisted him in guarding the camp entered the headquarters. Behind them were fifty of their comrades, belonging to the marauding companies that Joaquin had distributed through the state. The captain of each company turned over the product of his expedition to Joaquin. The total plunder amounted to about five thousand dollars. While the newcomers related their adventures, the others prepared for the feast that would follow, and end with a general fandango.

A bonfire was lighted in the center of the camp, and over it were roasted the two bears, which had been killed so opportunely. This unexpected barbecue would be the "piece de resistance" to the hungry bandits; this and the great number of provisions that the marauders had brought were the delights of the feast. Soon the camp cooks announced that the dinner was ready; conversation ceased and they all seated themselves about the glowing bonfire. Dinner did not last long, because the excitement of that day had diminished their appetites. After eating, they smoked and drank their favorite liquors, and then began to relate a thousand and one tales, each telling his own experiences, especially in love.

When everyone else had told his story, Joaquin turned to Antonio, who from the beginning had remained silent, and asked him to tell something.

"To tell the truth, my friends," said Antonio, shaking the ashes from his cigar, "today I find myself unable to tell you my reminiscences, because my spirit seems filled with fancies. At this moment a legion of grizzly bears are dwelling in my head, and they are revolving in it in an extraordinary manner. I will confess to you that while I was meditating, I just now dreamed that one of them was torturing me, tearing my bones apart. However, if you will allow me to substitute a song for the tale which you ask, I shall take great pleasure in doing that—all the more since singing dispels my foolish ideas."

"Yes, yes, a song!" they chorused.

"Come, what shall I sing you," asked Antonio. "El castillo de Santa Ana? La serenata de Monte-Sierra? Or perhaps . . . "

"Sing Nuestro país es México (Our Country is Mexico)," answered Valenzuela.

"Yes, yes," echoed the others, "Nuestro país es México, that's the one! Sing that one, Antonio, sing it!"

"With great pleasure; however, you must all join in the chorus. It is a charming song, one which Father Jarauta liked best of all; but it doesn't sound well unless you join in the chorus."

"All right, countryman, begin."

After a little preliminary humming to prepare his voice, Antonio sang the song of "Nuestro país es México" to the tune of "La Niña de Monterrey."

When the song was ended, the singer said; "Yes, indeed, Mexico is our country, and it is the only place in the world, my old friends, with the exception of Spain and Italy, where one can enjoy all the pleasures of life."

"Have you been to Spain?" asked Valenzuela.

"Certainly," replied Antonio, "and the proof is I was born in Madrid. In regard to Italy, I am proud of having served under the famous Carlotti."

"What!" exclaimed Guerra. "You knew Giovanni Carlotti?"

"The same, Giovanni Carlotti, descendant of the one who was an officer under the celebrated Massaroni. Friends, some day I will tell you my story; but not now as my throat is dry."

"Drink, drink, Antonio," said Joaquin, serving him some wine from the bottle before him. "Take two fingers of this wine to refresh your palate. Fill your glasses, friends, and let us drink to the memory of the valiant Massaroni." Then Joaquin sang a verse which Captain Massaroni was wont to sing, which was received with great enthusiasm by the troop. All drank a toast to the never-to-be forgotten Massaroni.

"Silence," said Joaquin suddenly, "I think I heard a signal."

"Oh, yes, they are some of our comrades who are returning," said Valenzuela, "and if I am not mistaken, it is Sevalio's signal. Isn't that right, Margarita? In less than ten minutes your lover will be holding you in his arms."

"My word! I believe it is. You know his signal better than I."

Joaquin drew from his breast a magnificent silver whistle, which he put to his lips; a prolonged whistle echoed through the mountains, and a few minutes afterward Sevalio appeared, accompanied by two bandits who were leading the horses by the reins. The three men were so overcome by exhaustion that one would have taken them for invalids escaped from a hospital.

Joaquin walked toward them with Antonio and Valenzuela, while the rest of the company jumped up to greet them, and make a place for them around the fire.

"What news do you bring us?" asked Joaquin, when they were all seated.

"Wait, Captain, wait, and you, my comrades, give us quickly a glass of wine as we are half dead."

Five or six bottles were placed before them, but they only drank a few swallows.

"Now," said Sevalio, putting his arm around his sweetheart, who had just seated herself beside him, "I can answer you. But first I must tell you that it is bad news that I bring. It seems to me that it might be better to wait until tomorrow, and not break up this happy meeting with the tale."

"No, no," replied Joaquin, "we must know now. Uncertainty is torture. Tell us what has happened. I see that you only return with two men, while you started with nine. The others are dead, are they?"

"Oh, yes, dead and buried."

"How did they die?"

"Two were killed in a fight . . . the others."

"And the other five?"

"Hanged, hanged till they died. Hanged on trees by the roadside. Comrades, hand me some more wine! I want to drown the memory of this terrible scene. It seems to me that I still feel the rope around my neck."

"What's that?" exclaimed Joaquin. "Around your neck?"

"Yes, the rope was around my neck, but not tied, and I was being led to the fatal tree, when I made a supreme effort, broke the rope, and amid the fire of the revolvers of my pursuers, I jumped into a thicket where two of my companions awaited me. Then we three began to run as fast as we could. Caramba! Those Americans are worse than Apaches. It doesn't pay to irritate them. Give me more wine, my friends, I am beginning to feel better. Those devils of Americans never do things by halves, and they always do them differently from anyone else. If they hang a man, they hang him on the highest tree in the country. Well, anyway, they didn't get to hang me. I am very bitter, though, and will avenge my murdered comrades without mercy."

"Where did all this take place?" asked Guerra.

"On the branch of the Feather River exactly fifteen miles below Pico Espanol. There is a company of miners, about eighty or a hundred men, whom I believe are the strongest Americans in the whole state. Caramba! And how they are armed! Each man has two or three revolvers, a knife and a rifle."

"Well, now that you have told us how the affair ended, we want to know how it started."

"Surely," said Sevalio, "it started like this."

Chapter XVIII

"A few days after leaving Red Bluff," said Sevalio, who was just finishing his fourth bottle, "we arrived in Shasta, and had the luck to meet a convoy of mules loaded with gold. We stopped the train about two miles from town, took the cargo and returned to Red Bluff. Each of us was carrying twelve pounds of gold. As you might imagine, we were anxious to reach headquarters. The individuals whom we had robbed were miners, and consequently, we were expecting them to follow us, and that very soon. We were just finishing our meal in Pedro's restaurant and were ready to leave when Pedro warned us to take care that we were not seen leaving town or we would be hanged, if only in suspicion. You see that the beginning wasn't exactly promising, but we set out, each one separately and all in different directions, agreeing, however, to meet in Oroville. A large company of Germans, Frenchmen and Americans followed us, but we were lost from view near Downieville. We followed four Americans down to the valley of Honey Lake, and then overpowered them, giving them their lives in exchange for the gold they were carrying. As we turned away from Honey Lake, we were attacked by the miners of Feather River. Two of our men were killed in the combat; the enemy had five of theirs mortally wounded. My own two companions had succeeded in hiding in the brush where they waited. We remained there three days without eating or drinking and finally we ventured out by way of Sonora Pass. Two miles from Downieville we buried our gold, helped ourselves to horses, and here we are."

"That description isn't very pleasant, but we must realize that accidents will happen once in a while," said Joaquin, "Come, friends, pass around the bottle; we must enjoy life while we can."

"Yes, yes, Captain, you are right," said Sevalio, "and we all heartily agree. Lopez, my friend, pass me a bottle or two, for I swear by all the saints that I have not yet recovered. The flight we had over precipices and ravines did me up completely."

"What's that, you climbed over precipices, you say?" asked Antonio. "Did you lose your way?"

"No, of course not, but we took the worst roads in order to escape from the enemy."

"Ah, but who was pursuing you? Come, Sevalio, what the devil?"

"What, haven't I told you that? The Americans followed us past Lake Mono as far as the mountains, and when we finally lost sight of them, they were only five miles away."

"The devil!" said Joaquin, leaping to his feet. "This thing looks very serious. If they only lost you five miles away, our fires could easily guide them here."

"Silence!" exclaimed Valenzuela suddenly. "It seems to me I hear the sounds of hoofs on that rocky road just below our camp."

"I do, too," said Murrieta, drawing his revolver. "Come boys, get up! Arms ready! You, Antonio, take thirty or forty men and guard the Pass on the left entrance. I will go to the right entrance with the rest of the company. Above all, men, go cautiously, so that none of those confounded Americans can boast of having come in this far."

These loyal bandits followed their leader silently, crawling over the rocks which protected the entrance. Each man hid the best he could, some behind rocks, others in curves of the mountain. The noise of the approaching steps became more distinct. From time to time a savage oath could be heard escaping from the lips of the besiegers (for it was indeed a siege) who tripped over the rocks. In spite of all this the enemy approached gradually and soon could be seen twenty feet below the place where Joaquin was stationed, the tall figure of Arkansaw at the heal of forty well-armed Americans.

"The devil take me if I like this ugly place," murmured Arkansaw. He had scarcely uttered the words when out from the rocks came sixty or seventy bullets, causing great destruction to the Americans. One bullet grazed Arkansaw's hat, and he saw that twenty-five or thirty of his men had been killed.

"Scale the rocks, boys," called the intrepid Arkansaw. "With all your might! It is your last chance." Every American began to climb the wall which protected the bandits. But vain hope! A second discharge as destructive as the first shook the mountain and the assailants fell wounded and dying at the foot of the rocks. Some of the bandits went to the camp and returned with torches. The scene appeared in all of its horror; nothing is more terrible than the ghastly light of a rosin torch shedding its pale light over the livid countenances of the dead. Even Joaquin could not endure it for long and left as soon as possible. Those who felt it less remained to despoil the victims, taking all of the money and weapons that they could lay their hands on and finishing any who still showed a breath of life. The most desperate of all was Sevalio. He rivaled Jack Three Fingers in his vengeance, cutting off the heads of the dead, stabbing his knife into the hearts of the dying, while Jack looked on with a sinister smile, almost as though he enjoyed it.

"By the soul of Judas! If you aren't depriving me of half of my greatest diversion, Sevalio," exclaimed Jack, "but it is all right as long as you don't become a too powerful rival. If things get to that point, we will have to have an understanding." Raising his torch in the air he glanced over at Sevalio with a look half sardonic, half sinister. Then he began looking among the Americans as if for someone he knew.

The other bandits had returned to camp, so that Garcia was alone on the battlefield. With a torch in one hand and a huge knife in the other, Jack continued his minute search, lowering the light at times to see the features of the victim. Sevalio suddenly appeared on the scene.

"Oh, it's you," murmured Jack. "At first I thought it was a grizzly bear."

"Whom are you looking for?" asked Sevalio with a smile which looked more like a grimace.

"For a man I can't find. If he escaped this time, he must be the devil himself."

"If you mean the leader of these men, he is in camp a prisoner with one of his men."

"Caramba! Who was so clever as to take him?"

"Murrieta. And I came to tell you that he wants to see you right away. Come on, I am anxious to know what he wants, and also to see that brave American once more."

When they entered camp, they found all of their men sitting around the fires, which they had rekindled with dry logs, celebrating their easy victory. Wine was passed freely, and the men who were drinking seemed much more lively than before the combat. The few prisoners lay stretched out on the ground, bound by some of the bandits' silk sashes. They seemed very much disgusted at the delay of their punishment.

"Thanks, my friend," said Joaquin as Jack sat down by the fire. "I want you and Sevalio to flip a coin to see who has the pleasure of killing one of these men."

"Which one? The chief?" asked Jack.

"No, the other one. I want to spare Arkansaw's life a few days."

"Well, but he might escape," objected Jack. "It would be better to let me finish him right now." And while he spoke he drew out that huge knife that he always carried, and thrust it before his enemy's face.

"No, no," replied Joaquin, "I have my reasons for saving him until later. He must be guarded."

"Oh, very well. I won't insist. Let Sevalio take care of the other one. I have no appetite for that now."

Just at that moment a moan was heard. Sevalio had just coolly broken the neck of Arkansaw's companion.

"A very simple matter," said the murderer, again seating himself and forthwith emptying a glass of wine.

"Very simple indeed," added Valenzuela. "It couldn't be more so, and it was executed with an energy that our friend Jack Three Fingers couldn't help appreciating."

"Come, comrades," exclaimed Antonio suddenly, "another song. Everyone is going to sleep." The lieutenant's suggestion was without response; the wine had had its effect, and four-fifths of the bandits were sound asleep. The others were not long in doing the same, the celebration ending in a chorus of deep and heavy snoring.

Chapter XIX

Not more than ten days from that night, Joaquin awakened his men and ordered them to pack up their tents and break up camp. Although surprised at this sudden resolution, all obeyed without answering, and before the sun appeared on the horizon, the party had gone out from Lake Mono in the direction of Sonora Pass. Arkansaw was not with the bandits. An hour before the departure, Jack Three Fingers, who did not wish to allow such a good chance for vengeance to escape, had killed without telling anyone, the man who had almost conquered him in a remarkable combat.

Joaquin had not failed to see the new crime committed by his assistant, but what could he do with a nature like that? The chieftain had preferred not to say anything about the matter, making a resolution not to think any more about Arkansaw. Nevertheless, in his heart he was only half angry at what had just passed. Joaquin was reserving for the American a special punishment.

When they arrived at the south branch of the Tuolumne River, Joaquin formed his people into companies of ten or fifteen men, who were to go forward by different roads to the Arroyo Cantova. Joaquin left the women in the care of Antonio and Guerra, and taking fifteen resolute men, he went with them toward the southwest, near Coulterville.

On the road which led from Don Pedro to Snellings Bar, he met three Frenchmen, two Germans, and two Americans, who were leading some mules loaded with provisions, blankets, and implements for use in the mines. Joaquin did not hesitate to speak to them, and while his men were talking at the side of the caravan, ready to fire their revolvers at the first sign, he advanced toward one of the Frenchmen, who did not dare to use his revolver, seized him by the neck, and told him to tell where the sack was which contained the gold. The Frenchman delayed in order to give his companions time to defend the treasure, but the bandits were too able, and were not to be surprised in this way. In a few seconds three of the miners rolled on the ground, bathed in their own blood. Joaquin, angered by their resistance, raised his dagger and threatened to cut the throats of the four men who remained if they did not hand over at once the money which they had on hand.

The miners had to give up, and taking from under the blankets a small canvas sack, they gave it to Joaquin, assuring him that it was all the fortune which the company owned. The sack contained four thousand dollars.

Murrieta continued on the way in spite of the petitions of Jack Three Fingers, who wanted to finish with the Germans and Frenchmen, and ordered that they should advance as before.

The four miners did not wait for this to happen twice. If Joaquin had ventured a more careful examination, he would have found six sacks like the first, containing almost twenty-five thousand dollars in gold dust.

After the new robbery the bandits crossed the Merced on the side of Snellings, going east to return to Mariposa. Two miles from Mt. Ophir, Joaquin was obliged to interfere to prevent Jack Three Fingers from killing a Chinaman called Chung Vo, as he had compassion on seeing him, such was his weakness and debility.

Some hours later they arrived at Mariposa. Joaquin and his men were obliged to separate and go into the town two by two in order not to excite the suspicions of the neighbors. They remained there eight days, eating and gambling with the money which they had stolen from the Germans and Frenchmen. At the end of a week they left the city and crossed the Mariposa River, the Clowchilla and the Frezus.

Ten or twelve miles from Coarse Gold Gulch, four Russian miners were killed and robbed. Several Indians, witnesses of these murders, approached after the departure of the assassins and despoiled the corpses of their clothing. Some time later these clothes were found in the possession of the Indians, and they, having been pointed out to other Russian friends, were persecuted and suffered for the crimes committed by Murrieta and his men.

The latter had crossed the San Joaquin River about twenty-five miles above Fort Miller. After remaining in an Indian village two or three days to rest, they continued their march. On the morning of the third day they entered the Arroyo Cantova, where the majority of their comrades were just pitching their tents on the plain. Joaquin, calm on account of the death of Arkansaw, had decided to stay again in his old headquarters, more comfortable and more secure than any other.

When all were settled in camp, the bandits took some rest for fifteen days, after which Joaquin sent them away by companies more or less numerous, and each with a different mission. It was necessary that they should supply themselves with horses and with money; also it was necessary that some expedition should be planned which should render the company some reasonable benefits, and obtain exact information. When all the companies had gone to carry out the orders of their leader, Joaquin found himself in camp with only a dozen men, among whom were Antonio, Sevalio and Guerra.

Murrieta and his companions passed a month agreeably, eating, sleeping, smoking, making love and hunting in the mountains. While they passed the time there, the rainy season arrived, which, disagreeable everywhere, is, as is well known, especially inconvenient in the mountain regions. Therefore, Joaquin decided to go out into the country himself in order to find a place favorable for the execution of the enterprises which he was planning. Two days after having made this resolution, he went toward the north of the state accompanied by Sevalio, who wished to find the gold buried by himself and his comrades at the mouth of the Feather River. After some very short stops in Mariposa, Sonora, Murphy's, Mokolumne Hill, Jack, Brytown, Rangetown, and Fiddletown, the chief and his assistants arrived at Hangtown.

The first thing which they did on their arrival was to dine happily and comfortably in one of the restaurants of the village. Then Sevalio mounted a horse and set out, while Joaquin went into a dance hall, where he was very soon seen surrounded by beautiful Spanish girls who were very fond of the fandango. Joaquin danced with one of these several times. A little later he felt tired and sat down between two beauties of the place, talking with them with much mirth of various interesting things. The sound of the conversation and the laughter of the young people soon called the general attention to that small group, and our hero noticed that he was watched very closely by various Americans who seemed to be with marked intention near the door. In the midst of them he recognized presently the driver of the stagecoach which he had stopped near White Rock House. From the expression of the man it was seen that he had recognized Joaquin, but without appearing the least bit pre-occupied, Joaquin got up very coolly, said goodnight cordially to the girls, put on his cap and went out.

"Excuse me, sir," said a voice at his side as soon as he reached the sidewalk in front of the house. "I wish to see your face."

Before the stranger had finished these words, Joaquin had thrown himself upon his horse, which was tied at the door of the restaurant.

"Well," said the Mexican, imitating the voice of the one who had just spoken, "you are at liberty to see me."

He spurred his horse and in a few minutes was lost to view, riding along the road. After a rapid run, which lasted about five miles, he arrived at Junction House, where he spent the night, assuming rightly that, if he were pursued, his followers would not undertake the pursuit before the following morning. When it began to dawn, he mounted his horse and directed his escape toward the Taylor Ranch, with the intention of describing in his flight a half circle and arriving at Fiddletown at the right time to meet Sevalio. A light covering of snow had blanketed the plain during the night, but this did not disturb Joaquin, who continued his way peacefully, considering the consternation which had overcome the inhabitants of Hangtown at the first news of his visit. He was just passing the ranch when he heard behind him the galloping of several horses, and at the same time he saw that a large number of well-armed horsemen were running at full speed toward him. He knew at a glance that he would have to make the best of it. Then he gave his horse the reins and fleet as the wind, he began to run at highest speed. The Americans dug their spurs into their own steeds, shouting and swearing, and on seeing that their prize was escaping them, their fury knew no bounds.

Abandoning his original idea, Joaquin turned suddenly to the southeast and hurled himself into the midst of the mountains at a trot, hoping that at least there the Americans would not overpower him. The slipperiness of the ground made his flight more difficult than he had thought in the beginning. Several times in climbing the very steep hills his horse had fallen, and several times on going down them the noble brute had taken false steps.

At the foot of one of the hills was found among the rocks a hollow, in the middle of which ran a torrent which went to join the American River. That place was very difficult to cross, even for a good horseman, and even Murrieta hesitated before crossing it, but seeing his pursuers at the top of the hill at a distance of some hundred yards, he advanced toward it. A few moments later he found himself on the other side of the torrent. The leader of the Americans wished to go across but fell into the water with his horse. Immediately, his men climbed up. Then they fired twenty or thirty shots, none of which touched him, and seeing the outcome of their enterprise, they abandoned it.

Chapter XX

Joaquin continued journeying among the mountains in sheltered places until he found himself completely out of danger. Then he cleared Carson Pass and four days later arrived near a mining camp situated at the mouth of the Walker River. He passed the night there, but fearing to be recognized, he set out at daybreak, and the next day at the same hour he found himself inside of a second camp, which he supposed belonged to some Indians. After drawing near he was surprised to find himself face to face with Valenzuela and Jack Three Fingers, who were not less surprised than their leader at the meeting.

While they were breakfasting, the chief heard from the lips of his subordinates the result of their travels, and why they happened to meet at that moment. On going out from the arroyo, Valenzuela had directed his company toward Weaverville in conformity with the orders of Joaquin. Before arriving, they had seized a number of horses, which had been taken to headquarters by fifteen of the men.

Valenzuela had remained alone with Lopez, Pedro, Castillo, Rafael and Garcia. Pursued by various ranchers from whom they had just stolen several horses, the six bandits succeeded in escaping by swimming across a very rapid torrent. Wounded by the bullets of the enemy, Lopez, Pedro and Rafael had been drowned. Castillo succeeded in crossing the stream, but suddenly found himself face to face with a Missourian who knocked him down with a heavy blow. At last, Valenzuela and Jack Three Fingers were the only ones who succeeded in saving themselves.

On arriving at Weaverville, Jack had wished to go into a dance hall, in spite of the objections of the prudent Valenzuela. Four Americans leaning on the bar of the saloon were drinking and talking about the horse thieves. One of them expressed his opinion that Joaquin was probably not a stranger to the robberies which they had lately perpetrated, and added that he would gladly exchange his head for a ball to see the robbers hung. Garcia planted himself in front of him, and in a brutal tone said, "It is possible that you may exchange your head for a pistol ball."

"Who are you?" the miner asked.

"If you can count," answered Jack, showing his mutilated hand. "This ought to be enough."

"Are you Jack Three Fingers?"

"The same."

And without more preamble Jack Three Fingers drew his dagger and plunged it into the heart of the American. A fight followed. Several Americans joined the first one, and had it not been for the horses of the outlaws, they would not have escaped from the hands of their pursuers. Finally, they succeeded in reaching the place where Joaquin found them.

The day following this unexpected meeting the three Mexicans continued their journey in the direction of Arroyo Cantova. They crossed the canyons of Sonora and Tuolumne on the south bank; then, dismounting from their horses at Rattlesnake Bar, they went into a house and sought to eat supper. The house was occupied by an old woman, her son and daughter. The appearance of the three Mexicans, well dressed, and armed, surprised them and with reason. But they did not say anything and soon supper was served by the girl, as beautiful and ladylike a creature as could be.

Murrieta, who under the habiliments of a bandit carried the soul of a gentleman, spoke pleasantly with the lovely child while she served him and his comrades very graciously. The old lady observed with a suspicious air the hunger of the guests, but she kept her observations to herself.

When he had finished supper, Valenzuela got up from his chair, advanced toward the girl who was sitting by the fireplace, and, threatening her with his revolver, asked her if she would object if her house were searched.

"If you have any objections, speak quickly," said the bandit.

"Sir," exclaimed the old lady, "I have suspected that these men were bandits." And she began to scream so that Jack Three Fingers found it necessary to gag her. The girl consented for them to search the house, which was very soon put in complete disorder. Finally, the bandits went away, taking with them several hundred dollars.

Near Mariposa Joaquin reflected that the lack of prudence of Jack Three Fingers would probably cause them some difficulty as had happened to Valenzuela when they were in Weaverville. So he resolved to enter the town alone. Consequently, he ordered his two companions to proceed together to headquarters, while he would remain one or two days in the home of one of the members of his gang, called Juan Berreyesa.

This man had furnished some excellent information to some of the members of the company, and from time to time loaned them money, so they considered Berreyesa a sincere and faithful friend. Nevertheless, he was not. Without showing it, Berreyesa had a mortal hatred of Joaquin, and at all times had sought a favorable opportunity of freeing himself from him, delivering him over to his enemies. At that time, persuaded that the occasion which offered itself to him was an excellent one, he employed all of his energy for carrying his treason to an end.

It was three or four days since Valenzuela and Jack Three Fingers had left their leader. One night Joaquin was visiting the dance hall in the hope of meeting some of his friends, when he happened to notice that his revolver holster was empty. He thought that probably he had left his revolver on his bed and went to look for it. First, he stopped at the stable, situated at the side of the house, to see whether his horse had enough feed. Then he entered through the back door into a small room next to the kitchen, which Berreyesa had given to his guest. While he advanced in the darkness, seeking a candle and a match, he heard the voices of two persons who were talking in the next room. One of these persons, as he showed by his accent, was an American.

In any other circumstances Joaquin would not have paid any attention to them. But his name pronounced distinctly by the two speakers, and in a manner not at all friendly, made him suspicious. In spite of the fact that he considered it absurd that his friend would conspire against him, he had a curiosity to know why his name had been pronounced, and this seemed to him a sufficient reason for listening to the conversation. He crossed the kitchen walking on tiptoe, and put his ear against the wooden partition which separated the two rooms.

"Yes," said Berreyesa, "in this way my vengeance will be complete. He has mortally offended me several times, here as well as in Mexico, and I owe it to myself to pay him for it. Furthermore, I need the money. My gambling losses have obliged me to sell my ranch for half of its value, and . . . . But what is the amount you offer as recompense?"

"That is what I do not know," said the other. "Wait. I believe it is five or ten thousand dollars."

"Give me a thousand and you shall have him tomorrow."

"But are you sure that it is he? If you can prove it to me, I am able to collect the sum as soon as you ask it, and certainly it would be a good business deal. But are you sure that you are not deceiving yourself?"

"How could I fail to be sure that it is he? I have known him too long to be able to deceive myself."

"Where is he now? You have told me that he is within several miles of here, but where?"

"Caramba! Perhaps you take me for an idiot!"

"It might be better to take you for an accomplice, a member of his gang and as such to lynch you."

"Is that so? But you do not even have proof that I have spoken to him once."

"Good! Good! I have no desire to fall out with you. If this same night you wish to deliver him to us . . . ."

"Excuse me, what do you mean by 'deliver him to us?'"

"Oh! A thousand devils! Perhaps you suppose that I am going to take him alone. No! No! I have heard of too many of his exploits recounted to risk myself with him. There will be three of us, and one of my companions is exactly the one who should deliver to me the sum which you have stipulated."

"Oh, then, very well. I understand. The matter is all settled. You will pay me the sum mentioned when you have him in your power, dead or alive?"

"Exactly, if you are in earnest in your promises."

"I speak seriously for once in my life. But for my bad luck at monte I would have asked three times more for his head than the amount mentioned. At this miserable price it is a bad day's work that I am undertaking."

"Where and when shall we find him?"

"In this same house, before two hours, provided that you have the money soon."

"Very well, I will have it before ten minutes, and in the morning the career of Joaquin will have ended. Wait for me."

The American immediately went out, closing the door after him. A second later Joaquin dashed into the room where the preceding conversation had taken place, and like a wild beast, drawing his dagger, he seized by the neck the miserable Berreyesa, who seemed to be petrified by the apparition. "Silence," said Joaquin at the first effort the other made to speak. "You have already spoken your last word on earth."

"But Joaquin . . . ."

"Why do you wish to be a traitor to me?" continued Murrieta after a pause of some seconds, squeezing with more force the throat of his accomplice. "To be a traitor to me for money and vengeance. To avenge yourself of what? Have I not always been your best friend? Do you need money and would you sell me for a few ounces of gold, making your purchaser believe that your principal motive was vengeance? In whom of my band can I now trust? They, like you, have always appeared to be attached to me, and are able at any moment to deliver me over to my enemies, and cause me to be hanged on the first tree. And it is you, Berreyesa, who work thus. You, whom I have supposed incapable, more than anyone, of such lowness and cowardice. Berreyesa, you are going to die." And he buried his dagger in the heart of the cowardly Mexican.

Then, the door opening, he found himself face to face with the American, the accomplice in the contract to which there had been a secret witness. The American, seeing the terrible scene which had just taken place, let the sack of gold which he was carrying to Berreyesa fall from his hands and drew his revolver.

"Who are you?" he said to Joaquin.

"I am the man that you have bought for that sum," said Murrieta, pointing to the sack.

"Then you are Joaquin? Well, surrender or you are a dead man."

"Very well, but in that case, head for head! And be sure that when you have fired a shot, I shall make use of my dagger."

"I should prefer to hang you alive, and it is better that you surrender at once, for you will not be able to escape from us. My two companions will be here before five minutes. I wished them to be present when I delivered the money to the man who was just killed."

"Who was just punished, you wish to say?"

"Well, well, words do not have any weight in this matter. Drop your dagger or I shall fire."

"Fate is against me," said Joaquin, "and I see that my career is ended."

Joaquin kills Berreyesa, who betrayed him.

"Put up your weapon!"

"The only thing which I beg of you is that if I have to be hung, you will deliver me to justice and not to the people."

"I will do it for you with much pleasure," answered the other, extending his arm to take the dagger.

Taking advantage of the moment when his enemy held out his arm, the daring bandit leaped on him with the agility of a panther, threw him to the floor and stabbed him in the breast. Then, seizing the revolver, which had fallen to the floor, he went from the room, just as the two companions of the American arrived. Joaquin took his horse, and, without even saddling it, he fled from that place as fast as possible.

He was hardly a mile from Mariposa when the populace had already gathered; several horsemen left to pursue the outlaw in different directions, but all their efforts failed before the speed of Joaquin's horse, which penetrated into the mountains.

Two weeks after this dangerous adventure Murrieta arrived at headquarters, where he found almost all of his men collected and, besides, something like four hundred horses, which they had stolen in different parts of the state. The young outlaw explained to his men the cause of his long absence; then he retired to his cabin with Clarita, who told him all that had happened in the camp since his departure.

Among other news, Joaquin learned that one of his men from San Luis Obispo, called Texas Jack or Jack Texas, had appeared in the company of two other individuals, who, although they were complete strangers to the band, had been presented by Jack as excellent and congenial comrades. He was supposed to have been on a campaign to get horses, and they had met by chance near the headquarters. A majority of the members of the gang were almost on the point of throwing the two intruders out, and there were even those who would try to murder them, persuaded that they were nothing but spies; but others who had been with Texas in Lower California several times had faith in his words and defended his cause with such valor that their comrades consented to save the lives of the three new arrivals until Joaquin returned.

As soon as he knew what had happened, Murrieta ordered Antonio to bring in the three prisoners. They had been put in a secure place apart from the others, so that they should not be able to participate in the secrets of the band and cause it any trouble in case they should be set free.

Chapter XXI

Jack Texas or Texas Jack was a great rascal in every sense of the word. At the time of the Battle of San Jacinto he was twelve years old. When his father, a very daring man, enlisted in the army, Jack wished to follow him, but was not allowed to do so. Desirous of proving that he could fight as well as anyone, he lay in wait for an Indian laborer of theirs, caused him to fall into a trap and killed him by cutting off his head, which he presented to his father when he returned from his campaign.

Texas Jack was in San Francisco in the month of June 1851, in company with a Louisianian named Indian Fred and Bill Flanders, a consummate rascal who had been obliged to leave Maryland suddenly in company with a Mexican known by the name of Montezumito, or Little Montezuma, as it would be in English. The four outlaws had with them a number of horses and mules, which they had stolen in the valleys of San Joaquin and San Jose. They put them in a corral on Mission Street near First Street, and at once set out together toward a saloon situated at the side of an old jail. In this house lived several policemen, among others one named McCarthy, who was confined to his bed with sickness.

From his room the police official heard and recognized the voice of Indian Fred. He sent for him and advised him to leave town immediately for there were heavy charges of robbery against the three; and furthermore he was suspected as the author of a murder which had just been committed in the next county. Fred told Texas what had happened and left for Stockton with his two companions. The three bandits had hardly gone when the best one of the horses was sold to the owner of the canteen; then Texas led the others to the public plaza and sold them at auction.

Then he went fifteen miles from San Francisco on the Santa Clara Road, and broke into the ranch where the saloon-keeper had put the horse which he had just bought. Texas took possession of it for the second time and set out toward the Mission of San Luis Obispo. That was where he scraped acquaintance with Murrieta and some of his men in a disorderly house owned by a certain Victor Narigon, situated between the Mission and the docks where the sailors embarked who sailed on the coastwise ships.

Texas had the good luck, on a certain occasion, to perform a service for Joaquin, giving him information about certain individuals who were pursuing our hero. In recompense, Joaquin made him a present of a magnificent horse worthy in every way of rivaling the famous "Black Bess" of Dick Turpin. In the course of his travels Jack had a habit of camping during the night and sleeping with his head between the front feet of his horse. One night, while he was reposing in this way near the cabin of San Antonio, he was awakened suddenly by his horse, which pulled his hair with his teeth. He had hardly got to his feet when he saw three or four men, Mexicans and Indians, who were advancing cautiously toward him, with the intention, no doubt, of robbing and killing him.

He mounted his horse and began to run with all speed. At the same time he heard some bullets whistling by him, losing themselves in space. He reached San Benito and soon lay down on the grass at the side of an adobe house. The horse imitated his hero and neighed as if congratulating him on having escaped so happily from that danger.

Texas was finally arrested as a thief and sent to San Quentin, where he remained until 1857.

When Texas Jack and his friends were presented before Joaquin, the chieftain freed them and permitted them to leave at once. Some members of the company showed that they were not of the same opinion as their leader, so pointedly that Joaquin, fearing that those three men would be killed, judged it wise that Valenzuela, Jack Three Fingers and two other Mexicans should escort them to the middle of the San Joaquin River. They had hardly gone sixteen miles from camp when Jack Three Fingers attacked one of the Americans and discharged his revolver in his mouth while he was speaking. Seeing this, Texas Jack and his other comrade spurred their horses, riding as fast as they were able, to escape the clutches of the ferocious Jack. Only Texas succeeded in saving himself. His companion was overtaken by the bloody Three Fingers and in spite of all resistance he perished under Jack's dagger. Seeing presently that it was impossible to overtake Texas, Jack contented himself with firing three shots at him, saying at the same time, "Good luck, comrade! You should be proud of your escape from danger."

After these words the ruffian went to join his comrades, who at the first shot had remained dumfounded in the middle of the road, without knowing what to do and incapable of helping the prisoners.

"You have just committed a piece of foolishness," said Valenzuela, "but I suppose that you have received orders from our chief for this."

"Orders!" exclaimed Garcia. "Certainly not! I have not received any more orders than those which he gave, to you."

"What! Have you taken the responsibility for the death of those men?"

"Yes. Caramba! And the third one would have had the same luck if I had been able to get hold of the d.... fellow, but he flew as if he had been pinched."

"What was your object finally," continued Valenzuela, "in letting us in for such useless bloodshed?"

"Useless! What is it that is useless? Come! Come! I advise you to go back to Mexico and become a hermit. It seems that you are dismayed because a little blood has been shed. Suppose that those men had escaped—what would have happened?"

"Well, what would have happened?" the other one said.

"They would have betrayed us."

"Yes, but you forget that one of them has escaped, and that now by your action you have turned into an enemy a man who, I am sure, has always been one of our best friends. Texas will think that you have done this in accordance with Joaquin's orders."

"You may think what you please," murmured the brutal Jack. "I have to laugh at him and at you, too."

The men returned to camp, but they were very careful not to tell what had happened on the road. Each one of the outlaws had the same reason for fearing the wrath of their leader, for Jack's companions had been made his accomplices by not preventing the crime. A week later, that is on the first day of March 1853, the men under Joaquin began a series of depredations, which filled the whole country with terror. The bandits had chosen for their field of operations the three richest counties in the state of California: El Dorado, Calaveras, and Tuolumne. There was never seen a devastation like it or one so swift. Companies of four or five men, and sometimes even of a dozen, were scattered all over these counties, and such was the number, the variety and the rapidity of their operations, that it would be impossible to try to give an account of them.

The thievery, murder, incendiarism and pillage were the theme of every conversation and what everyone feared. Some of these abominations were committed by daylight, and others remained wrapped in the most profound mystery, but always the hand of Joaquin was recognized in it. It was seen that all of those calamities were the fruit of his own invention, which had germinated and ripened in his brain, and it was known that this great dramatist was always the principal factor in those tragedies. Although the numerous ramifications of this plot, so vast and so complicated, diverged widely among themselves, they were always united by a common thread; they started from the same point and had the same tendencies which Joaquin guarded in his heart as his secret.

In all the state there was not a single town of any importance which did not have one or more spies, according to the needs of the cause. Joaquin never lacked places of refuge for the wounded and for the stolen horses, and indeed many ranches might be named, inhabited by men honored and respected by everyone, where the Mexican chief went as much as was necessary.

Stealing and plundering along all the highways, Murrieta and eight of his men arrived one night in the month of March at one of the banks of the Tuolumne River. The boat for crossing the river was moored to the shore in such a manner that they were not able to move it to the other side, as they were accustomed to do. Because of this, they went to the cabin of the boatman, who was sleeping so soundly that the outlaws had to break down the door to awaken him. The poor man went out completely terrorized and asked Joaquin what he wished.

"We wish to cross the river," said he, "but before you take us there, we wish you to lend us all the silver money which you have on hand. This will show you the need of a speedy answer." At the same time the Mexican drew his revolver and pointed it at the face of the poor wretch.

"Yes, sir," said the boatman, "the demonstration was not necessary. I will give you everything I own."

At the same time he lit the light and drew from under his pillow a purse, which contained nearly a hundred dollars.

"Come, come," said Jack Three Fingers, who was one of Joaquin's party and did not lose the opportunity to fire a shot under the nose of the boatman in order to frighten him, "you have more money than that; show it to us."

He was preparing to shoot in earnest when Joaquin ordered him in a severe tone to be quiet. The boatman answered trembling, "It is all that I have, but I give it to you willingly."

"I do not want it," said the leader, moved by a stroke of generosity. "You are poor and you have done me no harm. Take us to the other side of the river and I will pay you for your work and the trouble which we have caused you."

We have narrated this incident to demonstrate that Murrieta had not lost all the noble sentiments he possessed before he took up the life of a highwayman. We also wish to answer those who believe that he had lost every generous idea, every human thought.

The little party arrived near Stockton without any further adventure, after having continued for two days, and camped three miles from the city in an immense grove of oaks such as are only to be found in California. One Sunday morning while the bells were calling the faithful to church, and the men, well shaved, carefully dressed, stood on the street corners watching the pretty girls go by, suddenly a stranger appeared in the city. He was a good-looking young fellow with black expressive eyes; his hair was also black, and thick, and fell about his shoulders. He rode calmly along, looking indifferently at whatever attracted his attention. The man was dressed very elegantly; he was mounted on a horse so handsome and well harnessed that, in spite of no one knowing him, he was the object of all the glances and all the conversation.

"What a good-looking young man!" said the women. "Look at him. Perhaps it is some highborn Mexican who is traveling for pleasure," said one.

"I believe," added another, "that he is the son of General Vallejo."

"I do not think that the general has a son," objected a third.

And the girls were so absorbed in watching the bold horseman, that we suppose that day the priest delivered his sermon for the walls to hear, and went to the expense of lighting the candles for himself alone. This youth who had attracted so much attention in the city of Stockton, in passing in front of a corner where several flaunting posters were nailed up, stopped suddenly. One of them had surprised him, and he read; $500.00 REWARD TO THE ONE WHO DELIVERS JOAQUIN MURRIETA, DEAD OR ALIVE!" The Mexican had no more than read these lines when he jumped down from his horse, took out a pencil and wrote some words under the sign, then remounted his horse and rode out of the city as coolly as if nothing had happened.

A dozen persons, more or less, excited by curiosity, walked up to see what the stranger had written with his pencil. This is what they found: "I will give $10,000.00. Joaquin."

Our readers may imagine the many exclamations with which the reading of these words was accompanied. In that whole week nothing else was talked about among the women. All wished they had guessed by his appearance, by his glance, by his carriage, that that horseman was no other than the famous Murrieta, in spite of the fact that none of them had ever seen him.

Chapter XXII

The strange deed which we have just related did not prevent Joaquin from coming to the city from time to time under different disguises, in order to learn for himself whatever it interested him to know. Joaquin was informed one night that at the hour of full tide a small schooner would leave Stockton for San Francisco. There were two miners on board, from Camp Seco, Calaveras County, who were going to sail, well provided with money or its equivalent in gold dust. Joaquin took three of his men who were inspecting the city, and with the aid of a small boat, they hid themselves on one of the banks of the river, covered with underbrush. The mosquitoes discommoded them so much that they were thinking of abandoning their undertaking; but the prospect of a good business made them reflect and persevere in their first idea. Murrieta regretted that he had not brought some matches with him, for with them he could have made a bonfire and let the smoke drive away the impertinent and bothersome mosquitoes; but the idea that perseverance always has its reward consoled him and he waited three mortal hours for the ship to appear.

The schooner finally came in sight. When it was opposite the bank, Joaquin and his companions directed their boat toward it, and laying hold of the side of the ship, jumped on deck and without saying a word, fired at the crew, which was composed of only two men. The poor fellows did not even have time to seize their rifles.

At the first shot they fell dead. The two miners, hearing the shooting, ran quickly to their comrades, firearms in their hands, and tried to defend themselves, but the sides were unequal. Bandits and miners shot at the same time.

Two of Joaquin's men fell dead on the deck. The two miners had the same luck. Joaquin and the comrade who was left took possession of the bags, which contained the entire fortune of the miners, then using some matches they found in the cabin, they set fire to the ship and it was devoured by the flames. At daybreak there remained no traces of the crime; there could hardly be discerned on the horizon a black point which projected from the surface of the water. By means of this audacious deed, Joaquin realized twelve thousand dollars in gold dust.

The next day, after he had sent Jack Three Fingers and four outlaws to the headquarters, Joaquin left with Valenzuela for Sacramento. There they remained about a week, and then sailed for San Francisco, where they arrived at eleven o'clock one night. As soon as they landed, they set out for a house on Pacific Street near Dupont. They called at the door several times and only after a quarter of an hour did they obtain an answer.

"Who calls?" a voice asked in a very low tone.

"We are friends, Senor Blanco," said Murrieta, "and very good friends."

"Ah, now I know you, countrymen," answered the voice. "Come in! Come in! I have been expecting you many days."

"Truly?" said Valenzuela, entering behind Joaquin, while Senor Blanco tightly closed the street door. "How would you be able to expect us? Are you such a magician that you can see even who is going to arrive at your house?"

"It could not be," added Joaquin, "that you have been visited by some spirit from the world of the devil!"

"No, no, nothing like that! My information is provided by a member of the company. Come here, I am going to show you the individual in person, although I suppose he will not recognize you; for forty-eight hours he has been as drunk as a grape. Come, come, you are a poor guardian. When I heard you call the first time, I supposed that it was an enemy, and tried to awaken the comrade. This is the reason that I was so slow in opening the door."

"Very well," said Joaquin, "but which of our companions is to be met here?"

"Come, see him yourself," answered Blanco. "Here, it won't take long. Be careful of those two steps. Here is the door. It is so long since you came to my house that it is no wonder that you have forgotten the corners. After you were here the last time, this house was burned; but I rebuilt it just as it was before, and now here is the man in question."

Joaquin and Valenzuela entered a very large room.

"Where is he?" they asked Blanco.

Joaquin went toward a table that was there, took the lamp which illuminated the room, and approached the man who slept.

"How is this?" he exclaimed, stepping back a few paces. "Garcia here!"

"Yes," responded Blanco. "He told me that you had ordered him to return to headquarters; but he had the good luck to find more money in his purse than he was accustomed to have, and he wished to come to San Francisco to seek distractions."

"This is all very well," objected Valenzuela. "Let us see if we can wake him." And, approaching the bed, he administered to his companion some well-directed blows, which far from producing the desired effect, only drew from Jack Three Fingers a muffled exclamation, and some short oaths such as "Caramba!"

Joaquin, knowing he would not be able to watch Garcia all the time they were in San Francisco, tried to avoid his company as much as possible. With this end in view, he bought a camping tent, which he had set up on one of the hills of the city, not far from the Hotel Fremont, that is today near the corner of Battery and Vallejo streets. Every night Joaquin and Valenzuela went from their tent to visit the Bella Union, Diana, El Dorado, and other gambling houses. They lost and gained quantities of gold with an ease so calm and gracious that they excited the admiration of the assistants, and even of the bankers themselves, who are, as is well known, the most unfeeling men in the world. One night the two outlaws went into the Bella Union, and were ready to seat themselves at a table where they were playing faro, when their attention was attracted by a great number of curious people who surrounded a table at which there was just beginning an interesting game of monte. Our men drew near and saw Jack Three Fingers seated almost in front of them, with five to six thousand dollars in front of them. He had just lost a sum almost equal to that, and the banker was coolly dealing the cards to commence a new game. At last he let fall on the table a king and a jack; Jack, without hesitating, placed his money on the king. The banker continued drawing out the cards, and finally came to the jack; in a few minutes he caused the stacks to pass from Jack to his side without the least flash of satisfaction appearing on his face. Garcia asked the waiter for a glass of brandy, which he drained philosophically, then he went out of the gambling parlor without uttering a single word.

Joaquin and his comrade had not been seen by Garcia. They still remained in the Bella Union, going from one table to the other, gaining here and losing there. Then they went away without having had any disagreeable adventure. On leaving the gambling house, they set out for a Mexican fandango on Jackson Street, where they found some compatriots, men and women who were dancing in an atmosphere of powder and smoke to the sound of tambourines, a poor violin and a flute as screechy as a whistle. The bandits mingled with the crowd and spent part of the night.

It was after two o'clock in the morning when they went from the dance hall to return to their tents. Joaquin had lost in gambling such a considerable sum, that after searching all the corners of their baggage they could only find a hundred dollars between him and Valenzuela. This sum was very paltry for men who in the space of a week had made more than twelve thousand dollars. Valenzuela proposed to his chief that they should go to San Jose Mission, where one of their associates lived who would have no objection to lending them several thousand dollars, if they would pay sufficient interest.

Joaquin rejected this proposal, for reasons which he did not judge it prudent to make known to his assistant, preferring to return to Sacramento, where they had left the horses in the custody of one Pradillo.

Passing in front of a wooden house on the way, the two Mexicans heard the sound of voices, in the midst of which one was distinguished who was swearing violently, whose oaths were answered with boisterous laughter. Our men stopped in front of the hut.

"It is Garcia's voice," said Joaquin, who had just heard one of his habitual oaths. The chieftain leaned over and looked between two of the boards of the cabin, poorly joined together; his companion imitated him. Then they witnessed, without being visible, a scene very interesting and very difficult to describe. In the atmosphere of the room the vapors of rum and whisky stood out, together with the acrid odor of the smoking of pipes. Various groups of men were seated around a half-dozen tables; their aspect alone indicated them to be the most depraved and vicious creatures—in a word, capable of anything. On each table there was a game of "barajas," and in front of each man was a tin cup, which he filled from time to time with the liquor, or better said, the poison from a barrel located in one end of the room. A fire, half extinguished, reflected on the faces of those men of such repulsive mien, forming a curious contrast with the single candle which illuminated that scene.

At the table nearest the blaze were seated four scoundrels of the lowest class. One of them was no other than Jack Three Fingers, and the others who were with him were Pedro Sanchez, Juan Borilda and Joaquin Blanco. The three belonged to Murrieta's gang and operated as spies: Sanchez in the territory of Sonora and Columbia, Borilda in Stockton and the third at the Mission of San Luis Obispo. The other groups were composed of English, Irish and Americans, and all appeared to have drunk more than usual, which did not prevent their talking still more.

In spite of the tumult which reigned in that poorly disciplined crowd, Joaquin and Valenzuela were able to hear certain phrases flung out heatedly by Jack Three Fingers, whose feelings in no way surprised the leader of the outlaws.

"You have already more than your share," Garcia suddenly shouted, "and I am not going to give you a single dollar more. There were not more than six thousand dollars in all, and each one of you has received a thousand. Caramba! You hardly think that I am going to give you the same part as myself, when you have only had the work of getting the man, while I was the one who killed him? No, no, this business is finished. In the future I will work on my own account."

Then, to better emphasize his assertions, the bandit gave the table a violent blow with his fist, which seemed more like a blow with a mace, such was his strength. This showed at the same time that it was not expedient to play with those fists.

Chapter XXIII

While Jack was settling with such energy the question of the division of the spoils, another scene no less curious was taking place in the end opposite the table where the bandits were seated. One of the men who was on that side got up at the moment that Jack was making his statements in such a formidable manner, and moving toward the fire, looked at Jack Three Fingers stupidly, yet with some admiration. Then he returned to his table and spoke some words in the ears of his companions. Without doubt, these words were of some importance, for they had the effect of making six or eight persons who accompanied their informant leave the cabin.

Murrieta and his friend followed them into the darkness, and saw that they went toward a cabin situated about fifty feet from there. Believing that Jack Three Fingers must have been the cause of the sudden departure of these individuals, our Mexicans allowed them to enter the house, then drew near, and listened to what was being said within. Joaquin and Valenzuela had drawn their revolvers in order to be prepared to defend themselves in case of attack.

"Did you see him? Did you look at him well?" said one of the men inside the cabin.

"Perfectly," said another. "I will know him all my life. But are you sure that is the same person?"

"I don't know; what I do know is that I know him. I have seen him several times in the mountains, and I can swear to you that it is Jack Three Fingers, one of the main members of Joaquin's gang. I am also positive that Joaquin himself is in San Francisco, for whoever sees one sees the other; you always find them in the same places and seldom are they separated. Therefore, the three men who are sitting with Jack must belong to the crowd."

"Then boys," said a third speaker, whose accent showed that he was a son of Ireland, "everything is clear; here is the one by whom the game we have been hunting disappeared last night."

"What do you mean, Dumps? Explain yourself."

118

"You know well enough—the crowd of miners that we met, one of whom had his pockets full of gold. Here you have the whole mystery. At least that's the way it ought to be; and as they beat a retreat, I don't believe that they did a very good business, for I saw our men gambling and losing their dollars by the hundreds at the monte tables of the arcade."

"To hell with the Mexicans! As if they needed to go out from the mountains to stop the white people from earning a poor living for themselves."

"That is what I say," murmured another. "The devil take them! What are they here for? For five days and nights we have been waiting around here and we have hardly come across the least little bit of money."

"In fact," Dumps added.

"I am going to tell you what I think," said the one whom Dumps had just interrupted. "It is sure to rid us of them completely. We will send them to the devil, and when the business is over, then we will be the bosses."

"Do you think that a surprise?"

"Oh, no, Grippy, nothing like that. Are you crazy? I'd like to know what you would do with only your dagger? Besides, you know very well that we have never come out well in a battle with them; they know how to manage steel arms a lot better than we do. Here is what I propose; we will set a watch on their trail, and if they do not go away, we will divide ourselves into different groups and give chase to Joaquin. You know a big reward has been offered to the one that takes him, and when we have him . . . ."

"Oh, when we have him . . . when we have him . . . but we haven't got him yet!"

"Don't say any more, Dodge. You are very drunk and you don't know what you are saying. As I was saying, when we have Joaquin."

"I can get him any time, and if this happens I know how to handle a dagger very well. Oh, yes!"

"And I, Dodge, I will know how to handle you very quickly if you are not quiet. You say . . . Oh, I'm dying!"

Dodge had just buried his dagger in his companion's heart. Immediately, all the men jumped toward the assassin. Joaquin and Valenzuela had no interest in seeing the end of that row, so they abandoned the place where they were posted and traveled on toward their cabin. A few steps below the Hotel Fremont they met two escaped convicts from Botany Bay, who had just gone out from the bar to join their comrades. The two seemed to be very drunk.

"Who is this sly fellow who is loafing around here?" said one of the drunks, stopping almost under Joaquin's nose.

"I don't know," said the latter.

"You lie, you know very well...."

Before he had finished the phrase, the drunk was lying on the ground, half dead and in agony. Murrieta's dagger had passed through his heart. His companion ran toward the top of the hill, followed by a revolver shot, which Valenzuela sent after him, but it did not hit him, and he quickly disappeared.

The two Mexicans continued quietly on their way, as if nothing out of the ordinary had happened, when suddenly they were confronted by a policeman who asked them what the shot meant that he had just heard. Joaquin tried to shade his face with the brim of his hat, and carelessly grasped his revolver. Then, seeing that another person, probably another policeman, was coming rapidly toward them, he answered in a courteous tone, "That shot, sir, was the result of an accident. My friend was going to put his revolver in his pocket when the trigger caught on his belt."

"What made you run so fast?" said the second policeman to the first, when he was near the group.

"Oh, nothing," said the other. "I heard a pistol shot, and I thought that they were killing someone."

Then, turning toward Joaquin, he added; "You say that your friend was putting his revolver in his pocket when it went off? Then why was he carrying it in his hand?"

"Because at this hour of the night, sir, it is dangerous to walk through the streets, so many scoundrels are met. My friend wished to be prepared for anything."

"Then why did he not keep on carrying his revolver in his hand?"

"Because I laughed at his fears and told him that we had nothing to fear."

"But right now you just told me that there is danger in going through the streets at night. It seems to me that your answers are evasive, and I do not know whether I ought to believe what you tell me."

"Excuse me, sir, I wished to say that my friend ought to wait until the danger appeared."

"How does it seem to you, Charley. Wouldn't we do well to

arrest them? There are certainly a lot of rascals around. It seems to me that the wind tonight is very favorable for a good fire, and this side of the city is situated just right for the beginning of a fire. I believe that it would be wise to arrest them."

"No, that is not my opinion. Leave them in peace. There is nothing to say. Go on, boys, don't wait another minute. Ned, you ought not to question them more. You know that you talk and argue like a lawyer from the New York Tombs who has been bribed."

"That's all right, I know what I'm saying."

"Without any doubt in the next election you will be nominated a candidate for judge."

"Be still! You are worse than Billy and Mulligan. And you, who fire your revolvers carelessly, go to sleep! Come with me, Charley, I want to go back to Mill House to take a whiskey grog."

Joaquin courteously said goodnight to the two policemen and with his companion went on to the tavern where they had left Jack Three Fingers.

"If that man had insisted on taking us to jail," said Joaquin, "his fate was settled. I would have killed him like a dog."

"And I would have done the same with the other one," said Valenzuela.

The noise which the Mexicans heard, on reaching the door of the tavern, was a good proof that the fiesta was continuing. Joaquin looked through the keyhole and saw Jack Three Fingers seated in the same place, but so drunk that he could hardly hold up his head. Murrieta told Valenzuela to watch outside, and entering the tavern, he went to the table where his unruly henchman slept, shaking him by the shoulders. Garcia straightened up, furious, and partially drew out his revolver.

"Ah," he exclaimed, "Murrieta!"

"The same. Come! I wish you to leave the city in a few hours."

"Why? What's new?"

"Because the police are on our trail, and perhaps in a few minutes they may come here to catch us."

"Caramba! Here's some news to the point. How many are there?" asked Garcia, drawing his dagger.

"Too many for us to fight against, as hundreds of citizens are joining them to take us. Come! Come with me!"

"All right. Just as you like." And Garcia went out of the tavern, followed by his three companions.

Joaquin sent all of these men to the house of Senor Blanco, where they remained until daybreak. Then he sent Blanco (not the owner of the house but Jack's companion) to San Luis Obispo; Borildo and Sanchez went to Stockton and Sonora, which were their respective districts. Jack Three Fingers received orders to travel toward San Jose, and go to headquarters without loss of time. The same day Joaquin and Valenzuela went on board a ship for Sacramento. There they found their horses. Then they went to Stockton for the purpose of giving Borilda the necessary orders, reaching the other members of the gang who might pass through Stockton, and directing them to the Arroyo Cantova.

Three or four days after the departure of Joaquin there was spread all over San Francisco the rumor that the celebrated bandit had just been taken and put in the city jail. In fact, the police had seized a poor Mexican who was crazy enough to pass as Murrieta, and who was speculating on the terror that this move would inspire. A great number of curious people went to the jail in order to see how the bold outlaw looked, who was only known by the sure blows from his hands. All returned persuaded that he was the true Joaquin.

During this time Joaquin was traveling quietly. Jack Three Fingers stole a magnificent saddle horse and silver spurs from a rich Mexican at the Mission of Dolores; then he cut the throat of a Chinaman near Alviso, to steal his blankets, and then he killed and robbed a man named James Walsh near San Jose Mission. This murder was worth three hundred and fifty dollars to him, besides a gold watch and a revolver. Two Mexican ranchers, on suspicion of having taken a part in this crime, were arrested and taken to San Francisco, but were soon set at liberty for lack of proof.

A week later another member of the gang called Rafael Quintana stabbed in San Gabriel near Columbia, a man who had done nothing, a respectable citizen, absolutely inoffensive. This inexcusable murder caused a lively indignation in the whole county. The energetic constable, John Leary, undertook the pursuit of the murderer, but lost sight of him in the narrow mountain road. A few days afterward, Quintana emerged from his hiding place and killed a certain Samuel Slater, stealing some gold nuggets, twelve revolvers and some food. The body of the unfortunate man was not discovered until after several days, half devoured by coyotes.

Chapter XXIV

After having sacked the country during several weeks and having brought desolation upon the unfortunate inhabitants of California, after having lost by this work some of the most daring and useful men of the band, after having obliged their enemies to gather on all sides to pursue them, and after having collected by their enterprise a considerable sum, Joaquin resolved to go from Calaveras County, which he had invaded since his return from headquarters, to change the theater of his operations to Mariposa County.

This county suffered in its turn what its neighbors had endured. We shall not describe the long list of crimes; this would be the endless repetition of the bloody scenes which we have already related to our readers. The genius which directed and protected Murrieta seemed not to wish to abandon him yet; and in view of the numerous incidents which were changed for him in enterprises of an extraordinary ending, we are tempted to credit the ancient superstition of the Cherokees, to the effect that certain men have a charmed existence, and cannot die unless they are wounded with a silver shot.

The outlaws did not cease to devote themselves to murder and pillage. They always left behind them some bloody sign, which indicated their passing, and the most daring crimes were committed almost in sight of the very ones who were pursuing them. At any moment their pursuers heard at a short distance from them, desperate shouts; they hurried their progress, but only arrived in time to see the victims bathed in their own blood, and see the desperadoes, who, more daring than ever, went off on their horses, without appearing to have any fear of being overtaken. Joaquin's hordes were divided most of the time into small companies of five or six men. Murrieta was seldom favored with more than four of his assistants; Valenzuela and Jack Three Fingers never left him.

Guerra had in his charge the guarding of the camp. Sevalio also was in active service, and only the arrogant Antonio equalled him in valor and skill in carrying to an end the most risky enterprises. The latter had a certain predilection for the territory between Putah and Cache Creek; all the inhabitants who owned horses were robbed of them with the greatest effrontery. Every day he was pursued without rest, but thanks to the noble animal which he rode, he always succeeded in escaping.

That horse was the very animal which Texas Jack had received from the hands of Joaquin as recompense for his great services. Some days before Murrieta left Stockton, while he was resting in a house on Hunter Street, he learned from Valenzuela that Texas Jack had just been taken before the county judge and accused of an important robbery. Anxious to see his old friend, Joaquin went to the trial, coolly seating himself among the spectators. While the judge was pronouncing against the thief a sentence which condemned him to the penitentiary for a period of five years, Jack glanced around the room and saw the Mexican chieftain. An imperceptible signal was rapidly exchanged between them, and the condemned man felt his heart palpitate with the hope of an early escape. Unfortunately, Joaquin only had in the city three of his companions, whose strength wasn't enough for such a thing. Later he confessed to an American at French Camp that if he had been able to reach only a dozen of his men, he would have snatched the prisoner from the hands of the police within the space which extends between the jail and the wharf where the ship docked which should take him to the prison at Benicia.

Five months later there was spread the rumor of a strange discovery. There had just been found in a grave on a ranch which had belonged to Texas Jack, a man on horseback. The horseman was still mounted and his spurs were fastened to his boots. Everything indicated that this man must have been wounded in the head in the same position in which he was found, and that his death was not very recent. At his side were found some skulls and human bones, last remains of other victims of the same Texas. His ranch was situated in the depths of a valley on the banks of the Stanislaus River.

One night Joaquin was lying in bed in the cabin of one of the friends of his gang, three miles from the town of Mariposa, when he was informed that two of his men had just been hanged at San Juan for stealing horses. They had been pursued and arrested between

Gilroy and Pajaro; then they were tied with strong rope and taken to the town, where they were presented to Judge McMahon, and finally put in jail. The inhabitants, who had suffered so much in consequence of their numerous depredations, united in a mob, and took the prisoners from the hands of the police; immediately, according to "Lynch Law," they were hanged from two posts erected for that purpose.

On receiving this news, Joaquin mounted his horse and set out, accompanied by his four comrades as always, toward Monterey County, making his camp on the banks of San Benito, at a short distance from San Juan. There the outlaws remained about half a week, hidden during the day, but spending the night stealing the best horses they found on the ranches in that vicinity. When they thought that they had avenged sufficiently their two comrades, they broke up camp and went with the stolen animals to Arroyo Cantova. When they arrived there, they found in it the greatest part of the band. Almost all of the companies had finished their expeditions with good results, and they were awaiting new orders from their chieftain.

This was when they began Murrieta's preparations for the great and important work which should end his career as an outlaw in California. Joaquin had relations with the richest and most influential Mexicans of the whole state, and he was sure of their cooperation in the movement which he was planning. The inhabitants were not able to suspect their intentions, not recognizing in him anything more than a chieftain of outlaws, ignorant and cowardly bullies. Murrieta sent to Mexico the intelligent Antonio, who received the money and the instructions necessary for the arming and equipment of volunteers and partisans who were only awaiting the occasion for joining the band.

Guerra was dispatched to diverse ranches in California, where there had been established hiding places for their horses; he was to collect all of the beasts which he found in them, and bring to headquarters all the members of the company whom he should find along his way.

On his side, Joaquin had an important business to finish in San Luis, and that same day he set out for that place accompanied by only one man. The important matter was nothing else than an interview which he must have with the Mexican lady whom he had met by chance some months before in the Hangtown stagecoach, when it was attacked by Joaquin. This lady, sister of Joaquin's first sweetheart, the unfortunate Carmen, had been married to a rich rancher of Guadalajara, Mexico. When her husband died, she entrusted her ranch to the care of an old priest, well thought of in all the country, and went to California to encourage the feeling of vengeance in the heart of Joaquin and to abet him in the spirit of his sinister projects. This woman learned with regret that Joaquin was thinking of leaving California within a short time, but seeing that nothing could make him change his mind, after having consulted with Murrieta, she returned to Mexico the next day.

A week after this interview Joaquin undertook to protect the women from every danger, come what might. Therefore, he put at the disposition of Sevalio twenty of his most resolute men, armed to the teeth, confiding to this company the mission of escorting the women to the neighboring state of Sonora. Joaquin himself traced the road which they should take. They had to follow the coast of the gulf of California, going toward the missions of Santa Catalina and San Pedro; then they should travel to San Francisco Borgia, and to the Mission of San Gertrudis, cutting across a mountainous and wooded country very well known by Sevalio and the other men of the escort. Joaquin himself accompanied the women some distance from camp, embraced Clarita and the other girls, and, going back over the same road, soon entered Arroyo Cantova.

The Mexican chief, reflecting that it was best to await the arrival of his new forces from Lower California and from Sonora, before uniting all the contingent at his disposal, gave a reverse order to Guerra and sent some of his bandits who were found close at hand, to the neighboring regions.

He, with a company of six men, proceeded toward Calaveras County, plundering whatever they found on their way; thus, they arrived in the neighborhood of Jackson, and, breaking into the shack of a miner named Jewel while he was at work, they stole from him three hundred dollars in gold, a Colt revolver, and various other objects.

His inseparable companions Valenzuela and Jack Three Fingers formed a part of this expedition. Never did the bloody Garcia have more pleasure than during the stay of the gang in Calaveras and the neighboring counties. The best results had crowned all the enterprises of the outlaws in the northern territory of Calaveras during three weeks. The inhabitants had been despoiled of immense quantities of gold, to an extent that Joaquin considered it prudent to change from that country.

Before leaving, they joined fifteen of their men, who came from an excursion near Thom's Creek, in Colusa County; there they stole a large number of beautiful horses and four of the bandits had been sent on to take them to the headquarters.

Joaquin kept this desperate reinforcement with him, followed the Stanislaus, and in the rich valleys that river fertilized, made continuous the scenes of desolation and bloodshed so many times described.

Chapter XXV

After a sojourn of two weeks in the valleys which the Stanislaus crosses, Joaquin set off toward the Mariposa and Merced rivers. His passage along that territory was marked by colossal depredations after which he sent to the headquarters at Arroyo Cantova the men who accompanied him, with the exception of the six whom he had brought with him. With these he retired to a Mexican ranch near San Jose; killed a Frenchman on the highway, the owner of a public garden; and remained hidden some time in the house of a friend. The latter, named Francisco Sicarro, was secretly affiliated with the gang, which explains Murrieta's protection.

The extreme prudence of the chief in the manner of conducting his operations surpassed everything until this relatively insignificant case. One night, Joaquin, not wishing to go out to drink, sent an Indian from the ranch to San Jose to buy him a bottle of liquor. He had hardly gone when there came over Joaquin as a presentiment the fear that he might be betrayed by that man; and after mounting his horse, he overtook the Indian on the road which passes near Coyote Creek and killed him.

Such were the troubles imposed on the citizens of the whole state, such were their violences, their marauding acts—in short, their crimes—that justice was seriously disturbed. A petition, covered with signatures, was presented to the legislative houses, for the purpose of obtaining the authorization for Captain Harry Love to form a company of horsemen with which he should be able to arrest, drive out of the country or exterminate the numerous gangs which continually placed in danger the life and property of all the citizens. To this end, a decree was approved and signed by the governor of the state the 17th day of May, 1853.

The 28th of the same month, a company had already been organized by Harry Love. The payment for each man had been fixed at a hundred and fifty dollars per month; the legal existence of the company was limited to three months; the number of men who composed it could not exceed twenty. In spite of the fact that the pay was not much, each horseman had to provide himself with a horse, provisions, and the equipment, without having the right to any reimbursement for it.

Love did not hesitate a moment. He immediately took command of twenty men, taken from among his valiant comrades, all of whom had served with him during the war of Texas. When they were collected together, Love put himself at their head and set out at once, fully determined not to return to San Francisco until he had met the most formidable outlaw who has ever figured in the annals of crime.

History should preserve the names of the twenty who accompanied him on his expedition: Captain P. E. Conner; C. F. Bloodwith; G. W. Evans; Captain W. Burns; Deputy John Nuttall; W. S. Henderson; C.W. McGowan; Robert Masters; Mayor W. H. Hardy; Col. McLane; Lieut. Geo. A. Nuital; Lafayette Black; Dr. D. S. Hollister; Hon. P. T. Herbert; John S. White; P. E. Vetser; James M. Norton; Charles Young; E. B. Van Dorn; D. S. K. Piggott.

While this intrepid although small company passed on horseback through the cities and towns of the interior, the inhabitants followed them with uneasy looks, as if they were victims destined for the slaughter-house. But they were forgetting that there was at the head of the group a leader with the authorization of the state, whose experience was the product of the daring battles which he had had in Mexico and in Texas—a leader whose mind was as severe, as inflexible, as the discipline through which he had had to pass, whose strength of will was as much alive in danger as that of the bold outlaw against whom he was going to fight.

The third day of June, Pedro Sanchez, who was in San Francisco three months before with Jack Three Fingers, was killed at Martinez, not far from Columbia, by a Spaniard named Albino Teba. Both were disputing over the division of a sum of money which they had stolen together, when Sanchez, irritated by the obstinacy of his accomplice, jumped on him, dagger in hand. Teba took a few steps backwards, and drawing his revolver, gave his adversary four shots; only one shot touched Sanchez, but it was enough to make him fall dead at the Spaniard's feet.

By a queer coincidence, Borilda was executed the same day at

Stockton for having murdered a miner named James. The outlaw had received an order from Joaquin to kill a Mexican who had offended him, and in trying to execute the commission, he had mortally wounded James, who was in the same house, by the side of the Mexican condemned by Murrieta. Borilda was declared guilty of the murder of three men and of other crimes more or less important. One or two days before the execution, he saw a revolver on a table. He took it and was going to commit suicide, but the weapon did not go off.

Joaquin Blanco, Jack Three Fingers' third companion in San Francisco, was killed near Stockton the following year by a Mexican named Eugenio Corral.

On the night of June ninth, four bandits, taking with them forty horses, reached the ranch of Andres Ibarra, situated some twenty miles from San Luis Rey, and without the least provocation they fired on his family, wounding one person. Then they tied up three men who were living in the house and took possession of everything they found, in gold or valuable objects. They set out at once for San Marcos and killed two steers.

The next day a small company set out from San Diego to pursue the bandits; but seeing that they were unable to follow their trail after sunset, they did not go further. Messages were sent to several tribes of Indians to try to arrange with them to follow the marauders; but they had already had time to hide in the mountains. Some days afterward, it was learned that in Santa Margarita eight horses had been stolen, one of which was taken from the ranch of Ibarra, near San Marcos.

Joaquin, hunted on all sides, and by resolute men, into whose hands he feared to fall, to suffer a defeat which would compromise his great projects and destroy his hopes cherished for such a long time, resolved to retire to a solitary place alone and to remain there hidden until the arrival of the reinforcements, which he was expecting from Sonora. At the beginning of the month of July, Murrieta got into the ranch of Andres Pico, situated in San Fernando, Los Angeles County, and stole fifty horses. He proceeded toward the San Francisco ranch, which is in the same county. There he met a rancher who accused him of having stolen Don Andres' horses, and warned him that he would be pursued. Murrieta then turned over to the rancher forty-three horses, commissioning him to take them to the San Fernando ranch, adding that he needed the other seven. Then he passed through Santa Barbara County and crossed the high part of the coast of Santa Ines, from where he was able to proceed without difficulty to the Tulare Valley.

Captain Love had received secret information in which the presence of Joaquin in that part of the country was given as a certainty. He, therefore, went out in that direction with twelve of his men. The rest of the company was engaged in investigation in another direction.

On reaching the plain of Tulare, at dawn, the captain saw a little smoke at some distance to the left. This detail, common in appearance, and not important in itself, our man believed should not be underestimated. In virtue of this, he advanced toward the place where the smoke was coming out. At first he only saw some horses, which were grazing quietly some hundred yards from that place; but later, approaching near and climbing a small hill, he discovered in a little grove, the Mexican leader and six of his comrades, all seated around a fire. One of them, occupied in preparing the meal for the others, saw the visit which was being paid them and gave the alarm, when the Americans were still about a hundred yards from the camp.

The bandits mounted their horses. After them ran Love's hunters at full speed and they did not stop pursuing them and firing at them until Joaquin and Jack Three Fingers fell wounded, while two of their companions were made prisoners. The bold Mexican fled with such speed that he was finally almost on the point of escape; a few steps more and he would have been out of range of the revolvers. But Captain Love, seeing that he was not able to overtake the horseman, tried to shoot his horse, which he succeeded in shooting in the side.

The noble brute felt weakened immediately; then recovering his strength again, in spite of the wound which he had just received, he advanced more quickly than ever and crossed the space of fifty yards. Suddenly, Joaquin saw that blood was running from its mouth and nostrils, and the poor animal fell to the ground, unable to carry him further.

Murrieta ran a few moments on foot, but seeing that the captain and one of his men were approaching nearer all the time, he turned and fired in their direction the last two bullets he had left in his revolver. At the same moment, several shots wounded him; he realized that his hour had come and begged the Americans not to shoot

Joaquin and Jack Three Fingers' deaths.

anymore.

"You have taken me by surprise," he said, "but it does not matter; I die contented; I have already avenged myself enough." And growing pale because the blood was streaming from three or four wounds which he had received, he remained yet a few seconds leaning on his right arm, and then he gave his last breath.

Jack Three Fingers, followed by two or three, fled at full speed, and in spite of having received eleven shots, he still ran a mile and a half across the country. His horse ran like the wind; minute by minute he was gaining ground over the enemy, whose horses, unaccustomed to such exercise, struggled frequently against the irregularities of the ground. Finally, believing that he was about to be taken, the ferocious Jack threw a savage look at the Americans and fired six revolver shots; one only went off. Everything conspired against him. In spite of this, he did not wish to fall alive into their hands and he refused to surrender. At last a bullet struck him to the ground and he died almost instantly.

In the meantime, the conflict was being waged in different places. Captain Love's hunters managed to join their leader, bringing two prisoners with them; one of the bandits, whose name we do not know, escaped, but only one got away alive and safe. His companion succumbed on the highway as a result of the wounds which he had received.

Chapter XXVI

After this bloody encounter, Captain Love collected the spoils of the enemy; these consisted of some magnificent horses, which were later returned to their owners; six excellent Mexican chairs; six Colt revolvers; a silver spur; some capes of fine cloth and a pair of rifles.

While Love's huntsmen were returning to San Francisco, one of the prisoners broke his chains and threw himself into a pool of water, where he was drowned. His comrade was put in jail in Mariposa county; there he remained until the company disbanded, and then he was taken to Martinez. In that place he made revelations that proved that he had taken part with a great number of his compatriots, in the crimes committed by Joaquin; this man was prepared to make revelations still more important, with the object of escaping extreme punishment, when a singular incident occurred. In the middle of the night the doors of the jail were broken down by a band of Mexicans who took him with them and hanged him. These Mexicans were undoubtedly members of Joaquin's gang, and his secret agents, and some ranchers who wished to prevent the compromising revelations of their old accomplice.

Love's huntsmen from that moment had but one object in view—to obtain the rewards promised throughout the country to whomever should take the celebrated leader of the outlaws, dead or alive. And certainly these rewards were well earned, on account of the courage which they had shown and the dangers which they had run, together with the daring with which they had followed Murrieta even into the mountains, demolishing his whole party.

First, it was necessary to show the public the reality of their deeds. Without that, none would have believed that Joaquin had been killed; unworthy suspicions would have tarnished Captain Love's reputation. Consequently, he did what he would never have done except under the circumstances cited; he sent and had Joaquin's head cut off; it was immediately taken to the nearest town, situated a hundred and fifty miles from the place where Joaquin had died, and there it was put in alcohol to preserve it.

The 14th of August, Mr. Black and Mr. Nuttall arrived at San Francisco with the head of the famous outlaw, whose numerous crimes had won him a reputation without equal in the history of crime. The surprising rapidity of his movements, the number of his accomplices, the extent of his operations in an exceedingly vast territory, had made his name notorious at the same time in places very far from each other, to a degree that many people thought him an imaginary person, a myth, to whom were mistakenly attributed all the diabolical acts of the evildoers taking refuge in the country.

Even after his death, the rumor was spread that he was in the southern counties, continuing his regular system of bloody tragedies and thefts like those which he formerly made on the ranches and in the miners' camps.

Besides Joaquin's head, Mr. Black and Mr. Nuttal took with them numerous certificates and declarations made by persons who had known the outlaw well. It was, therefore, impossible to doubt his identity and not believe the assertions of Captain Love and his men.

The head was exposed to the public so that the whole population could see it and judge it for itself. Signs were posted which indicated the place where it could be seen. The signs themselves were expressed in these terms: "Joaquin's head is to be seen at King's corner, Halleck and Sansome Streets, opposite the American Theatre. Admission, one dollar."

Among the numerous statements, vouchers and certificates intended to prove the identity of the head were the following:

"State of California, U.S.A., County of San Francisco. Ignacio Lizarraga of Sonora, after having passed judgment, declares: that he has seen the pretended head of Joaquin actually in the possession of Messrs. Nuttall and Black, assistants of Captain Harry Love, which is exhibited in the establishment of John King, Sansome Street; that the deponent knew perfectly Joaquin Murrieta and that the head aforesaid is truly that of the celebrated outlaw Joaquin Murrieta. (Signed) Ignacio Lizarraga.

Certified before me, this day, August 17 of the year 1853. Charles D. Carter, Notary Public."

"State of California, U.S.A. The eleventh day of the month of

August of the present year 1853, before me, A. C. Baine, Justice of the Peace of the said county, there has appeared in person the Reverend Father Dominic Blaive who declares under oath, according to the requirements of the law, that he has known the famous bandit Joaquin; furthermore, that he has just examined the head which is in the possession at this moment of Captain Conner, one of the assistants of Harry Love, and that he believes truly that said head is that of the same Joaquin, whom he has known two years, as he declares above. Signed, Dominic Blaive.

Certified and signed before me, the day mentioned above, A. C. Baine, Justice of the Peace."

The crowds thronged to see Joaquin's head: it was truly a handsome head, which well justified the excitement with which the people went to King's establishment to examine it.

After having remained in San Francisco as long as was necessary, Joaquin's head was taken to all the towns of the state for exhibition. The mutilated hand of Jack Three Fingers was also displayed: and great was the terror of superstitious persons upon noticing that his fingernails had grown an inch after the hand had been cut off.

After a very careful investigation, Colonel Bigler, governor of the state, paid Captain Love the sum of one thousand dollars, which he had offered personally to the one who should deliver Joaquin dead or alive. A short time later, May 15, 1854, the California Legislature, considering the important service which the captain had rendered the country, in liberating it from such an audacious criminal, and deciding that he had not been sufficiently rewarded, ordered that an additional sum of five thousand dollars be given him.

Although Joaquin's death caused his gang an irreparable loss, and although it obliged the members to disperse instantly, nevertheless, the outlaws, formed in small companies and commanded by bold leaders, continued their depredations and their murders to a degree that some began to doubt that the true Joaquin had ceased to exist.

Furthermore, many inhabitants of the state of California asserted that Joaquin wrote from the republic of Chile, contradicting the news of his death, and that this took place in the District of Altar, state of Sonora, when he was ninety years old.

Toward the end of 1854, Joaquin's head was sold by Deputy Sheriff Harrison because of attachment for debts pronounced against the person charged with exhibiting it to the public. The sale was made at auction. While the auctioneer was raising the price, an Irishman exclaimed with the greatest indignation, "Oh! Is it possible that you are going to sell the head of your fellow creature? You will certainly never have good luck! You will never again have good business for the rest of your life!"

The bids had at the moment reached the sum of sixty-three dollars. Disturbed by the Irishman's remark, the auctioneer had not the courage to go farther, and let the gavel fall. The head was then delivered for sixty-three dollars.

Some time later Harrison killed himself. He accidentally discharged a loaded revolver in placing it on the desk in his office.

Such is the history of the most famous bandit chief who has ever lived on this earth. On tracing it according to authentic facts and documents almost official, sometimes, perhaps, we have given some color to the deed. But we have not related a single thing which did not have for a foundation the most rigorous exactitude. This narrative, then, may be considered as an integral part of the truthful history of the early days of California.

As a curious fact, we will add that there actually live in the city of Los Angeles, California, Rosa, Herminia and Anita Murrieta, daughters of Antonio, brother of Joaquin Murrieta.

Additional books in the Recovering the U.S. Hispanic Literary Heritage Series:

Recovering the U.S. Hispanic Literary Heritage

Volume I
Edited, with an Introduction,
by Ramón Gutiérrez and
Genaro Padilla
ISBN 1-55885-063-5, $34.95
ISBN 1-55885-058-9, $17.95

Volume II
Edited, with an Introduction,
by Erlinda Gonzales-Berry and
Chuck Tatum
ISBN 1-55885-139-9, $34.95

Volume III
Edited, with an Introduction,
by María Herrera-Sobek
and Virginia Sánchez Korrol
ISBN 1-55885-251-4, $39.95

The Account: Álvar Núñez Cabeza de Vaca's Relación
Edited and translated by José Fernández
and Martin Favata
ISBN 1-55885-060-0, $12.95

Las aventuras de Don Chipote, o, Cuando los pericos mamen
Daniel Venegas; Edited, with an Introduction, by
Nicolás Kanellos
ISBN 1-55885-252-2, $12.95

Black Cuban, Black American: A Memoir
Evelio Grillo
With an Introduction by Kenya Dworkin-Mendez
ISBN 1-55885-293-X, $13.95
Contains an eight page photo insert

Cantares: Canticles and Poems of Youth
Fray Angélico Chávez
Edited, with an Introduction, by Nasario García
ISBN 1-55885-311-1, $12.95

The Collected Stories of María Cristina Mena
María Cristina Mena
Edited by Amy Doherty
ISBN 1-55885-211-5, $12.95

Conflicts of Interest: The Letters of María Amparo Ruiz de Burton
María Amparo Ruiz de Burton; Edited, with an
Introduction, by Rosaura Sánchez and Beatrice Pita
ISBN 1-55885-328-6, $17.95

El Coyote, the Rebel
Luis Perez
With an Introduction by Lauro Flores
ISBN 1-55885-296-4, $12.95

Jicoténcal
Félix Varela; Edited by Luis Leal and Rodolfo J. Cortina
ISBN 1-55885-132-1, $10.95

El Laúd del Desterrado
Edited by Matías Montes-Huidobro
ISBN 1-55885-082-1, $10.95

Lo que el pueblo dice
Jesús Colón
Edited, with an Introduction, by Edwin Padilla
ISBN 1-55885-330-8, $12.95

Hispanic Periodicals in the United States, Origins to 1960: A Brief History and Comprehensive Bibliography
Nicolás Kanellos with Helvetia Martell
ISBN 1-55885-253-0, $69.95

History and Legends of the Alamo and other Missions in and around San Antonio
Adina de Zavala; Edited by Richard Flores
ISBN 1-55885-181-X, $12.95

The Real Billy the Kid
Miguel Antonio Otero, Jr.
Introduction by John-Michael Rivera
ISBN 1-55885-234-4, $12.95

Selected Poems/Poesía selecta
Luis Palés Matos; Translated from the Spanish,
with an Introduction, by Julio Marzán
ISBN 1-55885-303-0, $12.95

The Squatter and the Don
María Amparo Ruiz de Burton
Edited by Rosaura Sánchez and
Beatrice Pita
ISBN 1-55885-185-2, $14.00

Tropical Town and Other Poems
Salomón de la Selva
Edited, with an Introduction, by Silvio Sirias
ISBN 1-55885-235-2, $12.95

Versos sencillos/Simple Verses
José Martí
Translated by Manuel A. Tellechea
ISBN 1-55885-204-2, $12.95

The Woman Who Lost Her Soul and Other Stories
Jovita González; Edited, with an
Introduction, by Sergio Reyna
ISBN 1-55885-313-8, $12.95

Women's Tales from the New Mexico WPA: La Diabla a Pie
Edited by Tey Diana Rebolledo and
María Teresa Márquez
Introduction by Tey Diana Rebolledo
ISBN 1-55885-312-X, $17.95